African Theatre
10

Series Editors
Martin Banham, James Gibbs,
Yvette Hutchison, Femi Osofisan
& Jane Plastow

T0335010

Reviews Editor

Jane Plastow
Workshop Theatre, School of English, University of Leeds LS2 9JT, UK

Associate Editors

Omofolabo Ajayi-Soyinka
Dept of Theatre, 1530 Naismith Dr, University of Kansas, Lawrence, KS 66045–3140, USA

Awo Mana Asiedu
School of Performing Arts, PO Box 201, University of Ghana, Legon, Ghana

Eckhard Breitinger
Forststr. 3, 95488 Eckersdorf, Germany

David Kerr
Dept of Media Studies, Private Bag 00703, University of Botswana, Gaborone, Botswana

Amandina Lihamba
Dept of Fine & Performing Arts, PO Box 3505, University of Dar es Salaam, Tanzania

Patrick Mangeni
Head of Dept of Music, Dance & Drama, Makerere University, Kampala, Uganda

Olu Obafemi
Dept of English, University of Ilorin, Ilorin, Nigeria

Titles already published in the series:
African Theatre in Development
African Theatre: Playwrights & Politics
African Theatre: Women
African Theatre: Southern Africa
African Theatre: Soyinka: Blackout, Blowout & Beyond
African Theatre: Youth
African Theatre 7: Companies
African Theatre 8: Diasporas
African Theatre 9: Histories 1850–1950
African Theatre 10: Media & Performance

In production:
African Theatre 11: Festivals

Articles not exceeding 5,000 words should be submitted preferably on disk (as a Word file). Typewritten submissions may be considered in exceptional circumstances if they are double-spaced.

Style: Preferably use UK rather than US spellings. Italicise titles of books or plays. Use single inverted commas and double for quotes within quotes. Type notes at the end of the text on a separate sheet. Do not justify the right-hand margins.

References should follow the style of this volume (Surname date: page number) in text. All references should then be listed at the end of article in full:
Surname, name, date, *title of work* (place of publication: name of publisher)
Surname, name, date, 'title of article' in surname, initial (ed./eds) *title of work* (place of publication: publisher).
or Surname, name, date, 'title of article', *Journal*, vol., no: page numbers.

Reviewers should provide full bibliographic details, including extent, ISBN and price.

Copyright: Please ensure, where appropriate, that clearance has been obtained from copyright holders of material used. Illustrations may also be submitted if appropriate and if accompanied by full captions and with reproduction rights clearly indicated. It is the responsibility of the contributors to clear all permissions.

All submissions should be accompanied by a brief biographical profile. The editors cannot undertake to return material submitted and contributors are advised to keep a copy of all material sent in case of loss in transit.

Editorial address
African Theatre, c/o Workshop Theatre, School of English, University of Leeds, Leeds LS2 9JT, UK • j.e.plastow@leeds.ac.uk

Books for Review & Review articles (as from *African Theatre* 11)
Professor Martin Banham, Reviews Editor, *African Theatre*, 4 Oakwood Gardens, Leeds LS2 2JE • martinbanham@btinternet.com

African Theatre 10
Media & Performance

Guest Editor
David Kerr

Reviews Editor
Jane Plastow

JAMES CURREY

James Currey
is an imprint of Boydell and Brewer Ltd
PO Box 9, Woodbridge, Suffolk IP12 3DF, UK

and of

Boydell & Brewer Inc.
668 Mt Hope Avenue, Rochester, NY 14620, USA
www.boydellandbrewer.com
www.jamescurrey.com

British Library Cataloguing in Publication Data
Media & performance. -- (African theatre ; v. 10)
1. Theater--Technological innovations--Africa.
2. Videorecordings in the theater--Africa. 3. YouTube
(Electronic source)
I. Series II. Banham, Martin.
792'. 096'09051-dc23

ISBN 978-1-84701-038-4 (James Currey paper)

Papers used by Boydell and Brewer are natural, recyclable products
made from wood grown in sustainable forests

Typeset in 10/11 pt Monotype Bembo by Long House, Cumbria, UK
Printed and bound in the United States of America

Contents

Notes on Contributors

Christy Adair is Professor of Dance Studies at York St John University. Her book, *Dancing the Black Question: the Phoenix Dance Company Phenomenon* (Dance Books: 2007) offers a significant critique of key issues in performance. Her research interests, developed in *Women and Dance: Sylphs and Sirens* (Macmillan: 1992), continue to focus on gender and ethnicity in relation to dance studies and performance. Her current writing draws on her research in East Africa.

Gbemisola Adeoti is a Reader in the English Department of Obafemi Awolowo University, Ile-Ife, Nigeria. He was once a reporter/researcher with *The News* Magazine, Lagos. His areas of teaching a research include: Dramatic Literature, Poetry, Literary History/Theory and Popular Culture. He is the author of *Naked Soles* (poems), *Voices Offstage: Nigerian Dramatists on Drama and Politics* and *Aesthetics of Adaptation in Contemporary Nigerian Drama*. He is the Editor of *Muse and Mimesis: Critical Perspectives on Ahmed Yerima's Drama*. Adeoti was a British Academy Visiting Fellow at the School of English, University of Leeds, UK, and a Postdoctoral Fellow, African Humanities Program of the American Council of Learned Societies (ACLS).

Nehemiah Chivandikwa is a full-time lecturer at the University of Zimbabwe. He teaches applied theatre, acting and playmaking. His research interests are in applied theatre, gender, performance and the connection between religion and theatre. Currently, he holds an M. Phil in Theatre Studies and he is pursuing an M. Phil degree programme in Theatre for Development and Disability. Nehemiah Chivandikwa has been involved in several projects in Theatre for Development, Community Theatre and Mainstream theatre as a producer, consultant, actor, director and stage manager. These projects have been carried out in Zimbabwe, Mozambique and the USA.

Akinwumi Isola studied at the universities of Ibadan and Lagos and made his name through outstanding contributions as a dramatist, poet, essayist, reviewer, script-writer, actor, director and professor. He is celebrated for championing the cause of literature in the indigenous languages of Nigeria, particularly in

Yoruba, his mother tongue, and also for promoting women's issues. *The Campus Queen* is one of three video film scripts he has written so far.

Samuel Kasule is working on post-colonial musical theatre, politics and theatre, the development of home movies, and Black British theatre. He is also interested in African theatre practice and theory, and the influence of African thought on contemporary theatre. He has published articles on Black British theatre, East African musical theatre, colonial and pre-colonial performance in Uganda, and politics and the influence of Idi Amin on Ugandan theatre. He is a Reader in Postcolonial Performance and Theatre Studies at the University of Derby, UK; and a founder member of the African Theatre Association (AfTA).

Moratiwa Molema holds a BFA (University of Hartford, Connecticut, USA) and an MFA (University of Cape Town, South Africa). She has produced and directed several in-door and out-door shows in Gaborone, Botswana. She participated in the Maitisong Festival, staging 'The Rebirth of the Ostrich' (based on a San story collected by Arthur Markowitz in an anthology of the same name), and incorporating dance, video-projection, and a live band and choir. She has participated as choreographer in a training workshop run by students of the Julliard School of Music, Drama and Dance, New York, for Botswana secondary school students.

Ngonidzashe Muwonwa is an Assistant Lecturer at the University of Zimbabwe, who has recently completed an M. Phil in Cultural and Television Studies. He teaches scriptwriting, directing, acting and topical issues in African theatre such as racism, ethnicity, gender and politics. His research interests are in identity issues in cultural spheres and particularly in media spaces such as television. He is currently working on his D. Phil on social uses of television in Zimbabwe, and represents one of the emerging new generation of theatre and cultural researchers in Zimbabwe who aspires to adopt a multi-disciplinary approach to his research.

Samuel Ravengai is a doctoral candidate in South Africa at the University of Cape Town in the Drama Department where he doubles up as a Visiting Scholar and is also a board member of the International Federation of Theatre Research (IFTR/FIRT) where he works closely with the African Theatre and Performance (AT&P) Working Group of which he is one of the founding members. He is particularly interested in the interconnection of race, nation, empire, migration and ethnicity with cultural production. Samuel Ravengai's most recent publications are in *African Theatre 9* (2010), *African Identities Journal* 8 (2) 2010, as well as *Trends in 21ˢᵗ Century African Theatre and Performance* (2011). Apart from his research, he is a director and lecturer in drama and theatre at the University of Zimbabwe.

Torsten Sannar is a doctoral candidate in the Department Theater and Dance at the University of California, Santa Barbara. His research, funded in part through an ASTR Dissertation Research Award, focuses on the intersection of race, politics, and spectacle at the South African tourist resort, Sun City.

Torsten has also written articles for *The Brecht Yearbook* and *SAGAR*, an annual journal sponsored by the South Asia Institute at the University of Texas at Austin. His dissertation, 'Playing Sun City: The Politics of Entertainment at a South African Mega-Resort', will be completed in September 2011.

Vicensia Shule Apart from teaching at the University of Dar es Salaam, Tanzania, Vicensia Shule conducts research and consultancies on theatre, film, radio and television programmes. Her areas of interest include the political economy of creative industries, dramaturgy and media criticism. She is a contributor, reviewer and a critic for various performing arts journals, books, programs and productions. Independently she works as a producer and a director for film, radio and television programmes. Vicensia holds a Dr Phil (Theatre Studies) from Johannes Gutenberg Universität Mainz, Germany, MA (Performing Arts) and BA (Fine and Performing Arts) from the University of Dar es Salaam, Tanzania.

Sarah Woodward has an MA in Theatre and Performance, specialising in Theatre Voice praxis from the University of Cape Town, and is currently the portfolio holder for Voice in the Drama Division at Wits University. She has always been fascinated by media culture, and her research is primarily focused on the relationship between subculture and student vocal choices. Die Antwoord has been an obsession for a while now, and elements from their live performances have been echoed in her own directing work.

Obituaries

Ulli Beier, 23 July 1922, Chotwitz – 3 April 2011, Sydney

Ulli Beier's remarkable work in Nigeria was motivated in part by two deeply held convictions. The first was profound suspicion of official institutions, and the second, closely connected to this, was scepticism about the rigidity of formal education, particularly in the arts. Beier was distrustful of colonial institutions and favoured the self-taught artist over the academically trained scholar-artist. This mattered because he was a man of enormous creative energy who 'found himself' in Yorubaland and helped to establish structures there through which local artists could express themselves and reach wider audiences. Inevitably, Beier's success in promoting creative Africans with strong links to indigenous conventions led to criticism, much of which originated in the very institutions that he regarded with most suspicion.

Ulli Beier was born into a Jewish middle-class family in Chotwitz in what is now Poland, and emigrated to Palestine in 1933 after the Nazis came to power. Palestine did not prove to be the promised land for Beier, and the British interned him as an enemy alien. Although he was not admitted into the secondary school system, he matriculated and took an external University of London degree in English Literature, History and German. After the War, went to London where he did the only course open to him at that time – a post-graduate diploma in phonetics.

In 1950, after a brief period in London, Beier was appointed a Junior Lecturer in Phonetics at University College, Ibadan (UCI), where he immediately encountered – and challenged – elitist and colonialist attitudes among the British staff. His responses included co- founding a forward-looking, Pan-Africanist literary journal, *Black Orpheus,* whose editorial policy reflected belief in the potential of West African creative intellectuals. Beier's drive, sometimes referred to as his 'ferocious energy', ensured that, under his editorship, the journal appeared regularly and more or less on time.

In the same period, he promoted the ground-breaking Mbari Club in Ibadan, and waged a campaign to liberate visual and theatre artists from domination by European influences. The success of this campaign was seen particularly clearly in Oshogbo, where he taught after he transferred to UCI's Extra-Mural Studies department and where he encouraged artists to begin a dialogue with traditional aesthetics and a variety of new materials.

In December 1966, as tensions in Nigeria increased, Ulli Beier left Nigeria for Papua New Guinea – only to return for three years in the early Seventies to take up a post at what was then the University of Ile-Ife. From the mid-Seventies, his influence was somewhat distanced, but he remained a vital presence on the African cultural scene and continued to offer challenges and create opportunities. This was particularly the case between 1981 and 1996 when he gave enlightened leadership to Bayreuth's Iwalewa House.

The precise nature of Beier's cultural legacy has recently been discussed in relation to the destination of his remarkable collection of Nigerian art and of his archive from the time he spent in West Africa. Significantly, the Ataoja of Oshogbo purchased part of the archive, including an extremely rich photographic record of performances by Duro Ladipo company.

Beier's photographs represent a very significant visual record of Beier's long and productive working relationship with a supremely creative drama group, and draw attention to the amount of time, skill and energy that he devoted to African theatre. Beier played a variety of roles and enabled Ladipo's company to travel widely and perform in Europe. Another of his creative partnerships was with the redoubtable Segun Olusola, and led to the establishment of Theatre Express, an enterprising travelling theatre company.

Beier wrote profound and powerful plays that he published under the penname 'Obotunde Ijimere', a 'nom de plume' that took in many students of African theatre. 'Ijimere's' scripts added to the repertory of plays that have proved popular across swathes of the continent. Among the best-known are *Eda*, a re-writing of Hugo von Hofmannsthal's version of *Everyman*, and *The Fall*, a dramatization of the creation story. The depth of Beier's sympathy for Yoruba thought and his ability to find theatrical expression for it is shown by *The Imprisonment of Obatala*, and the serious discussion it has prompted.

In a brief obituary, it is impossible to do more than hint at Beier's qualities and achievements, the paths he negotiated, and the controversies he sparked. For a wide-ranging account of his life and a bibliography of his prolific output readers are directed to Wole Ogundele's *Omoluabi, Ulli Beier, Yoruba Society and Culture* (2003). That volume shows what a significant cultural pioneer Ulli Beier was, how he opened doors and encouraged cultural cross-fertilisation.

Eckhard Breitinger and James Gibbs

Sunbo Marinho (1942–2010)

Sunbo Marinho, set- and lighting-designer, teacher, director, actor, producer, and technical consultant, made a great contribution to the Nigerian theatre largely, but by no means exclusively, through his work at the University of Ibadan.

Born in 1942, Henry Olasunbo Marinho received his primary education in Ebute-Meta and proceeded to St Gregory's College, Ikoye, and then to the School of Drama at the University of Ibadan. He graduated in 1967 and worked for a time at the Mbari Club, Dugbe, Ibadan, before returning to the university where he was employed in the Technical Unit of the Theatre Arts Department. In due course, he started to teach Scenic Design and Technical Production in the Theatre Arts Department, where he was known to generations of students as 'Sango'.

At the end of the Seventies, when I got to know him, and to admire his contribution to numerous productions, he was a member of a strong Theatre Arts Department that included Dapo Adelugba, Kinni Olusanyin, Tunji Oyelana, Bayo Oduneye, Zulu Sofola, Bode Sowande, Esohe Omoregie, Jide Malomo, Femi Fatoba, Laolu Ogunniyi and Felix Begho.

Although initially and primarily a set- and lighting- designer, Marinho was also involved in film work from early on. His credits during the Seventies included work on the Calpenny production of *Kongi's Harvest* , and on *Harvest of Ants*, a cinematic treatment of Chinua Achebe's *Arrow of God*.

Although his commitment was primarily to the Ibadan Theatre Arts Department, Marinho was also called on by the University of Ile-Ife, where he designed the lighting for Derek Walcott's *Dream on Monkey Mountain*. In 1980, he was deeply involved in the theatre company Gbakanda Afrikan Tiata that Yulisa Pat Maddy had taken to Nigeria. For example, he not only did the lighting- and set-design for Maddy's *Big Breeze Blow* (July 1980), but also took the role of Sammy.

Many groups that brought productions to Ibadan at the time called on his services – though they didn't always spell his surname correctly! The credit for lighting Derek Bullock's FGC Kano productions of *Macbeth* and *The Road* in Ibadan was given to 'Mr Sumbo Merhenini'.

In his funeral tribute, Femi Osofisan provided a vivid sketch of Marinho, together with a reflection on the fate of the designer. He wrote: 'Sunbo … was a spectacle by himself, a marvel to watch during the hectic preludes to opening night. You would see him wrestling with ladders and lanterns, sawing up sheets of wood and knocking them together again, painting canvasses and carpets, aligning lamps and dimmers, all without seeming to tire. And then he would retreat silently into the background, as was the custom, leaving the actors and the playwright to lap up the applause. For such, regrettably, has always been the fate of the designers on our stage, to toil unacknowledged. The public sees the décor and the costumes and the dazzling set; but those who design them are rarely seen or sung. In time Sunbo came to earn the sobriquet of "Sango", the Yoruba god of lightning; but this was from informed admirers, in the restricted circle of theatre specialists; the larger public remained broadly ignorant of his significance.'

Marinho's emergence as a director was only a matter of time, and, significantly, it came through his work on Osofisan's texts. After regularly being involved in the technical side on Osofisan's productions, Marinho's directorial credits include *Aringindin and the Night-watchman*, premiered in Ibadan during January, 1988.

In addition to demonstrating all-round theatre skills, Marinho in his mature years took forward the involvement with other media glimpsed in his early work on *Kongi's Harvest*. Responding to opportunities in television, he both co-produced and acted the role of Major in the sit-com *Sura de Tailor*. In his active retirement, he moved on from the university campus and his skills were employed by a multimedia Company offering creative lighting, sound, stage design, and set construction services to Z-Mirage. As 2010 moved towards a close, the last switch was thrown.

Sunbo Marinho, teacher and creative technician, warmly appreciated by colleagues and students, born 16 July 1942, died November 2010, leaving a widow, children and grand-children.

James Gibbs

Introduction

DAVID KERR

A collection of articles, interviews and a screen-play, reflecting issues of African performance and media inevitably carries some aesthetic and ideological baggage. A common perception of innovation in Africa places media firmly in a tradition derived from exposure to colonial and post-colonial ideologies. The perception is perhaps inevitable, given that most twentieth-century electronic media technology (cinema, radio, telephone and television) was introduced to Africa through colonial importation. More significantly, the early development of these media tended to be influenced by Northern economic support, training and cultural influences.

Such a narrowly technocentric interpretation of media, however, needs to be interrogated. Although this collection deals with electronic communication, the history of Africa's engagement with it has been strongly influenced by indigenous oral performative media: dance, masquerades, mime, puppetry and oral narrative. The problem with a technocentric viewpoint is that it tends to situate innovation within a paradigm dominated by technology, so that 'progressive' or 'avant garde' cultural innovations are projected as those associated with the latest media technologies. This perspective ignores the adaptive genius of much African creativity, which has often been expressed in such performative modes as improvisation or the synaesthesia of mixed art forms. Economic constraints make it rare for African entertainment media to be at the fore-front of technical innovation, but the programme creators are able, in an ingenious way, to graft African motifs and techniques on to Western genres such as video drama (Haynes and Okome 1997: 26) radio-drama (Kerr 1997: 134-170) or television sit-coms (Roome 2000).

Inevitably, in a collection of articles on a very broad topic, there are important gaps – not just in genres but also methodology. One of the big genre gaps is that of radio drama, which is arguably the most widely consumed form of electronic media in Africa. A less surprising lacuna is that of the impact of digital technology. Obviously the use of digital cameras, recorders and editing suites has become an established part of African video and radio industries and its impact is described by several authors. However, this collection (with the exception of Woodward's paper) does not explore the potential of such phenomena as video/computer games with their built-in ability to create virtual, participatory communities, nor of blogs as a more democratic alternative to conventional criticism by trained 'experts'. Some African communications specialists, such as Ansu-Kyeremah feel that internet-based platforms like social networking sites and blogs provide in the 21st century, potentially more Afro-centric and participatory interaction than face-to-face or analogue modes of communication (2005 : 242-248).

One surprising gap is the lack of articles about Francophone or North African performance, especially as the best known and most prestigious African cinema has come from those regions. Equally surprising is the lack of reception analysis. Three of the authors are practitioners discussing their own work (as are the interviewees in Sam Kasale's interviews), while several other authors are close to the producers; there is thus a strong bias towards analysis of performance production rather than reception. Only Woodward's article on the Afrikans pop group Die Antwoord provides a personal, viewpoint on consuming performance (and criticism of the performance). A side-effect of authors' interest in production is a reflection on the ever-changing face of technology (for example in the articles by Adair, Adeoti and Shule). In particular, the changes to the production and distribution of music and video films, caused by the digital revolution, is a motif running through the collection. On the issue of reception it is important to remember that the atomised audiences which are common with the reception of electronic media in North America and Europe (Scannel 2007:138) are not necessarily widespread in Africa, where communal and participatory audiences for both public and private performance reception are normal (Kruger 1999:109, Okome 2007: 6-7).

The authors who do show some interest in reception issues are the first two, dealing with popular music as performance in South Africa. Sannar's article, 'I ain't Gonna Play Sun City' (the title of a global hit song and music video of 1985) adopts a bi-focal viewpoint in analysing both the song and the campaign to encourage artists and audiences to join the cultural boycott of South Africa by refusing to perform at or consume products from Sun City. One perspective is that of the American producers of the song/campaign in which their aims are linked to the words of the song and the images of the associated video. The other is a more complex reinterpretation of the campaign made with the hindsight of almost two decades. This demonstrates that the images and words sometimes undermine the simplistic message of the campaign by marginalising the black population of South Africa, through their depiction as helpless victims, rather than the actors that was a historically accurate interpretation of their role.

Sarah Woodward's article tries to interpret the performative image created by Afrikaans pop group, Die Antwoord, two and a half decades after the 'I ain't gonna play Sun City' hit. By 2010 the ANC had been in power for 18 years, and many Afrikaaners, though reconciled to the reality of the new dispensation, felt themselves to be marginalised. Die Antwoord's post-punk music and rebellious, profane, hybrid image is the result of multiple historical ironies. They have recast their marginal role through identification with subaltern black identities, but they are so successful at creating this image that they are able to articulate their rock radicalism with the lucrative global star mechanisms of international festivals and fan-based internet communication. Woodward's analysis of these contradictions is supported by her familiarity with social networking sites and fan-based, highly inter-cultural, critical blogs.

The hybridity displayed in African entertainment video industries relate to rather different historical transformations which have initiated their own forms of cultural ambiguity. Technological changes in the last four decades can be related to wider changes in ideology, particularly the move from the statist economic policies, Pan-African ideologies and one-party politics of the 1960s, 70s and 80s towards a capitalist, commercial economic base with its (often spurious) links to an ideology of pluralism, democracy and individualism.

This transition has given rise to an interesting debate about African cinema and video industries. Critics such as Diawara (1992), Ukadike (1994) and Pfaff (2004) champion traditions, practices and narrative modes established by the pioneers of celluloid film industry in Africa (such as Ousmane Sembène, Souleymane Cissé and Med Hondo), with their concern for African authenticity, history and oral culture as sources of cinematic inspiration. A more recent critical tradition has challenged established aesthetic and ideological viewpoints, on the grounds that such authenticity constitutes a nostalgic chimera in an Africa articulated so closely with global, urban cultures, technologies and modernising consumerism (Papaioannou 2009). African cinematic 'authenticity' has also been challenged by authors who see the digital video revolution coming out of Nigeria, Ghana, and more recently, Cameroon, Kenya and Tanzania, representing, despite its technical, artistic and ideological deficiencies, a less elitist, democratic cultural tradition in tune with indigenous systems of creativity (Okone 1997, Larkin 2002).

One interesting theoretical insight developed recently is a recognition that video technology, especially digital editing software, has produced huge benefits in popular distribution, and rather than condemning the video film industry in Nigeria and other countries, it makes sense to use the same technology and distribution systems to create more artistically polished and politically correct films. In other words, the opposing camps described above could be reconciled by creating links between the cinematic achievements of the 'classic' early cinematographers and the democratic accessibility of digital video technology, thus producing a popular but aesthetically pleasing and culturally authentic film industry. Both Adeoti's article on Mainframe films and Isola's screenplay, *The Campus Queen*, illustrate this attempt to combine the best of both film/video movements.

The subject of Adeoti's article, Tunde Kelani, was trained in celluloid cinema techniques in the 1970s. Unlike many of his Nigerian and Ghanaian contemporaries who gave up making films when social, financial and technological developments almost wiped out the embryonic celluloid film industry, Kelani saw the potential, first of analogue and later digital video technology, for making and distributing intelligent, well-crafted popular films. Adeoti points out that Kelani's awareness of the cross-cultural influence of Nigerian videos encouraged him to introduce multi-cultural, multi-linguistic incidents, characters and motifs in his films. In addition, links with NGOs and human rights agencies, both broadened his financial support base and helped him project a more sympathetic understanding of women's issues than the stereotypes Nollywood usually projects.

Isola also straddles several generations of theatre/film practitioners. He made his reputation in the 1970s and 80s with popular Yoruba theatre, sometimes including links to University travelling theatre experiments. His move into video drama was a logical transition to a medium which was becoming increasingly popular with subaltern audiences. *The Campus Queen* shares some motifs with Nollywood. These include the beautiful young woman threatened with rape or tempted by the seduction of money and material gifts, and the sinister group of roughnecks working on behalf of a greedy, manipulative, political leadership. But the scenario differs radically from the usual Nigerian video fare, in that the heroic, wily protagonist is a woman refusing the status of victim. Moreover, the series of conflicts in the plot are linked to a class-conscious, dialectical analysis of Nigerian society, which pitches a grossly corrupt political leadership against a coalition of exploited manual workers and class-conscious, marginalised university students. The play structure itself, with its frame of a music festival shows its strong links to indigenous theatre traditions.

Nigeria and Ghana are considered the pioneers of commercial African video drama, but the films' popularity in neighbouring and even more distant countries has encouraged the emergence of similar industries. East African film-makers have been particularly industrious in their production of video dramas in English, kiSwahili and other local languages. Sam Kasule provides insight into Ugandan Luganda language films through his interviews with Mariam Ndagire and Ashraf Simwogere. Kasule focuses much of his interviews on issues of gender, since such videos in both West and East Africa have been much criticised for perpetuating male chauvinist views about women's role in society. The interview with Ndagire, Uganda's only well established female video drama director is particularly interesting for the light it throws on attempts to project a progressive gender viewpoint within an industry where established formulaic plots undermine such insights.

Both Ndagire and Simwogere have a strong awareness of the history of Ugandan film and video industries. Vicensia Shule, a Tanzanian film-maker has even more strongly expressed views on the shift from centrally controlled, Ujamaa-themed films of the 1970s, through the doldrums of the 1980s and 90s when very few films were made, to the 2000s, when a rapid expansion of commercial videos, mostly in kiSwahili, started to reach wide audiences. Shule is sensitive to the multiple constraints that prevent the industry producing artistically and technically competent films. These include the lack of cinema training of actors, script-writers and directors, and the economic imperatives which lead film-makers to concentrate on quantity rather that quality in order to maximise profits. Shule, as one of Tanzania's first commercial female film directors, is aware of the obstacles to women entering the rough entrepreneurial waters of the African video industry. The recent founding of a Pan-African organisation, Women Film-makers in Africa (WFA), may go some way to smooth that career path in future.

There are two articles in this issue on Television drama in Zimbabwe. Clearly, television shares some similarity with video, but there are important differences in that there are for more stringent demands on quality, and there is a need to fit into an existing broadcast format – soap opera in the case of *Studio 263*, and the drama series in that of *Sinjalo*. Ravengai raises issues which have plagued Theatre for Development for the last four decades, the contradictions between the thematic demands of the non-government organisation (NGO) sponsors and the aesthetic choices of the artists. Population Services International (PSI), a US-based multi-national NGO, which has supported stage, radio and television drama on HIV/AIDS issues throughout Southern Africa, has a reputation for programmatic briefs and very meticulous monitoring (Kerr 2007). Ravengai gives his experience as a script-writer for *Studio 263* to explain how artistic interference by the sponsors at the level of plot and characterisation can defeat the very aims of the soap opera to convey health messages in a culturally relevant and entertaining way. Ravengai interprets this interference as a form of neo-colonial cultural control.

The concerns of Cont Mhlanga's *Sinjalo* as explained by Chivandikwa and Muwonwa are rather different. Cont Mhlanga's stage plays, from *Workshop Negative* (which was the featured play-script in AT6), through to *Good President* (2007), though popular with audiences, have frequently challenged Zimbabwean government ideologues. The same is true with *Sinjalo*. Chivandikwa and Muwonwa show how the simple story about two friends, one Shona-speaking, the other Ndebele, trying to cover up their sexual infidelities, is really an allegory about the need for cultural tolerance between different peoples in Zimbabwe. Although this appears to conform to official Government policies, in fact, the series, coming at a time of growing cultural nationalism among many Ndebele citizens, proved to be politically very sensitive. Chivandikwa and Muwonwa also make interesting comments on the gender implications of the allegory and the way stylised techniques carried over from Theatre for Development relate to television drama's more realistic conventions.

The final two articles focus on performances which mix stage techniques with video or other electronic media. There is, of course, a long Euro-American tradition of mixing live performance with film, slides or video (Piscator and Brecht through Brook to Mnouchkine and the Wooster Group). In Africa, popular Yoruba theatre playwrights like Hubert Ogunde and Moses Olaiya experimented with mixing performance and film. It is mainly in South Africa, however, that well equipped theatres have allowed a strong avant garde tradition to develop mixing multi-media and live performances. The most famous South African example is the Hand-Spring Puppet Company, especially in the plays of Kentridge, but much experimentation has also taken place at university art centres. The two last articles in this collection show that this mixing of live and electronic performance is beginning to take root outside South Africa.

Adair's article about a dance performance by Lailah Masiga needs to be read within the context of East African women's dance in general. A strong tradition throughout East Africa is the ghettoisation of women's so-called traditional dance into the realm of the erotic, aimed mainly at tourist audiences (both external and internal). The style conjures up an imaginary, pre-industrial arcadia of supple, male warriors and compliant, hip-shaking maidens. Masiga's solo dance breaks the tradition of group dancing, but more obviously, those of touristic voyeurism. It focuses instead on the brutal and controversial facts of female genital mutilation through the juxtaposition of a realistic documentary on the topic and Masiga's expressive and stylised, choreographic commentary. Adair's attitude is to point out the controversies, but to allow the non-prescriptive dance-narrative to speak for itself.

Much of the theorising about video's incorporation into performance deals with enhanced perspectives in dealing with time. Matthew Causey (2006) feels that experiments with mixing video and live performance create a 'para-performative, tele-theatrical phenomenon wherein the immediacy of performance and the digital alterability of time, space and subjectivity overlap and are combined'. Moratiwa Molema describes this flexibility in an account of her 2008 mixed media production, *Water Feels*. Her concept of 'layered time' is expressed by rooting her performance in the indigenous cultural bedrock of African humanism (*uBuntu* or *Botho*) as well as spiritual respect for ecological balance. This indigenous culture is overlaid and interacts with later traditions of resistance to colonialism, apartheid and economic globalisation. Thus stylised, post-colonial techniques of *Water Feels*, such as inter-racial casting and the overlapping mixture of live and video performance, are able to probe the ambiguities and complexities of several recent cultural epochs, layered over pre-colonial sensibilities.

Water Feels thus illustrates, as do several of the performance descriptions in *African Theatre 10* an easy relationship with electronic media, which reflects neither unthinking acceptance of Euro-American media techniques, nor an essentialist repudiation of them. They portray the output of a generation of African performance artists who are able to use electronic performance media as flexible, accessible, entirely African technologies.

REFERENCES

Ansu-Kyeremeh, Paul A.V., 2005, 'Indigenous communication in the age of the internet', in Ansu-Kyeremeh, Paul A.V., (ed.) *Indigenous Communication in Africa: Concept Applications and Prospects* (Accra, Ghana University Press).

Causey, Matthew, 2006, *Theatre and Performance in Digital Culture: From Simulation to Embeddedness,* (London and New York, Routledge).

Diawara, Manthia, 1992, *African Cinema, Politics and Culture,* (Bloomington and Indianapolis, Indiana University Press).

Haynes, Jonathan. and Okome, Onookome, 1997, 'Evolving Popular Media: Nigerian Video Films', in Haynes, Jonathan (ed.) *Nigerian Video Films*, (Jos, Nigerian Film Corporation) 21-44.

Kerr, David, 1997, *Dance, Media Entertainment and Popular Theatre in South East Africa,* (Bayreuth, Bayreuth University Press).

Kerr, D. 2007, 'African Performance, Knowledge Formation and Social Change', in Arndt, Susan & Berndt Katrin (eds) *Words and Worlds: African Writing, Literature and Society – A Commemorative*

Publication in Honor of Eckhard Breitinger, (Trenton and Asmara, Africa World Press).

Kruger, Loren, 1999, 'Theatre for Development and TV Nation: Notes on an Educational Soap Opera in South Africa', *Research in African Literatures*, 30/4,116-26.

Okome, Onookome, 2007, 'Nollywood: Spectatorship, Audience and the Sites of Consumption', *Postcolonial Text 3/2*, 2007, http://www.postcolonial.org/index.php/pct/article/view/ 763/ 425. [Accessed 23rd May 2008] (Retrieved, November 17th 2008).

Papaioannou, P. Julie, 2009, 'From Orality to Visuality: the Question of Aesthetics in African Cinema', *African Cinemas*, 1/2, 141-57.

Pfaff, Francoise, 2004, 'Introduction' in Pfaff, Françoise, *Focus on African Films*, (Bloomington & Indiana, Indiana University Press) 1-11.

Roome, Dorothy, 2000, 'Humor as "Cultural Reconciliation" in South African Situation Comedy: "Suburban Bliss" and Multicultural Female Viewers', *Journal of Film and Video*, 51/3-4, 61-87.

Scannel, Paddy, 2007, *Media and Communication*, (Los Angeles, London, New Delhi, Singapore, SAPES Publications).

Ukadike, Nwachukwu, F., 1994, *Black African Cinema*, (Berkeley, University of California Press).

'I Ain't Gonna Play Sun City!'
Anti-apartheid solidarity & its consequences

TORSTEN SANNAR

A hip, young veejay[1], sporting an outfit reminiscent of Don Johnson in his glory days, holds up a piece of fan mail and directly addresses the camera with a wry smile: 'We'll see if we can read this when we come back from the video, which is *Sun City* by Artists United Against –' He breaks off his introduction and turns to his co-host to refresh his memory. 'Apartheid', she finishes. He nods in approval. 'That's it. Be right back.' And the new video begins.[2] The veejay's momentary loss for words can be excused. In 1985, the year the video in question premiered, 'apartheid' was still something of a foreign word to the producers and consumers of American popular culture. It would not remain so.

Earlier that year, Steven Van Zandt, Bruce Springsteen's back-up man and future *Sopranos* cast member, wrote and produced one of the most influential American protest songs of the decade. 'Sun City', released by the non-profit collective Artists United Against Apartheid (AUAA), combined the talents of fifty-four musicians and singers in an effort to make the South African mega-resort of the same name an anathema for international performers. While Van Zandt's single and subsequent album never achieved vast commercial success, his project significantly affected the anti-apartheid movement throughout the world. A comprehensive cultural endeavour, the 'Sun City' project included an album as well as fact sheets about apartheid, a music video, and a book on the making of the record. Through this multi-media platform, Van Zandt intro-duced the politics of South Africa to a new generation of US citizens, advocated for the cultural boycott of South Africa and vilified the apartheid regime, all in a slick and marketable pop culture package.

My introduction to the project came as a youngster. I vividly recall watching the video on MTV with my sister. At that point in our lives, we were more interested in spotting the various celebrity musicians in the video than in contemplating its political content.[3] The catchy beat and contagious chorus had us singing along in time: 'I ain't gonna play Sun City!' However, the overtly political intentions of AUAA differentiated the song from the cultural fare on offer from Duran Duran, Madonna and other pop icons of the 1980s. The message was difficult to ignore: white perpetrators of the apartheid

1

regime were violently repressing black South Africans, and the situation outraged this group of Western artists. Just as it did for many young Americans, this initial encounter with South Africa profoundly influenced me. The song and video dictated the little I knew about South Africa at the time and awakened me to a political world outside the US that suddenly seemed vibrant and important.

A US-produced music project such as 'Sun City' may seem an odd means of approaching African media and performance. Yet the past dismissal of seemingly trivial objects of analyses has left an unexamined treasure trove of pop culture material related to South Africa. As the literary critic Rita Barnard comments in her reading of Walter Benjamin: 'A critical reader of culture should ... prick up her ears when a text, idea, or practice is habitually and as a matter of course dismissed as silly, uninteresting, or passé; for it is in the fertile loam of the marginal that we may find the structures of power revealed in peculiarly fascinating ways' (Barnard 2001: 347). It is also worth recalling that in pre-internet 1985, popular music and the relatively new concept of music videos functioned as the contemporary means of communicating with and sometimes politicizing a young American populace, a group that would ultimately adopt apartheid as one of its major political causes of that decade. Without an overt military war of our own to condemn, Van Zandt's project encouraged us to look to foreign shores to stoke the political fire within.

Revisiting Van Zandt's project now, twenty-five years after its release, I argue that the symbols of apartheid and the anti-apartheid movement, while promoted as fixed and transnational, transformed as activists disseminated them to various audiences around the world. The divergent and sometimes conflicting interpretations of *how* and *why* people opposed to apartheid should act revealed the innate instability of cultural signifiers as they circulated within the global cultural economy (Appadurai 1996: 27-47).[4] The complex interplay between Sun City, the resort, and 'Sun City' the album, reveals an interdependence of symbols, places and products on a global scale, even within a nation purposefully isolated from the rest of the world.

In past academic treatments of 'Sun City', the project has been lauded for its contribution to the global anti-apartheid movement and its innovative musical aesthetic (Nixon 1994 and Ullestad 1987). Measured in terms of its ability to generate popular awareness in the West, 'Sun City' was an undeniable success. The record, in spite of its overtly political message, cracked *Billboard*'s Top 40. Presaging Bono's emergence as a rock ambassador of political import, Van Zandt testified before the UN Special Commission Against Apartheid and headlined other political events in conjunction with the release of the record (Marsh 1985: 114, 118). While these efforts emanating from the USA and Great Britain contributed to the demise of National Party (NP) rule in South Africa, they should not be dismissed as entirely benign. In conjunction with its contribution to the end of apartheid, the 'Sun City' project introduced two nettlesome variables to a complex cultural/political calculus: 1) the essentialism inherent to a commercial media project designed to 'sell' the anti-apartheid cause; and 2) a conflation of

American and South African antiracist political movements.

Regarding the first phenomenon, the 'Sun City' project – especially the music video – often depicts South African culture as an essentialised racial feud between blacks and whites. The drawback here is that by embracing and propagating the simplified moral ideology set out by advocates of the cultural boycott, AUAA could not avoid the same traps on the international level that had already ensnared numerous South Africans domestically. Namely, as South African cultural and literary theorist Njabulo Ndebele has noted in his criticism of the protest movement in his own country: 'moral ideology tends to ossify complex social problems into *symbols* which are perceived as finished forms of good and evil, instead of leading us toward important necessary insights into the social *processes* leading to those finished forms' (Ndebele 2006: 15, italics in original). The 'Sun City' music video was an aesthetically crafted collection of such symbols designed to motivate, educate and entertain its American fans. However, in its eagerness to accomplish these goals, AUAA also risked misinforming Western audiences about the intricacies of South African race and cultural relations.

In my reading of the video below I also analyse how AUAA implemented a variety of visual and aural strategies to portray the anti-apartheid protesters in the US *and* South Africa as racially integrated and politically unified in their opposition. These strategies led to a conflation of national resistance movements (the US Civil Rights Movement and the South African anti-apartheid movement) that obscured internal domestic divisions and promoted the faulty impression to US audiences that the racial dynamics within South Africa were analogous to those within their own country. Throughout my analysis I ask: What are the repercussions of the mistranslation of a South African cultural and political idiom for the benefit of an American audience? Perhaps all of these dangers are simply the worthwhile cost of an effective and entertaining activist campaign emanating from one country on behalf of the people of another. Still, praising the success of a political campaign without examining its fallout – voices silenced or misinterpreted in the – can perpetuate historical inaccuracies and the erasure of differences between political and racial dynamics in the US and South Africa.

The cultural boycott

Even the cultural boycott of South Africa, of which 'Sun City' was one component, exacerbates a simplification of South African history and culture. While seemingly a deterrent to global connection, the boycott functioned as a powerfully unifying political issue. Ironically, the very concept of excluding and isolating a particular nation galvanized like-minded activists from different parts of the world.

In practice, the boycott was an especially coarse but effective means of forging together the political and cultural spheres within South Africa. It mandated that artists and audiences regard live performances and other entertainment media from a political perspective, for the boycott policy presented an ultimatum to those who created and witnessed aesthetic works. Framed as a binary opposition by ANC Arts and Culture Secretary, Barbara Masekela, artistic work in South Africa could ostensibly accomplish one of only two outcomes: it would either 'betray or support our struggle for national liberation' (Masekela 1986: 7-9). For better and for worse, 'the struggle' against apartheid became the predominant prism though which South African art and art about South Africa was apprehended.

Anti-apartheid activists in South Africa initially conceived the cultural boycott as a means to staunch the influx of performers from the US and Britain. Local activists feared that performances of foreign origin within South Africa would be perceived as evidence of international support for, or at least tacit acceptance of the NP regime. Writing to a British public in 1954, Father Trevor Huddleston initiated the boycott when he beseeched 'those who believe racialism to be sinful or wrong ... to refuse to encourage it by accepting any engagement to act, to perform as a musical artist or as a ballet dancer – in short, to engage in any contact which would provide entertainment for any one section of the community' (Huddleston, 1990: 67). By 1968, the United Nations General Assembly had officially endorsed Huddleston's request. It adopted Resolution 2396, which implored its member nations to suspend 'cultural, educational, sports and other exchanges with the racist regime' (British Institute of Human Rights 1976: 59).[5] Consequently, South Africa was officially deemed a pariah state in the eyes of the global cultural economy. As such, according to the ANC, the leading resistance party within South Africa, the government and its supporters deserved nothing less than complete cultural isolation.[6]

Gradually, as the anti-apartheid movement met tangible political goals and realised material benefits, the politicisation of performance intensified, and the aims of the boycott became more politically radical (Spector 2004: 149). This trend of escalation culminated in a complete separation of cultural realms. The ANC announced to its supporters in South Africa and around the world the existence of two cultures within one nation: an emergent democratic South African culture (what Masekela would term the 'people's culture') pitted in direct opposition to the dominant 'apartheid culture' (Masekela 1988: 18-21). Within this paradigm, the people's culture was vaguely defined, but strictly regulated. Adherents were to follow certain tenets to remain members in good standing: 1) support the economic and cultural boycott of South Africa absolutely; 2) support 'the struggle' within the content of any artistic expression; and 3) liaise with the ANC before performing to ensure compliance with these agreed upon standards. Thus, the cultural boycott policy in effect thrust the act of performance and recordings of these performances into a permanently political context and established the ANC as a primary cultural gatekeeper. Any artist who wanted to engage with South Africa in a politically responsible manner needed the approval of the resistance. Conversely, those who broke the boycott would bear the wrath of an empowered and increasingly vocal opposition.

Performing against apartheid

AUAA popularised the ANC position on the boycott by making the case to an international audience in song and video. 'Sun City' provided a specificity of place around which Western artists could concentrate the disjointed boycott policy. American artists and citizens suddenly had a tangible location upon which to focus their scorn. If the political protest within South Africa throughout the 1980s was meant to make the country ungovernable, this cultural expression of protest emanating from outside was meant to make its stages unplayable. As such, Van Zandt and his fellow rockers established Sun City as a metonym for all of apartheid – a bound and identifiable tourist resort and yet one that acquired meaning beyond the confines of its physical borders.

Throughout the various components of the 'Sun City' project, two objectives structure much of the content. In the comprehensive paperback book that documented the creative development of the album, Dave Marsh explains that the project, initially catalysed by Van Zandt's political activism and creative vision, was 'born out of *outrage* and a desire to *educate*' (Marsh 1985: 5, my italics). I also discern these intertwined goals within the structure of the song and music video. As such, I utilise these categories as tools of analysis below. The more I listened to the music and watched the artists perform on video, the more clearly I recognised a pattern, one that took me back to my initial conception of 'Sun City' in the mid-1980s and then onward toward a more politically and historically informed reading. On the surface, the artists convey their ire; the message of the chorus is simple and the images from the video violent and shocking. On a deeper level, the artists prompt an examination of the political issues at hand through the verses of the song and a visual documentation of racism overcome. The challenge Van Zandt faced as a result of his dual-strategy is the same as that of all artists: the assorted pieces of the 'Sun City' puzzle were discrete, and Van Zandt could not ensure that his audience consumed the project as a whole. Viewers of the video might have felt outrage at the sight of racial hatred, but they did not necessarily receive the accompanying education that would elucidate the historical specificities of the South African anti-apartheid struggle. For AUAA, value and meaning were tied directly to audience interpretation. The very success or failure of the project depended on the receipt of its political component, for as Marsh contended, 'Sun City' would be judged by virtue of 'the activity it stirs toward ending apartheid' (Marsh 1985: 77).

The repetition of the chorus-slogan, 'I ain't gonna play Sun City!' served as the memorable and dominating centerpiece of AUAA's efforts.[8] Belted out in unison by all fifty-four participants, it was a revealing declaration of political intention, which, to an as yet uninformed American public, prompted a series of fact-based queries: What is Sun City? Why do these artists vow not to play there? The verses to the song and the images within the popular music video became the potentially educational explanation of the outrage implied by the chorus. Thus, Van Zandt and company pleaded their case deductively. The

Fig 1   *Record sleeve,*
AUAA Sun City Album

political conclusion presented to us near the beginning of the video (apartheid deserves the condemnation of the international community) simplified a relatively complex political and cultural logic embedded within the chorus: 1) Sun City stood in for white racist apartheid; and 2) to 'play' Sun City was to align oneself with the wrong side of history (the ignorant foreign celebrities who broke the cultural boycott and the oppressive white regime of South Africa). While AUAA's supplementary material implicitly acknowledged the educative limitations of this declaration of outrage, I question the potential for audience members to transcend what Ndebele refers to as our 'gut response' (Ndebele 2006: 30) to political pleas like that in 'Sun City'. Take, for example, the dramatic beginning to the music video, as below.

The viewer is first presented with a mocked-up promotional video clip for tourists considering a trip to Sun City. Pleasant Muzak underscores the mellifluous voice of a commentator describing the luxurious resort on the screen. The voice (touched with a white South African accent) assures the viewer that at Kerzner's Sun City, visitors will be privy to shows from some of the world's 'headline entertainers' and unapologetically notes that the relocation of black South Africans to Bophuthatswana is 'one of the realities of apartheid', almost as if the location itself might give the tourist a snippet of what authentic apartheid is like – a perceptible and (desirable?) commodity to be consumed during a stay at the resort.[9]

As tourists (all of whom appear to be white) lounge poolside, Vegas-style dancers traverse a glowing stage, lit by a giant sign that announces arrival at our destination: 'Sun City'. It all appears remarkably pleasant to the prospective guest. But just as a spectator might settle into this alluring comfort, the music of Van Zandt's 'Sun City' takes hold. The first eerie strains of Miles Davis' trumpet and a breathy 'Ahh, Sun City' spill out, both in recognition of the political target at hand, and a shaming of the name, like a parent to a naughty child. The rifle shot of a South African police officer unalterably disrupts the visual and aural flow. A brief clip of a white woman sunbathing is quickly interrupted by the snippet of a frenzied white policeman using what appears to be a whip to disperse a gathering of black South Africans. As his whip strikes, its impact is timed to coincide with a musical blast of outrage. The second-long montage of the image of the striking whip, the sound of its impact and a dispersing black crowd rewinds and replays four, five, six times to emphatically drive home the point that we have strayed from the path of tourist leisure and blissful political ignorance. The repeating whiplash spurs the audience member and scholar out of his/her comfort zone and into an engaged political perspective.

In this new politicised context, even the seemingly simple proclamation 'I ain't gonna play Sun City!' resonates with meaning. Since this personal commitment takes place in the public sphere, the declaration is simultaneously a call for solidarity. As an announcement to one's peers (fellow performers) and to the consumer public (the viewers of MTV and the radio listeners), 'I ain't gonna play Sun City!' invokes a subtle peer pressure. The celebrities' statement implies that while the individual artist vows not to play Sun City, anyone listening should readily agree, provided the individual has an appropriately enlightened political consciousness.

The scattershot approach to filming, favoured by director Jonathan Demme, increased the likelihood that these visual depictions of engaged artists affected the audience.[10] So many celebrities populate the video that almost inevitably an MTV viewer of the 1980s would encounter someone s/he recognised. At the moment of recognition the power of celebrity testimonial takes hold. However, celebrity endorsement and sloganeering inherently show a spectator little about the process by which apartheid developed and how it was subsequently combated. Instead, black and white Americans reduce intricate cultural and political processes to loudly voiced promises. More troubling, these American activists surrogate for the black protestors they strive to protect.

If apartheid perpetrators in the video were fixed as referents for iniquity, then black South Africans were initially fixed as anonymous victims. Although the video depicts an amorphous group of black dissenters, the project's various components make it clear that these insiders were in need of help from the outside. The video tells a story of gathering political will. Early on, black South Africans cannot sustain their protest when faced with the violent threat of white South African police and military force. They disperse and their political power disintegrates *until* the intervention of Western artists refocuses their resolve.

When characters such as the black South African protesters in the 'Sun City' video lack personal history and definition, they are quickly subsumed by the collective political will of the group. As Ndebele has noted, this enforced anonymity 'becomes the dialectic equivalent of the anonymity to which the oppressive system (apartheid) consigns millions of oppressed Africans. Thus, instead of clarifying the tragic human experience of oppression, such fiction becomes grounded in the very negation it seeks to transcend' (Ndebele 2006: 15). One potential way out of this vicious circle is to educate the reader/ spectator about the political context in which these strategies take place.

I see 'Sun City' as a project caught between its allegiance to a broad political cause and the unwieldy realities of promoting that cause within a competitive global cultural economy. Granted, 'Sun City' was a significant innovation during its time, a precedent for what contemporary audiences expect from commercially successful media projects. Van Zandt engaged his audience through a variety of media formats and exhibited the foresight to contact his audience members wherever they happened to exist along a spectrum of political consciousness. For those who sought a good song and easy-to-remember political stance, 'Sun City' delivered. However, in order to move beyond this 'mere articulation of grievance', (Ndebele, quoted in Nixon 1994: 95) Van Zandt and company imagined a commercially viable product that was simultaneously full of topical information related to apartheid.

The paperback book that accompanied the album and Van Zandt's extensive media appearances evidenced AUAA's commitment to an educational component. Dave Marsh's recounting of the making of the 'Sun City' record was to be a 'rock book', available to fans and fellow activists who took an interest in the project. But the book would simultaneously provide a history of apartheid as a reader friendly, visually compelling narrative. For example, in the opening, readers are confronted with a definition of apartheid printed in stark white font on an otherwise all-black page. Recalling a textbook glossary entry, it reads:

> Apartheid is a word meaning 'apart' or 'separate.' It is the system of legalized racism in the Republic of South Africa. Under apartheid, all persons in South Africa are classified by the color of their skin...Although there are only 4.5 million whites, under the repressive system of apartheid, they control every aspect of life for the 24 million blacks (including Africans, Coloreds, and Asians). (Marsh 1985: 2)

While such moments retain educative potential, they are at least as much aesthetic gestures as analytical pursuits.

The risks of solidarity

The conflation of American liberalism and South African radicalism that takes shape at the end of the video further complicates the impact of the 'Sun City' project. Long before 1985, when the record was produced, the US had already realised the political goals of the Civil Rights Movement and the dream of racial integration. As such, 'Sun City' forever emanated from a historical place that had already (putatively) solved its own problems in regard to race. To then claim that the US's lingering racial tensions were analogous to South Africa's apartheid nightmare is to confuse a partially realized US present for a hoped for South African future.

In the wake of apartheid atrocities such as the Sharpeville Massacre in 1960 and the Soweto Uprising of 1976, some South African activists associated Western liberalism with negotiation and reform, tactics that had proven ineffective against the stranglehold of NP rule. Black leaders such as Stephan Biko, political parties such as the Azanian People's Organisation (AZAPO) and the Pan African Congress (PAC), and even the ANC's military wing *Umkhonto we Sizwe* connected the principles of nonviolence (as espoused by political figures like Martin Luther King in the US) with a *right-of-centre* mentality that had largely failed and was distinctly at odds with the radical politics of the Black Consciousness Movement. This emergent radicalism, at its zenith during the tumultuous 1980s, later gave way to a more conservative, pragmatic political ideology as the ANC negotiated a peaceful end to apartheid. I regard the 'Sun City' project as a possible contribution to and effect of this transition. While 'Sun City' advocated a political position well to the left of American President Ronald Reagan's disingenuous policy of 'constructive engagement', it simultaneously modelled a position to the right of that of South Africa's black radicals.[11]

By the end of the 'Sun City' video, any distinctions between the USA and South Africa, or between the ANC and more radical political strains within South Africa, are deliberately obscured. In his speech to the UN Special Committee Against Apartheid, Van Zandt urges Westerners' political involvement on the grounds that 'All [black South Africans] ask is that we look at them and see them, because by seeing them we see ourselves', implying an innate sameness that American viewers could ascertain through the act of perceiving. He continues, 'Once informed, we all might take a closer look at our own consciences and the disease of racism in our own culture' (Marsh 1985: 118). Such statements demonstrate AUAA's clear commitment to goodwill. Van Zandt intended to bring together the scourge of racial discrimination in the US and South Africa as a way to perform good works and level a cultural playing field skewed in favour of the West. However, the cross-cultural connection Van Zandt proposed might, in fact, work inversely. Instead of looking at ourselves *after* we have been informed, Western audiences make ascertainments about the foreign world *reliant upon* accessible and already known parallels to their own experience.

The video attempted to establish an international signification of race, yet one that was defined by Americans and legitimated by American historical imagery. Specifically, 'Sun City' focused on a transnational 'black' race that signalled Van Zandt's conviction that the casting of black South Africans and/or African-Americans would not matter in the context of the video's over-riding political message (O'Brien 2001: 117).[12] The video solidifies the connection and ostensible similarity between the US and South Africa with images of Martin Luther King marching during the Civil Rights era and brief snippets of his 'I Have a Dream' speech intercut with footage of black South African protestors. In this edited version of history, the South African protestors become the audience for one of history's greatest proponents of nonviolence. The implication is clear: South African protestors, anonymous and undifferentiated from African-Americans, might learn from our great national leader and racial reconciler. The black South Africans remain silent dancers whose cause is left to be articulated by American artists.

Moreover, the AUAA video equates Martin Luther King to South Africa's Nelson Mandela. By drawing on iconic references to King, AUAA establishes the American Civil Rights leader as an authoritative point of reference for its viewers. When images of Nelson Mandela follow, American viewers return to the King references in order to ascertain the meaning of Mandela and to con-textualise his significance to the anti-apartheid movement. Thus, from the per-spective of an American viewer, AUAA represents Mandela as South Africa's MLK. Given Mandela's international prominence since the end of apartheid, it is difficult to imagine a Western audience unfamiliar with the South African leader. However, in 1985 Mandela remained imprisoned by the NP regime and lacked the global celebrity that has been foisted upon him since his release in 1990. Interchanging political celebrities may be expedient, but such a practice is ultimately damaging to both Americans and South Africans, since the analogy relegates South African history and its leaders to derivatives of the American 'originals'.

The frenzied celebration of protest and defiance depicted near the end of the video also reveals the underlying nature of the relationship between AUAA and those who would benefit from its intervention. Filmed in New York's Washington Square Park, the closing moments of the video show American and British musicians fist-pumping in unison. These images are intercut with those of thousands of black South Africans who seem to have taken up the *Westerners'* cause by *toyi-toyi*ing in the streets.[13] But who is dancing with whom? Who is dancing for whom? At first glance, the rhythm of movement and the beat of the song make it appear that protesting black South Africans are dancing with the predominantly white group of American artists.

However, a closer look reveals a fundamental difference between the two groups. AUAA performers are passionately celebrating injustice overcome while the South Africans are resisting ongoing injustice. Frequently, smiles appear on the faces of the AUAA performers. The Western artists revel and dance as if the political change they seek has already been achieved. Indeed, while government sanctioned racial discrimination had been overcome in 1985 New York, it raged on in 1985 Johannesburg. The faces of the South African protestors are framed in close-up less frequently. When we do see them, they are grim and determined. As a result, the AUAA performance loses some of its political potency when read in the context of celebrity, celebration and the post-Civil Rights safety of an imperfect, but relatively stable and racially inte-grated society. Perhaps these final images are AUAA's snapshots of what South Africa could and, to some degree, would become: another 'Western' nation dedicated to racial tolerance and a relatively free and stable cultural and economic marketplace. My objective is not to pine for the radical 1980s or advocate for the return of political radicalism to ANC policy. Rather I urge us to remember that a specific kind of radicalism worked within South Africa long before the arrival of international anti-apartheid activists, and that traces of that particular radicalism still remain, lest we succumb to the narrative that South Africa has always been part of the Western family of nations.

Conclusion

While one can in part correctly attribute some changes in South Africa to Van Zandt's efforts, the project rested on the long-held premise of a beneficent West acting on behalf of a somehow needy Africa (in this case a wayward South Africa in need of the West's morally enlightened perspectives on race)[14] Recognising the asymmetry of power inherent in a foreign-instigated benefit for Africa, AUAA sought to educate its audience about apartheid through an innovative array of media platforms. Unity and solidarity were key components to the success of the project. However, through the performance of a static and cohesive anti-apartheid sentiment, 'Sun City' contributed to a conflation of the Civil Rights Movement in the US and anti-apartheid activism in South Africa. The differences between these movements need to be foregrounded, not obscured, for to leave the video on its own terms risks mistaking the good intentions and political success of the Van Zandt project for proof of a fundamental sameness between the two nations and South African dependence on US goodwill. Without critical inquiry, we risk reading projects like 'Sun City' teleologically. They appear as discrete units of culture that show us purportedly clear evidence of the linear progression toward apartheid's end and mistakenly suggest that the momentum toward a Westernised model of protest was ineluctable rather than a result of specific political events and choices.

NOTES

1 Media personality, or software video instrument mixer and sampler for realtime performances
2 The 'Sun City' music video can be viewed in its entirety at: http://www.youtube.com/watch?v=OjWENNe29qc (accessed 11 August 2010).
3 For a brief biography of all 54 participants see Marsh, 1985: 91-95.
4 For a reading of Appadurai in a South African political context see O'Brien, 2001: 41.
5 See also Reddy (1999) for a useful history of the anti-apartheid movement (AAM). The economic sustainability of the South African state throughout the 1970s and much of the following decade speaks to the patchwork nature of both the economic sanctions and the cultural boycott. Conservative Western leaders like Ronald Reagan and Margaret Thatcher, while denouncing apartheid rhetorically, fought against the full implementation of the boycotts politically.
6 The apartheid regime banned the ANC and other resistance parties and forced them to operate in exile until February 1990 when negotiations over a transition to multi-racial democracy gained momentum.
7 I have summarised these tenets of the ANC cultural boycott policy based on a variety of position papers and speeches by Masekela. These tenets were challenged over time and not adhered to uniformly. By 1989, ANC party leaders recognised the difficulty of maintaining an absolute boycott. The ANC addresses a less stringent policy in ANC Department of Arts and Culture (1990).
8 Anecdotally, when I have explained my research to curious friends and fellow scholars, some

would chant the 'Sun City' chorus back to me as a smiling response. However, subsequent conversation most often revealed little factual knowledge about Sun City beyond the slogan.

9 Bophuthatswana was one of the apartheid regime's 'independent homelands', a purportedly sovereign country according to the South African government. In an effort to attain racial homogeneity, the government forcibly relocated thousands of black South Africans to one of ten such homelands during apartheid based on their ethnic/tribal affiliations. Sol Kerzner, the white South African entrepreneur, exploited Bop's quasi-sovereign status to develop Sun City and provide a workaround to the cultural boycott, for as an 'independent' state, Bop was not subject to the conservative laws in South Africa prohibiting gambling, nudity, prostitution, and interracial performances. See Jones, P. S. (1999) and Knight, R. (1984).

10 Demme would later win a Best Director Oscar for another work at the intersection of art and social conscience, the feature film, *Philadelphia*. Van Zandt discusses the production of the video in (Marsh 1985).

11 See Nixon (1994): 77-97 for how the conflation of these political ideologies operated in several big-budget American films about apartheid.

12 O'Brien notes how the designation of 'black' works as primarily a *political* category and not a racial one, within both the anti-apartheid movement and the Black Consciousness Movement. The definition of blackness as a political concept is contentious as evidenced by the debates in both the USA and South Africa over how (or even if) non-black people might contribute to the eradication of institutional racism.

13 *Toyi-toyi* is a Southern African dance that typically includes militaristic high stepping, rhythmic stomps and choral calls and responses. The dance gained notoriety during the apartheid era for its role in the political protests of NP policies. See *Amandla!* (2003) for examples of the dance in action.

14 The 'Sun City' song and video were banned within South Africa. However, ANC leaders in exile, like Barbara Masekela, publicly praised AUAA for its adoption and promotion of the ANC's position on the cultural boycott. One of Sun City's entertainment producers confirmed for me that the release of the song detrimentally affected the resort's image. For a foreign tourist, a visit to Sun City had become something of a political act.

BIBLIOGRAPHY

Amandla! A Revolution in Four Part Harmony (2003) [DVD] directed by Lee Hirsch, Los Angeles: Lions Gate.

ANC Department of Arts and Culture (1990) 'An Internal Memo on the Cultural Boycott', 4 November 1990, South African History Archive, AL2457.H.5.10.7., University of the Witwatersrand, Johannesburg.

Appadurai, A. (1996) *Modernity at Large: Cultural Dimensions of Globalization* (Minneapolis: University of Minnesota Press).

Barnard, R. (2001) 'Contesting Beauty' in S. Nuttall, S. and C. Michael eds, *Senses of Culture: South African Cultural Studies* (Oxford: Oxford University Press), 344-362.

Biko, S. (1986) *I Write What I Like* (San Francisco: Harper & Row).

British Institute of Human Rights (1976) *The Human Rights Review, Volumes 1-3* (Oxford: Oxford University Press).

Feldman, H. Former Manager of Entertainment, Sun International, personal interview with the author, 6 July 2009.

Huddleston, T. (1990) *Makhalipile - The Dauntless One: Archbishop Trevor Huddleston Talks about His Life and Work* (Cape Town: Mayibuye Books).

Jones, P. S. (1999) 'From "Nationhood" to Regionalism to the North West Province: "Bophuthatswananess" and the Birth of the "New" South Africa', *African Affairs*, 98, 393: 509-534.

'Keynote Address by Cde Barbara Masekela at the Lusaka Regional Cultural Workshop' (1988) 5 December 1988, South African History Archive, AL2457.H.5.10.7., University of the Witwatersrand, Johannesburg.

Knight, R. (1984) 'Black Dispossession in South Africa: The Myth of Bantustan Independence', [online] available at: http://richardknight.homestead.com/bophuthatswana.html (accessed 30 March 2010).

Mandela, N. (1986) *Nelson Mandela: The Struggle is My Life - His Speeches and Writings* (New York: Pathfinder Press).

Marsh, D. (1985) *Sun City by Artists United Against Apartheid: The Making of the Record* (New York: Cloverdale Press).

Masekela, B. (1986) 'Isolate Apartheid Culture', *Rixaka*, 3: 7-9, available at: http://disa.nu.ac.za/index.php?option=com_displaydc&recordID=Rin386.1684.811X.000.003.1986.5 (accessed 30 March 2010).

Masekela, B. (1988) 'Culture in Another South Africa', *Rixaka*, 4: 18-21.

Ndebele, N. (2006) *Rediscovery of the Ordinary: Essays on South African Literature and Culture* (Scottsville: University of KwaZulu-Natal Press).

Nixon, R. (1994) *Homelands, Harlem and Hollywood : South African Culture and the World Beyond* (New York: Routledge).

O'Brien, A. (2001) *Against Normalisation: Writing Radical Democracy in South Africa* (Durham: Duke University Press).

Reddy, E. S. (1999) 'AAM and the United Nations' available online at: http://www.sahistory.org.za/pages/library-resources/official%20docs/anti-apartheid-movement/aam-un-partners.htm ,accessed 23 May 2010.

Spector, J. B. (2004) 'Non-Traditional Diplomacy: Cultural, Academic, and Sports Boycotts and Change in South Africa' in Mills, G. and Sidiropoulos, G. (eds) *New Tools for Reform and Stability: Sanctions, Conditionalities and Conflict Resolution* (Johannesburg: South African Institute of International Affairs): 167-88.

'Sun City' by Artists United Against Apartheid [music video] available online at: http://www.youtube.com/watch?v=OjWENNe29qc accessed 11 August 2010.

Ullestad, N. (1987) 'Rock and Rebellion: Subversive Effects of Live Aid and "Sun City"', *Popular Music*, 6, 1: 67-76.

Ownership & Power
Debate & discourse around the subcultural phenomenon of Die Antwoord

SARAH WOODWARD

Prologue

The scene: Backsberg Wine Estate in Stellenbosch, in the Western Cape. Summer, Saturday the 18th December. There are four groups performing as part of the Sonic Summer festival: They are Locnville, Jax Panik, Goldfish and Die Antwoord. Die Antwoord have top billing, and I am here waiting anxiously for the chance to finally see this group perform live. The Goldfish set ends, and the crowd starts to chant. The Vuzu presenter has left the stage sobbing 'This job is hard', and her co-presenter looks eager to join her. This is not a friendly crowd. This is a menacing crowd, and they want blood. An image appears on the screen, it is the face of Leon Botha, a Cape Town artist and one of the oldest survivors of Progeria. His face is magnified onto a screen over ten metres high, and he stares at the audience, blinking slowly. Over the loud speakers there is a low rumbling chanting, a recording of Tibetan throat singers. The effect is chilling. The antic- ipation in the crowd is palpable. People are whispering things like 'Come on', Where are they?' And still we wait. It has been five minutes, then ten, and the tension is building. Suddenly there is a puff of smoke and the lights change to vivid yellow and red, and there they are in white tracksuit with pointy white hoods. Ninja, Yo-Landi Visser and DJ Hi- Tek. Ninja is tall. A cranky-looking guy with a Mohican and bad tattoos. Yo-Landi is tiny, with the ugliest hairstyle I have ever seen, while DJ Hi-Tek remains in the back- ground, masked. They are ferocious, and launch into 'Enter the Ninja' the first song to garner attention on the internet. The crowd bellows along with Ninja and so do I, we bounce up and down as one pushing and shoving – it is exhilarating. It is mad. It is dangerous. It is Die Antwoord.[1]

Introduction

This paper seeks to frame notions of identity, persona and ownership in the debate surrounding the subcultural phenomenon that is Die Antwoord, by analysing the performance identity of the band and deconstructing the elements that have given rise to their relatively short journey to global fame. I shall unpack the subcultural signifiers that have been appropriated by Die

Antwoord in order to illustrate their immense appeal among the internet community, and to illuminate a societal fascination both with the Carnival-esque and violence. Die Antwoord are, as the 21st century cliché would have it: an internet phenomenon. The band's name translated means 'The Answer'. They are a trio, made up of Ninja, Yo-Landi Vi$$er and DJ Hi-Tek. Their website has this to say about them in the 'about' section:

> *For those who don't know yet* Die Antwoord *are a futuristic rap-rave crew from South Africa who represent a fresh new style called ZEF.* Die Antwoord *crew is made up of zef rap master NINJA, fre$ futuristic (sic) rich bitch ¥O-LANDI VI$$ER and the mysterious beat monster DJ HI-TEK.*[2]

They describe their musical style as 'Zef', as Ninja says in an online interview with Michael Mechanic on the website Mother Jones:

> Zef is South African underdog kind of style. Zef has been an insult for long in South Africa. It means you're like a piece of shit. So not really bling. It's seen as an embarrassment… We've got like different styles, but it's like that too-fast-too-furious, WWF lifestyle. A kid wearing a 50 Cent t-shirt in North Africa for me is fokken zef. People say trashy; it's not really trashy. It's not having money, but still fokken having style. So we kind of embraced that.[3]

The YouTube video for their song 'Enter the Ninja' has garnered over 8.9 million 'hits' since January 2010, as of 4 January 2011. In this year, Die Antwoord have gone from being entirely unknown and having a few videos on the internet to touring the USA, most of Europe and recently performing in Japan (I have been following the tour on Facebook).[4] They also released an album through Cherry tree/Interscope Records in October 2010. Their trajectory from obscurity to notoriety has been incredibly fast and is an example of how the internet is changing the way an audience accesses, applauds and shares information that is exciting to them. The rise of Die Antwoord echoes the rise of the social networking phenomena and can be used as a lens to discuss performance identity, the 'mainstreaming' of subculture and the interactive nature of audience reception on the internet.

Performing identity

> *If the shaping of life and character is not only the highest art but one which all can practice, then aesthetics should pay closer attention to the concept of self-styling (Shusterman 2000).*

The first mention of Die Antwoord on Twitter was by Katy Perry when she posted the lyrics to 'Enter the Ninja'. This was followed by tweets from Fred Durst, and actor Jake Gyllenhaal (Coetzer, 19 Sept 2010). Ninja and Yo-Landi speak about their initial reaction to the popularity of their video:

Q: February 3, 2010 is the day the videos went everywhere. What was that day like for you?

Yo-Landi: It was messed up.

Q: Did you leave your computer that week?

Ninja: We just left to go to the bathroom and then came back. Or when the food ran out after the third day. We just laid down on the floor and looked at the sky and then went and looked at the computer again.

Yo-Landi: When you have like 5,000 emails in your inbox you just give up eventually. I didn't know what to do.

The common thread that has appeared on many message boards and chat rooms is that Die Antwoord are a 'work of genius, a brilliant, sardonic take on the stereotypical idiosyncrasies of low class, and also low-in-class, South Africans living in poor drug-, alcohol- and criminal-infested suburbs where profanity is part of everyday speech and punctures each sentence like a knife to the stomach' (Nagel 2010). Nagel is just one of many commentators on the net writing about and discussing Die Antwoord. Here, Ryan Dombal on 12 February says: 'Considering the mix of absurdity, genuine talent, and impressive production values, you can't help but think "are these guys for real?"' And it's that curiosity that made me temporarily obsessed with Die Antwoord on first glance; I spent a solid hour following links and browsing message boards for clues' (Dombal 2010).

One of the first articles to appear on the internet that revealed the 'true' identity of Die Antwoord was 'Die Antwoord And 'Zef' – South Africa's Biggest Non-Existent Scene', written on the 9 February 2010 by Jaimie Hodgson. The article reveals that Ninja is actually a man called Watkins Tudor Jones, who has been a frontman for a number of different bands over the years, most recently a group called Max Normal. This is part of his reaction to the revelation: 'Whilst it's kind've ruined my week that neither "zef" or Die Antwoord exist in this grey February real world, or at least if they do "exist" technically-speaking, that aren't what they claim to be, it hasn't stopped me watching 'Enter The Ninja' at least five times a day, every day since Monday' (Hodgson 2010).

The first comment in the Comments section to this article was: Scan2001 [Visitor] //February 10 2010 at 23:32 'My world is shattered, but I still love them' (Hodgson 2010). The comments debate continued, with many South Africans defending: (Moose [Visitor] //March 18 2010 at 11:15 'Fake? Er... that's not quite what I'd call them. They have captured something unusual and great about SA culture. Power to them' (Hodgson 2010).

This debate appears in many different incarnations whenever someone posts an article about Die Antwoord I was gripped with the same obsession as Ryan Dombal (mentioned above), and trawled the internet for information on what was 'real' about the group. I wanted to be the one who was 'in the know'. My obsession with veracity echoed the discourse I discovered in my research.

In an online article entitled 'Is Die Antwoord blackface?' written by Andy Davis, Rustum Kozain writes in the Comments section:

For me the depth of invention is probably the most troublesome, because it reveals an anthropological bent: it is not a persona that has emerged in any organic way, such as our identities change in different environments; rather, it is a persona invented but clearly based on detailed anthropological study. (Kozain 2010)

It is this *persona* of Ninja that Kozain refers to which 'troubles' critics of Die Antwoord_the most. Ninja describes himself on the opening track of their debut album 'o', (available as a download from their website in 2009 – Musica 2010 Online) as being all the cultures of South Africa 'f★★★ed into one' (YouTube, August 2010), and what has emerged is not the rainbow nation, non-racist idealism of a country united, which is an image perpetuated by the South African media. 'Rainbow Nation' is a term that was used by the Archbishop Desmond Tutu to describe post-apartheid South Africa and he has appeared on SABC TV (South African Broadcasting Corporation) in a number of slots in which he referred to South Africans as the 'rainbow people of God' (Baines 1998). The construction of a multi-racial identity in post-apartheid South Africa is continuously reinforced through the idea of a rainbow nation, as Baines writes:

> As public broadcaster, the SABC has apparently assumed some responsibility for communicating the message of national unity. This is epitomised by the repetitive jingle on SABC-TV: 'Simunye – We are one.' The content of certain radio and television programmes, and even some private sector funded advertisements convey the message of nation building. For instance, South African Breweries who are the chief sponsors of the national soccer team (the Bafana Bafana) have promoted Castle Lager with the slogan 'One Beer, One Nation'. As cultural carriers, the media have been crucial in disseminating the rhetoric of 'rainbowism'. (Baines 1998)

But within this ideal of the 'rainbow nation', government policy has also been to reinforce notions of 'multi-culturalism', seen in the constitution emphasising the rights of individuals over the rights of ethnic groups or race, but still allowing those individuals to operate from within the context of their ethnicity or racial grouping (Baines 1998). This uneasy relationship between the 'rainbow nation' (celebrating unity) and 'multi-culturalism' (celebrating diversity) is perhaps responsible for the uneasiness of South African identity. As Ninja says:

> South Africans generally, the culture – this is gonna be a little controversial what I'm going to say here – the entire culture is insecure a little bit. Americans, they're not insecure. You'll see the French also and they're like, 'Fuck everyone; we're the centre of the world.' We're kind of inspired by that attitude. There's cool fokken shit in South Africa. But the people, as a culture, as a whole, they haven't got a fokken style. Then we check in and we get to present it and stylize it with full-force. (Mechanic 2010)

In this re-imagining of a South African identity and the way that they portray themselves onstage and in their videos, Die Antwoord_have embraced aspects of what Stallybrass and White call 'carnivalesque', a term used to describe those aspects of culture that were not central to the emerging bourgeoisie of the 19th century, but belonged in the world of the carnival (1986: 383): that is, in a world where performance was central, reinvention of notions of the self could be explored, and a theatricalisation of identity could exist. 'It encoded all that which the proper bourgeois must strive *not to be* in order to preserve a stable and "correct sense of self"' (ibid: 387). This schism is reflected in Cultural Studies as the relationship between mainstream popular culture and what is termed 'subculture'. Subcultural studies are concerned with the relationship between the familiar and stable 'centre' and the novel, and unstable 'margins'. As Stuart Hall says in his lecture entitled 'Race: The floating signifier': "Every culture has a kind of order of classification built into it, and this seems to stabilize culture" (1997: online video). Many writers emphasise the distinction between parent and child/ young and old as the most significant factor in what should be classified as subcultural. Hebdige asserts that the relationship of subculture to mainstream is such that the 'youth' are in reaction to the discourses endemic to the centre, in order to mark the 'transition from childhood to maturity' (Hebdige 1979: 442).

In this state of reaction Die Antwoord are working with the subcultural signifiers available to them in South Africa, where they have renegotiated race, culture and class in opposition to the mainstream notions of South African white identity. The members of the band are white, well-educated and in the case of Jones (Ninja), English speaking. Die Antwoord have appropriated cultural aspects of Afrikanerdom, gangster identity and 'poor whites' of both cultures (English and Afrikaans), and have recreated a background story for themselves; a mythology in which they refuse to acknowledge that any *appropriation* has taken place. There is no acknowledgement of any other reality other than the one that has been carefully constructed out of these signifiers. When asked about whether or not Die Antwoord could be considered satire, Ninja replies: "Not really. I think it's just kind of new. A lot of people say that but it's not really our thing. It's very personal to us. It's just how we are. We've done other stuff before but I didn't really know what my fokken zone was. Then when it hit me with Die Antwoord it was like, 'This is the fokken shit. We can go full-force into this'" (Mechanic 2010).

To more fully understand the construction of these identities, I will firstly briefly explore the context of Afrikaner culture, followed by an investigation into what is known as 'Coloured' culture (a term in South Africa used to describe those of mixed race) and then the notion of 'poor whites'.

Afrikaans is spoken by 13.3 per cent of South Africa's population of 48 million (Census 2001). The language is spoken by white Afrikaners as well as by the 'Coloured' population mainly living in the Western Cape area. Afrikaans is officially the world's youngest language; a language that was known initially as 'Cape Dutch' or 'Kitchen Dutch'; both derogatory descriptions (Drennan 1920: 964). Afrikaans was in danger of dying out in South Africa after the Boer War, when children at school were forced to wear placards saying 'I am a Donkey' if they spoke Dutch (Hopkins 2006: 31). However, from 1905 onwards, Afrikaners began to start their own private

Fig 1 *Ninja and Yo-Landi Vi$$er (Reproduced with permission of Die Antwoord)*

schools, and in the intervening years Afrikaans nationalism grew, resulting in the Christian Nationalist education system (for whites only) and forced conscription (Hopkins 2006: 31-48). Part of the culture of Afrikaans music was something known as the 'Lekkerliedjie' or 'nice song', which is, according to Ingrid Byerly as cited in Pat Hopkin's book *Voëlvry*, a 'bland form of easy listening with lyrics centred around flora, fauna and geographical locations' (Hopkins 2006: 35). The Voëlvry movement was born in reaction to this music, during Apartheid in the 1980s. It was a movement that started out on 4 April 1989 at the Club Countdown on Bree Street in downtown Johannesburg and it evolved into a musical tour that criss-crossed the country (Hopkins, 2006:14). Voëlvry was an ensemble of artists such as Bernoldus Niemand, Andre Letoit, Johannes Kerkorrel and Koos Kombuis. As Letoit says:

> We did not merely dislike our parents, we despised them, loathed them, we wanted to torture and hurt and discredit them entirely. We had come to that terrible place in a neglected child's life when he loses the final vestige of respect for his abusive elders. (Hopkins 2006: 19)

Voëlvry were the forerunners of Alternative Afrikaans music, as Kombuis writes: '… there are still a myriad young Afrikaans music acts on the scene, many of whom draw inspiration from us old guys who "started it all"' (Hopkins 2006: 234). Ironically, Kombuis wrote an article in the *Rapport* newspaper against Die Antwoord where he writes: 'Ek wil nie vir hulle pa staan nie en ek distansieer my van hul nihilistiese filosofie … Ek veroordeel hulle nie op morele gronde, soos die kerk sou doen nie, maar ek verwerp hulle op estetiese gronde. As jy verby die skok en tinsel kyk, is hulle eenvoudig vervelig'

(Kombuis, 21 February 2010). [Translation: I don't want to be their father, and I am distancing myself from their philosophy of nihilism … I don't condemn them on moral grounds, as the church would do, but I reject them on aesthetic grounds. If you get past the shock and the tinsel, they are simply boring.]

And Ninja responded with: 'Koos Kombuis se ma's se poes' (Koos Kombuis' mothers c★★t) live at the Sonic Summer Festival in December 2010. I was there, I heard him say it.

Die Antwoord rap mostly in Afrikaans and heavily Afrikaans accented English, and they swear almost entirely in Afrikaans. Yo-Landi comes onto stage yelling "fok julle naaiers" (f★★k you f★★kers) and in interviews both their dialogue is punctuated with the word 'fok' or 'fokken'. One of their songs is titled 'Jou Ma se poes in vispaste jar" (Your mother's c★★t in a fishpaste jar), which in translation becomes very a shocking thing to say, but is almost an idiomatic expression among lower class Coloured Afrikaners (also known as 'bergies'). They are using the Afrikaans language to defy the historical construction of Afrikaans as a tool of nationalism and traditionalism, and are revelling in its vulgarity.

The Coloured identity is a result of construction of the Coloured community in South Africa and 'the spatialization of race and class through apartheid social and spatial engineering' (Hammett, 2009). There are nuances of coloured gangster identity in the adornment of Ninja's body; his tattoos are crudely drawn, as if they were hand-made, which echoes the prison tattoos of gangsters in the Cape Flats. The tattoo on his right arm is of Evil Boy, which is a symbol of the 28's gang, in the middle of his chest he has the symbol representing the 27's, and on his right breast he has a tattoo of Richie Rich, a symbol of the 26's (Davis: February 2010). The numbers gangs are some of the most cut-throat and ruthless gangs in the country, and they have created elaborate and violent initiation rituals for recruiting young members. Ninja is signifying his dangerousness by using these symbols, as he says: "If you break into the house that I live in, you're pretty much fokked. Because, like, you're not the enemy. I'm the enemy" (Mechanic 2010).

In terms of class, Die Antwoord have drawn on the visual stimulus of the group of people in South Africa known as 'poor whites' as seen through the lens of such artists as Roger Ballen and David Goldblatt. Roger Ballen's photographs from the late 'seventies to the 'nineties are portraits of poor people living in small communities in South Africa. Robin Cook describes Ballen's work: 'It opens us up to those uncertain, shocking and frighteningly banal aspects of the waking dream, twitching between animal and human, the clean and the unclean, the animate and the inanimate, the lived and the imagined, the natural and the performed' (Cook 2010). David Goldblatt is also a photographer working from the late seventies and his work is described thus: '… he reveals a much more complex portrait, including the intricacies and banalities of daily life in all aspects of society…Goldblatt's photographs are an intimate portrayal of a culture plagued by injustice' (Gergel 2010). That Die Antwoord has links to both artists from their website reveals the influence these photographers have on the visual aspects of the group's identity.

The final cultural signifier that makes up the performance identity of Die Antwoord is the word 'Zef'. In an article entitled 'The dummies guide to Zef', Magdel Fourie writes about how the origins of Zef are unclear and that the word is 'presumably derived from a car which was quite popular in South Africa until the early 1970s: the Ford Zephyr. The Zephyr later became a favourite among owners who liked to soup-up their engines and add fat tyres with shiny rims' (Fourie, 16 February 2010). The closest approximation to the word Zef is 'white trash', but it is a much more insulting term. Yo-Landi Vi$$er has been quoted as saying: 'It's associated with people who soup their cars up and rock gold and shit. Zef is, you're poor but you're fancy. You're poor but you're sexy, you've got style'(Hoby 2010).

Thus, the subversion of Afrikaans from a language that was born out a fervent nationalism to a vulgar crudity, coupled with the dangerous aspects of gangsterism and the embracing of a class that is traditionally marginalised and rejected by mainstream South Africa, make up the various aspects of Die Antwoord's performance identity, emphasising the carnivalesque – everything the mainstream aspires *not to be*. And the result is a violent one. *My* experience of their live performance was part exhilaration and part real fear. The appeal of Die Antwoord is part of a fascination with the 'other'. As Goldstein notes:

For the rebellious young, the mere fact that the topic is taboo is reason enough for engagement. Their curiosity about the forbidden is satisfied, and they learn to manage anxiety and defeat fear by distorting and exaggerating reality. At the same time, they bond with others, story tellers, and peers by sharing intense emotional experiences (Goldstein 1999: 276).

Debate and discourse

Unlike in classical film theory, reception theorists agree that the spectator's interaction with the text is a complex one, and viewers or receivers are constantly negotiating and renegotiating their relationship to the 'text' (Hall 1990: 508). In this instance the primary text is the music and videos of Die Antwoord, and the site of re-negotiation is the internet or 'interwebs' in the words of Ninja. If *meaning* is a constantly shifting site of common culture and associations, then the interactive nature of the internet acts as a site to contend with, debate and offer alternative ways of 'reading' the primary source material.

To illustrate, let us consider a particularly intriguing debate that occurred on the website Africa is a Country (available at http://africasacountry.com) between two prominent voices, Rustum Kozain and Andy Davis. What follows is a description of the debate, followed by an analysis of the significance of the exchange.

Kozain wrote an article which was put on the website by the webmaster (Kameraad Mhambi). In the article Kozain asserts that Die Antwoord are Blackface, with all the implications of satire, parody and as he writes: 'misdirected appropriation'. Andy Davis in the Comments section retorts with a rather heated response to the article in which he accuses Kozain of having done very little research and of being guilty of 'academic discourse'. Kozain counters with a rebuttal defending his position and refuting the academic discourse label as being evidence of resistance to change. Davis in his turn counters with evidence of complicit knowledge of gang identity, whereas Kozain responds with a 1,486-word reply wherein he deconstructs his argument with Davis and seeks counter arguments to refute Davis' claims. Davis replies witheringly ('I wish I had your time, Rustum') and ends by telling him to 'lighten up'. Within this exchange there are three throwaway comments which change the nature of the discourse: (1). Davis asks Kozain if he (Davis) still has his (Kozain's) Dillinger LP.(2). Kozain is puzzled by the comment and uses it as further evidence of Davis' lack of focus. (3). Davis replies by telling how he once DJ'd with someone called Rustum and stole his LP. To which Kozain replies with one line: "LOL, Andy, yes it's the same Rustum", which ends the 'conversation' (http://africasacountry.com).

This exchange is fascinating for a number of reasons. Firstly, the debate is being waged on the 'text' of Die Antwoord and the opponents are seeking ways of 'decoding' the message inherent therein. Kozain frames his understanding and negotiation with the text in terms of blackface, a position which reveals his grappling with notions of identity and society. If, as Hall asserts, the signifier of race works like a language, that is, through constantly shifting meanings in relation to cultural signifiers which can never be fixed in time (as we have discussed in the previous section), then the idea that Die Antwoord operates on the level of blackface is one which is appropriate to the question of identity and race in contemporary South Africa (Hall 1997, online video). Blackface operates at the level of the carnival, but it positions 'blackness' as the other and whiteness as the perceived norm. Much of the global idea of subculture is drawn from traditionally 'black' culture (Rastafarianism, rap, etc) and I concede that much of the power of Die Antwoord has been their appropriation of the 'blackness' of subculture. But I disagree with Kozain that it is done with a view to parody. I believe the myth that Die Antwoord has created in their performance identity has become so integrated into every part of their performance that it loses the knowingness of parody.

The second reason that this debate has such significance is that it highlights Foucault's notion of the discursive power of language to overcome and sublimate counter argument, revealing the dominant 'voices' in the critical analysis of Die Antwoord (Foucault 1984). Moseley asserts that the fight for status is one of the primal instincts of man (Moseley 2005:45). If one takes into consideration that all human interaction fundamentally comes down to the 'jostling' for status within a group, then the debate becomes an illustration of a fight for dominance and ownership of the interpretation of Die Antwoord. It echoes Dombal's question of 'are these guys for real?' – a question that I also have been intrigued by. Kozain's use of formal language is attacked by Davis as being academic (an increasingly common insult in the South African public forum). Kozain counters with a barrage of text that appears to be an attempt to dominate through the sheer number of words he uses. Davis rebuffs this by introducing a common experience, that of DJ-ing together, and it is at this point that Kozain retreats from his attack. What this status play indicates is the obsession with veracity that humans grapple with. These voices indicate the power struggle intrinsic to this 'obsession with veracity' that there is a belief that through *understanding* one can *own* and the struggle reveals that by its very nature Die Antwoord have deliberately placed themselves beyond that understanding. Otherwise it wouldn't provide such fuel for debate. The Kozain/ Davis encounter was the most eloquent of the discussions and it is why I chose to highlight it. But this 'comment war' is by no means an isolated incident. Much of the commentary, whenever someone publishes an article on the web about the band, is whether or not Die Antwoord are '*real*', who are they *really*, and what do they *really* mean.

In reply, ironically, Die Antwoord do not have that answer. The group have re-mythologized their identities and operate within a subcultural context, and they have done so deliberately but without ever once acknowledging that they have done so. They have taken self-styling to a level that integrates what Shusterman describes as the paradox of 'spontaneous nature and intentional striving … and the unformulable details of actual practice' (Shusterman 2000: 217). Die Antwoord refuses to answer the question about what is *real*. The official information on their website is evidence of their absorption of the personal mythology they have re-created:

> NINJA didn't do very good at school because all he did the whole time was write raps and smoke zol. After NINJA lied and cheated his way through high school, he moved to Alexandra Township in Johannesburg to smoke zol with the rastas. NINJA stayed in Alexandra in 19th Street down by the river for a few years living off boiled cabbage and zol. During this time NINJA started a rap group called The Original Evergreens which had a heavy stoned alien rastas in space vibe. (www.dieantwoord.com/about)

The 'facts' they have created for themselves have been woven into a new narrative to describe Ninja's existence. Every interaction on the internet with the public upholds the personas they have created, and the defiance they show in being 'unknowable' is part of the appeal of the group. And it is in the *actual practice* where Die Antwoord finds the integration of striving and spontaneity. As far as the kids watching are concerned, this is what it is all about: Everyone's smiles shining in the dark. Everyone around me soaking wet from sweat with hair hanging in strings over manic, starry-eyes. Brilliant. And all-of-a-sudden everyone wants to learn Afrikaans. How did this happen? I wonder' (Snyders, 14 August 2010).

Shusterman writes in a response to van den Haag's assertions that 'the gratifications of popular culture are spurious':

> Perhaps the most straightforward interpretation and justification of the charge of spuriousness is that popular art's art alleged gratifications are not real because they are only superficially and never deeply felt…but the experience of rock music, which can be so intensely absorbing and powerful that it is likened to spiritual possession, gives the lie to such a charge … (Shusterman 2000: 38)

NOTES

1 A first-hand account of the Sonic Summer Festival, S. Woodward
2 www.dieantwoord.com, accessed 2 January 2011
3 (Mechanic 11 October 2010, online)
4 www.facebook.com/DieAntwoord

REFERENCES

Books

Baines, Gary (1998), *The Rainbow Nation? Identity and Nation building in Post Apartheid South Africa*, available online at: <http://motspluriels.arts.uwa.edu.au/MP798gb.html> accessed 4 January 2011]

Census 2001 Available online at: Statistics South Africa. <http://www.statssa.gov.za/Publications HTML/Report-03-02-042001/html/Report-03-02-042001_18.html?gInitialPosX=10px&gInitialPosY=10px&gZoomValue=100> , accessed 2 February 2010

Coetzer, Diane (2010), 'A gangsta's paradise', *Sunday Times Magazine*: 19 September.

Cook, Robert (2010), 'About: Roger Ballen', available online at: <www.rogerballen.com>, accessed 4 January 2011.

Davis, Andy (2010), *Is Die Antwoord Blackface? Comments Section*, available online at <http://africasacountry.com >, accessed 30 August 2010.

Die Antwoord, available online at < www.dieantwoord.com>, accessed 2 January 2011.

Dombal, Ryan (2010), *Who the hell are* Die Antwoord, 12 February, available online at <http://pitchfork.com/features/articles/7766-die-antwoord/>, accessed 2 January 2011.

Drennan, C.M. (1929), 'Cockney English and Kitchen Dutch', in Eric Anderson Walker, (ed.) *The Cambridge History of the British Empire Vol. 1* (Cambridge: Cambridge University Press).

Foucault, Michel (1984), 'Space, Power and Knowledge', in Simon During, (ed.) *The Cultural Studies Reader* (London and New York: Routledge).

Fourie, Magdel (2010), *The Dummies guide to Zef*, 16 February, available online at <http://www.news24.com/Entertainment/SouthAfrica/The-Dummies-guide-to-Zef-20100216>, accessed 4 January 2011

Gergel, Joseph. 2010. *About David Goldblatt*, available online at < http://www.goodmangallery.com/artists/davidgoldblatt>, accessed 4 January 2011.

Hall, Stuart (1997), 'Race: The Floating Signifier', Lecture delivered at Goldsmiths College of London. Transcript: Sut Jhalley, Media Education Foundation, available online at <http://www.mediaed.org/assets/products/407/transcript_407.pdf>, accessed 30 August 2010

Hall, Stuart (1990), 'Cultural studies and its Theoretical Legacies', in During, Simon (ed.) *The Cultural Studies Reader* (London and New York: Routledge).

Hammett, Daniel (2009), Book review of *Gangs, Politics and Dignity in Cape Town*, by Steffen Jensen, available online at<http:// afraf.oxfordjournals.org, accessed 4 January 2011

Hebdige, Dick (1979), 'The Function of Subculture' in During, Simon (ed.), *The Cultural Studies Reader* (London and New York: Routledge).

Hoby, Hermione (2010), 'Die Antwoord: "Are we awful or the best thing in the universe?"' *The Observer*, 12 September, available online at <http://www.guardian.co.uk/music/2010/sep/12/die-antwoord-music-feature>, accessed 2 January 2011.

Hodgson, Jamie 2010, Die Antwoord And 'Zef' – South Africa's Biggest Non-Existent Scene, 9 February, available online at <http://www.nme.com/blog/index.php?blog=15&title=die_antwoord_and_zef_sooth_ifricah_s_mos&more=1&c=1&tb=1&pb=1>,, accessed 2 January 2011

Hopkins, Pat (2006), *Voëlvry: The movement that rocked South Africa* (Cape Town: Zebra Press, Struik Publishers).

Kombuis, Koos (2010), Die Antwoord *is geen Antwoord nie* (Die Antwoord *are no answer*), 21 February, available online at < http://www.rapport.co.za/Rubrieke/KoosKombuis/Die-Antwoord-is-geen-antwoord-nie-20100220>, accessed 4th January 2011

Kozain, Rustum (2010), *Is* Die Antwoord *Blackface?* Available online at <http://africasa country.com>, accessed 30 August 2010

Mechanic, M. 11 October 2010 Die Antwoord *on cultural overload, evil boy and the meaning of zef.* Available online at < http://motherjones.com/riff/2010/10/die-antwoord-ninja-evil-boy-interview>, accessed 2nd January 2011]

Moseley, Nick (2005), *Acting and Reacting* (London: Nick Hern Books).

Musica (2010), Online Music store. Available at < http://www.musica.co.za/cd/id/600966 1801487/Die_Antwoord-Sos_Zef>, accessed 4January 2011

Nagel, Andrea (2010), *The Zef side of the force*, 12 February, available online at <http://www.times live.co.za/entertainment/article303531.ece>, accessed 23 March 2010

Shusterman, Richard (2000), *Performing Live: Aesthetic Alternatives for the Ends of Art* (London: Cornell University Press).

Snyders, Marilu (2010), 'Afrikaans –in your face- in Japan!' *The Star, Tonight,* 14 August.

Stallybrass, Peter and Allon White (1986), 'Bourgeois Hysteria and the Carnivalesque', in During, Simon (ed.) *The Cultural Studies Reader* (London and New York: Routledge).

YouTube(2010). *www.YouTube.com* , accessed 30 August 2010.

Videos

Enter the ninja, available at < http://www.YouTube.com/watch?v=wc3f4xU_FfQ>, accessed 4 January 2011.

Zef side, available at < http://www.YouTube.com/watch?v=Q77YBmtd2Rw>accessed 4 January 2011.

Evil boy, available at <http://www.YouTube.com/watch?v=vTT6ehC-hdA> accessed 4 January 2011.

'Border-Neutering' Devices in Nigerian Home Video Tradition
A study of Mainframe films

GBEMISOLA ADEOTI

Introduction

Since its debut in 1988 with Isola Ogunsola's *Aje Ni Iya Mi* (My Mother is a Witch), home video film in Nigeria has enjoyed patronage across all social and economic strata nationally and beyond. Its international appeal has been widely acknowledged and well documented by scholars and critics (Okome and Haynes 1996, Larkin 1997, Haynes 1997, Adamu 2004, Jeyifo, 2009). The medium has benefited from modern advancements in technology especially in recording, editing, mass production and screening of people's narratives for consumption by the rest of the world. It is being sustained by its roots in the narrative, performative and oral traditions of the people, while also borrowing from foreign literary and cinematic cultures. Depending on the ethno-cultural background of the producers, Nigerian video films developed from the Yoruba Popular travelling theatre, literary drama in English, the Onitsha Market literary pamphlet tradition, Hausa *Wasan kwaikwayo* and Hausa written literature (*Soyayya* books). The television and radio drama series and photo–plays also provide antecedents that continue to energise the industry. Nigeria is a multi-ethnic and multi-lingual nation with over 250 indigenous languages, most of which have dialectal variations. However, Nigerian video films are mainly produced in major languages such as Hausa, Yoruba, Igbo, Tiv, Edo, Ijaw and Ibibio. Many are also produced in English, the inherited colonial language. In terms of classification, the films are in genres ranging from romantic comedies to adventure films, horror films, magical fantasies, thrillers, detective stories and melodrama.

However, the industry is still contending with a host of visceral problems in addition to preventive and punitive measures being put up by the Nigeria Film and Video Censor's Board (NFVCB), professional guilds and other stakeholders. Quite worrisome is the low quality of many stories and manner of their realisation on the screen. With poor conception and scripting of stories, some film makers pad out a thin story line with long establishing shots, boring irrelevances, daunting digressions and repetitive flashbacks. Some examples are Korede Soyinka's *Alani Kansilor 1&2,* Remi Surutu's *Senami Kerewa* and

26

Monsuru Obadina's *Ire Ayo*. Soyinka's *Alani Kansilor* for instance, features a merrymaking scene of tedious dancing and singing that lasts for over 15 minutes.

Critics have also pointed attention to the fact that by overblowing magic, rituals and murder, with sheer religious bigotry masquerading as evangelism, prompting distortions of African cultural practices, video films sometimes negatively portray the people of Nigeria (Adamu 2004, Ogunleye 2008). To tackle the problems highlighted above, some Nigerian filmmakers have responded with different strategies. In constructing stories, producers are reaching out for those narratives that would appeal to an international audience. Some filmmakers have gone to other countries such as Ghana, Kenya, Uganda and Benin Republic where they are collaborating with their counterparts to produce films. In the specific case of Ghana, Nigerian film producers bring in financial and technical resources, using a combination of Nigerian and Ghanaian artists to roll out titles in rapid succession.[1]

Mainframe films and trans-national (re)presentation

Mainframe Film and Television Production (henceforth Mainframe) is a leading player in Africa's motion pictures industry. It has responded to the challenges of global and local markets with a view to meliorating Africa's marginality in the world cine-market. The organisation believes that it is better to build a formidable popular culture at home before venturing into international markets. Since its establishment in 1992 by Tunde Kelani, a cinematographer with over forty years' experience, Mainframe has produced classics in Yoruba[2] and English (with French subtitles for *Saworo Ide*), most of which have received awards at various international film festivals and other fora such as the African Movie Academy Awards and the Festival of Pan-African Cinema in Ouagadougou (FESPACO).

Before establishing Mainframe, Kelani had worked with Western Nigeria Television and collaborated with members of the Yoruba popular travelling theatre movement as a cameraman in recording their television drama series in the 1970s and 1980s. He was part of the movement's transition from the stage to the celluloid medium as a cinematographer or director in works such as Akin Ogungbe's *Ireke Onibudo*,[3] Ola Omonitan's *Anikura*, Wale Adenuga's *Papa Ajasco*, Jimo Aliu's *Fopomoyo* (Confusion) and Awada Keri Keri Organisation's *Ogun Ajaye* (Victory). Kelani brought these experiences to bear on Mainframe video films which include the three part *Ti Oluwa Ni Ile* (The Earth is the Lord's) (1993), *Ayo Ni Mo Fe* I&II (Joy is my Desire) (1994), *Ko see Gbe* (Hard Nut) (1995), *O le Ku* I & II (Curious Wonder!) (1997), *Saworo Ide* (Brass Bells) (1999), *Agogo Eewo* (Gong of Taboo) (2001) *Thunder Bolt* (2000), *Campus Queen* (2005), *Abeni* I & II (2006), *Narrow Path* (2006) and *Arugba* (Votary Maiden) (2008).

Mainframe sees the film medium as a discursive space in which we can come to greater awareness of the problems of leadership which is widely acknowledged as the bane of Africa's postcolonial history (See Soyinka 1999). It is also a tool for the propagation of culture towards achieving a sense of cultural nationalism. Mainframe features stories that demonstrate the processes of socialising the African child into a responsible, honest and hardworking adult who is expected to shun corruption, materialism, greed, get-rich-quickly-and-by-all-means-possible syndrome and other vices. The organisation also explores folkloric elements and traditional belief systems of the Yoruba to address issues in contemporary politics and governance. Most of these issues, corruption, ethnic distrust, immorality, violence and religious bigotry are not peculiar to Nigeria.

Mainframe films use patterns of communication that rise above linguistic and cultural boundaries. Each film consciously employs devices aimed at tackling the problem of identity and representation by appealing to audiences beyond the boundaries of class, generation, gender, race, religion and other social constructs. The organisation tries to avoid most of the shortcomings identified above in terms of poor scripting, poor audio and visual representations and story-padding as found in a good number of Nigerian films. Rather, it adopts strategies that will enhance the rating of Nigerian video films among local and international patrons and critics.

Trans-border devices in selected Mainframe films

Abeni I & II

In *Abeni* I&II, Mainframe grapples with the problem of communication in foreign and indigenous languages with a view to achieving smooth inter-relations among Africans across geo-cultural boundaries that were erected by colonialism. Indeed, language is one of the major challenges to the trans-national aspirations of Nigerian video film makers. It is often a daunting task to communicate across ethnic and cultural borders in indigenous languages without using subtitles in English. Language in a multi-ethnic country presents phenomenal complexity. While some artistes resort to code-mixing and code-switching, involving English and an indigenous language, some adopt the Pidgin English option while for others, the solution lies in a curious mixture of these possibilities, that is, an indigenous language, pidgin English and standard English.

Abeni is a Yoruba language film, shot in Nigeria and Benin Republic. Yoruba people are found in both countries. While Nigeria was colonised by Britain, Benin Republic was a colony of France, hence the adoption of English and French respectively as official languages countries. Yoruba people who are separated by colonial history, however, find a re-connection in *Abeni*, as the film attempts to break down the barriers of communication across colonial borders.To produce the film, Mainframe collaborated with LAHA productions, a multi-media organisation led by Amzat Abdel Hakim, a Beninnois, which is based in Cotonou, the commercial city of Benin Republic. The film draws artistes across borders: Aboh Macelline Akinocho (Iya Akanni), Nolle

Funmi Agbandegba (Awa) and Amzat Abdel Hakim (Akanni) from Benin Republic feature alongside household names in Nigerian video films such as Jide Kosoko (Chief Bello), Kareem Adepoju (Chief Atiba), Lere Paimo (Baba Awa/Laku) and Bukky Wright (Fati).

The film presents the story of Abeni and Akanni, lovers who encounter and overcome parental hostilities to consummate their love at the end. *Abeni* Part I begins in Badiya, a residential area in Lagos for the low income group, with the 'face me-I-face-you' type of accommodation in order to establish the poor background of Akanni's parents. The image of poverty is immediately contrasted with the serene ambience and well kept lawns of Chief Bello's palatial residence. The Bellos are celebrating the tenth birthday anniversary of Abeni, their daughter. Akanni, the son of Bello's gardener reluctantly joins the celebration. At a tender age, he is already conscious of the class difference. At the celebration, a fight ensues between Akanni and Ogagu, one of the invited kids. Both kids are badly bruised, but more battered is Akanni's father who is sacked from his job for bringing his 'dirty and unruly' child to the upper-class event. Akanni's father relocates to Cotonou, Benin Republic, his country of origin. He dies five years later.

About two decades after the incident, Akanni is seen again. He has struggled through his education and he is now a top official in an accounting firm in Cotonou. He is rich and well connected. He also plays part-time as a musician in a popular night club. Abeni too is ripe for marriage and she is being pressurised by her father to marry Ogagu, the son of his friend, Chief Atiba. The marriage is to strengthen the friendship between Bello and Atiba and perpetuate their business empire, but more importantly designed to get the reckless Ogagu to be more responsible. Ogagu has returned from America after failing to qualify as a lawyer. Abeni rejects this marriage proposal because it is based on material consideration rather than love. Coincidentally, she runs into Akanni, her childhood friend in Cotonou where she goes on a research visit. Old verdant love is rekindled and so sweeping is the new affection between them that Akanni breaks off his engagement with Awa, his fiancée, two weeks before the wedding date.

However, Chief Bello, will not approve of a union between his daughter and Akanni, a foreigner who is also from a poor home, and he tries to frustrate the union. When persuasion fails, he employs blackmail and Akanni is framed for economic crime. The first part ends with Akanni imprisoned only to be released with the help of Abeni's mother who exploits her old love affair with a top prison official. The official is later revealed as the biological father of Abeni. The much-advertised wedding between Ogagu and Abeni ends in fiasco. The bride runs away with the connivance of her father's driver to Cotonou while all guests are anxiously waiting.

In Part II, Akanni and Abeni are married in a humble ceremony in Cotonou, devoid of pomp and parental consent. The marriage is conducted in French, a language that is both strange and familiar to the bride. French is used here to register her alienation and the struggle for inclusion, compelled by her experience of migration and exile. Ogagu, having parted ways with his father after the failed marriage, migrates to Cotonou with his rascally friend, Laku. They take to cyber-crime, defrauding equally fraudulent or simply gullible 'clients' abroad. In a welter of coincidence, Awa, who is Laku's sister, falls in love with Ogagu. Laku is opposed to the affair and to discourage it decisively, he frames Ogagu. But Laku is also caught in the web and both end behind bars for their cyber-crimes. It takes the intervention of Akanni, whom Awa inevitably approaches for help, to get the friends released from detention. They earn their freedom with a promise to sin no more. Ogagu and Awa decide to settle down in marriage. Abeni, who is already pregnant, has just put to bed in Cotonou. That brings her mother and her father to Cotonou in another coincidence. There, Bello finds his lost driver and discovers that Akanni is now rich and married to Abeni, the young mother. The new baby in the arms of Fati (Abeni's mother) tells the story more eloquently. With the new birth, old hostilities are buried. There is reconciliation amidst an atmosphere of merry-making.

In both parts I and II, *Abeni* raises universal issues of love, sex relations, class, migration, and popular youth culture. The film preaches against the desperation for instant riches among those African youths who negatively engage their intellect. The attempt to overcome barriers of communication in a multi-cultural and multi-lingual context in the film is worthy of note. It demonstrates that communication across colonial walls is possible with the use of English, French and dialectal variations of Yoruba language used in Nigeria and Benin. The film deploys visual, gestural and other non-verbal cinematic codes to generate meaning. The experience of Ogagu and Laku at a Restaurant – *Maquis La Vigeur* – in Cotonou is quite illustrative. While Ogagu and Laku speak Yoruba and English, with poor knowledge of French, the two Chefs speak neither English nor Yoruba, but French, apart from their mother tongue. The audience watches with amusement as both sides struggle to cross the linguistic walls to enter into economic relations. The non-French speaking customers are confounded by the menu. Their pronunciation of "rice" and "petit pois" with a Yoruba accent excites laughter.' The Chefs ask for the kind of drinks that Ogagu and Laku want, but drink (*bois*) is pronounced with Yoruba accent as '*Gboa*' like an aggressive punch landing on the cheek of a defenceless victim. *Poisson* is fish in French; to Ogagu, what is being offered publicly is 'poison' in English.Both sides succeed in communicating by resorting to visual and gestural representations.

Narrow Path

Bayo Adebowale's novel, *The Virgin* provided the source text for *Narrow Path*. It is another film that benefits from the border-neutering mechanisms of Mainframe productions. However, this is much more in the areas of scripting and plot than in the realm of language. Here is a story of love that turns sour, and consequently turns brother against brother. It is shot in Abeokuta, Western Nigeria and some villages in Benin Republic such as Itchede, Itofor, Ikpinle and Sakete.

The film centres on Awero, a maiden who is wooed by three suitors. One of them is Dauda, from the city; the others are Lapade, the rich gold trader, and

Odejinmi, the brave hunter. Awero chooses to marry Odejinmi, but as the bride price is paid and the wedding date fixed, she is lured into the bush by Dauda who rapes her. Ruptured along with her virginity is her pride and life dream of becoming a wife and mother in the home of a happy man whom she loves and who loves her in return. The path of public shame is wide open before her, in a culture that places emphasis on chastity before and after marriage. As she cannot call off the wedding, she faces the wedding night with anxiety. Her virginity test is to be conducted that night by Odejinmi and the result will shape her far fate for good or ill. As expected, she is discovered to be 'a broken pot' (a new bride with ruptured hymen). With a slur on her reputation, she finds herself caught up in a whirl of inter-communal hostility as Agbede village where Odejinmi hails from is up in arms against Orita, Awero's village. The former is seeking revenge over the humiliation brought them by the taboo of a 'broken pot'.

War is declared and destruction takes over. Awero however, declines to reveal the identity of the person who defiled her as required in the scheme of atonement rituals. She later leads a peaceful procession of women bearing leaves, to end the hostility. In between the warring groups of men, Awero offers herself to be killed, instead of men using her as the reason for killing and maiming. Moved by the woman's action, the men drop their weapons. The cleansing process begins with a new dawn, heralded by the Gelede masque performance. In Yoruba tradition, Gelede is a women's cult for social regeneration and female empowerment (Drewal 1992). In the concluding screen text summary of the plot, the two families and communities reconcile. Awero and Odejinmi are happily remarried in a more elaborate ceremony. The virginity test is abolished in Elerin Community.

In its gender discourse, the film seeks greater valuation for women in a patriarchal order, which is also a universal practice across the world, beyond the shores of Yoruba world. The woman is shown as the victim of war, yet she is the path that leads to the equilibrium that is often violated by male aggression. While the men are holding bows, arrows and guns (weapons of war), women are bearing green leaves symbolising peace, fertility and renewal. Awero's re-emergence as a new being at the end of the film, offering her life to be sacrificed on the altars of peace and unity is quite symbolic. Perhaps, this informs the dedication of the film to 'all African women who, often marginalised, play peace-keeping roles in traditional communities'.

Besides, *Narrow Path* articulates the imperative of unity and dialogue across identities of gender, generation, region and religion, since disunity has proved to be a major set-back to the developmental aspirations of post-independence Africa. The war between Agbede and Orita communities characterised by arson, murder and wanton destruction represents various inter-group hostilities in the contemporary world. War, love and politics presented in the film are universal subjects, but they are made more relevant in the way they portray the disjunction between the people and the authoritarian postcolonial State in Africa (see Kieh and Agbese 2008). The Elerin communities bear frequent harassment by city-dwelling government officials – police men, tax collectors and sanitary inspectors who besiege the village unannounced in search of tax defaulters or people maintaining an unhygienic environment. Apart from portraying clashes between tradition and modernity, it also raises the conflict between the rural and the urban. There is much suspicion and even hatred among the villagers for the city, as personified by government agents. The presence of their vehicle, a monster of sorts thundering through the dusty roads of the village, unsettles the peace and stability of the community as everybody scampers to avoid arrest by greedy government officials who insatiably extort taxes without caring about the people's income. The Land Rover is a symbol of imperial power and its arrival violates order and serenity of the village. Sopitan, one of the Elders of Orita village, pointedly articulates the people's disaffection with the government when he remarks:

> You said you people in the city and the government ... which Government? The government we never see except when your tax collectors come here to harass our people ... grab our money.

Abike reinforces this submission when she remarks: '*Our* men hate government officials. They hate *them* and they are always afraid of them' (emphasis added).

From the Chief's speech above and that of Abike, the use of second person pronoun 'your' in an oppositional relationship with the first person plural pronoun 'our', establishes the wide gap between the actions of the rulers in the urban centre and the aspirations of the common people in the rural areas, a situation that unmistakably hinders social development.

Besides, the film pillories post-independence African governments as being alienated from the citizens, just like their colonial predecessors whose relations with the people have been portrayed in earlier creative expressions as that of the few tyrannising over the majority (see Oyono 1958, Armah 1968, Ousmane 1970). Indeed, Claude Ake poignantly expresses this situation when he submits that 'In Nigeria ... much development that has taken place in rural communities has occurred not because of the state but in spite of it. To many rural dwellers, the state exists primarily as a nuisance to be avoided in their daily struggle for survival' (1994: 38).

In another vein, Dauda represents the meretricious allure of the African city and its trappings of modernity. In seducing Awero with mirror, powder and jewellery, the film evokes the memory of the encounter between Africa and Europe before the era of slavery and colonialism during which the latter was reported to have lured the former with gin, gun, gun-powder, umbrella, mirror, and so on. Embedded in the film is a postcolonial discourse in which the margin (country) engages the centre (city) in a drama of re-interrogation. With Dauda, the city has a destructive impact on the country. However, the city ends up destroying Dauda too and that is where a clarification needs to be added that the city has its undeniable attraction, but it destroys the unwary like Dauda who takes to smoking Indian hemp and committing crime until he is jailed.

Figs 1 & 2 *DVD covers for* Arugba *and* The Narrow Path (© *Tunde Kelani*)

Arugba

In the discourse of politics and governance, one perceives another significant paradigm by Mainframe. In handling the sensitive subject of politics, Mainframe acknowledges the authoritarian nature of the State in Nigeria, especially under military rule (1966-1979, 1983-1999) and the civilian regime that was in power between 1999 and 2007, headed by Olusegun Obasanjo, a former military General. Often, the conflict pitches certain individuals against the community, or conservative forces against forces of change. At the end, the latter triumphs while affirming a preference for the generality of the people. In *Saworo Ide* and *Agogo Eewo* those who represent the old militaristic order like Oba Lapite, Lagata, Seriki, Balogun, Bada and Iyalode all meet a disastrous end while the youths who represent the burgeoning democratic forces triumph (see Adeoti 2009).

Part of the rhetoric of politics in Mainframe films is the adoption of a monarchical framework which is rooted in Yoruba traditional political system. This system is still in constant struggle for accommodation in the present democratic experiment. Mainframe makes the institution of kings and chiefs occupied by anti-heroes, misfits and tyrants to justify their subversion or outright expulsion by youths and others who seek democratic change. This is true of *Saworo Ide*, *Agogo Eewo* and *Arugba*.

Arugba is a film on contemporary events, but grounded on Yoruba lore. The use of English subtitles prepares it for an international audience, just as the issues of gender, generation, public health, governance and development focused in the film are issues that many audiences in other African countries apart from Nigeria, can easily relate to. *Arugba* is a film maker's panoramic view of and commentary on socio-political events in Nigeria between 1999 and 2007.

The title, 'Arugba', is derived from 'Arugba Osun', which refers to the votary maiden who bears the spiritual calabash of Osun, the river goddess. She is the principal figure during the annual worship and celebration of Osun in Osogbo, an ancient city in the south-western part of Nigeria. The Arugba is usually a virgin from the royal household. She leads the ritual procession from the King's palace to the banks of Osun River, a distance of about a mile. As she bears the calabash, silently and forbidden from uttering any word to mortals, she is a symbol of fortitude, sacrifice and altruism; values and attributes that are required for the social transformation that Kelani and his audiences seek. The maiden's white attire is a symbolic affirmation of her serenity and purity and that of the water deity, which contrasts sharply with the corruption, deceit, violence and brazen contempt for rules that characterise national politics. The need to cleanse the polity of these abnormalities is well articulated in the film. Adetutu, the unblemished maiden who is the Arugba, is therefore, offered as the icon of a new era. She represents a new generation that is imbued with hope, vigour and vitality to confront underdevelopment.

In Arugba, the story of politics is blended with love, while paying attention to and affirming the import of African traditions in effectively mediating the challenges of modern life. For instance, the practice of sexual abstinence before marriage represented in the votary maiden is one habit that is believed to lessen the risk of exposure to unwanted pregnancies and sexually transmitted diseases among contemporary youths.

In representing the above thematic concerns, the film weaves its plot and conflict around gender and generational variables. But *Arugba*'s plot is episodic, lacking the firmness, solidity and economy already established in *Saworo Ide* and *Agogo Eewo*. *Arugba*'s plot has disparate incidents loosely strung together in a manner that severely strains its coherence.

The film is set in Ilu Nla (an anonymous contemporary Nigerian town or city) in 2008. In its anonymity, Ilu Nla (big town) refers to a city, a state or a country, showing all that is right or wrong with contemporary governance in many African nations. From the beginning, Ilu Nla is embroiled in political instability, looting of public treasury, mass poverty and hunger amidst the opulence of a few, with no social security system, unemployment, insecurity of life and property, inflation and other problems. Using the institution of monarchy among the Yoruba, the contemporary state is represented by Oba Adejare, his Chiefs and Jaayinfa, the Ifa Priest. But Ilu Nla is like a fish that is rotten from the head because Oba Adejare and some of his chiefs are soiled in graft in spite of an open declaration of a war against corruption by the Oba and his council. The Oba's double standard soon comes to the fore. Corrupt, greedy, short tempered, stubborn and vindictive, he is quite intolerant of opposition, priding in himself as 'the dreaded daemon'. He scornfully dismisses dissenting voices and always resists the slightest attempt to expose his shady deals; an attribute that closely identifies the Oba with Olusegun Obasanjo, Nigeria's former President who is the obvious target of the film's satire. So discredited is the Oba's council that one observes a parodic diminution of the high and mighty in the tradition of satire, where chiefs and village heads who are supposed to be the custodians of law and order openly engage in physical combat like lorry-park hooligans.

The heightened sense of insecurity felt by Oba Adejare climaxes in the open confrontation between him and his chiefs; Baba Kekere and Aare Onikoyi. He publicly dishonours the former while the latter resists the Oba's move to humiliate him. But the Oba overreaches himself when he wants to go against the dictates of the gods, by stopping Adetutu from performing the role of Arugba for another year. He wants to impose one of his own daughters on the people for the role; a move that is successfully rebuffed through popular will and Adetutu's proven chastity.

The process of choosing an Arugba is through divination. By implication, the maiden is a choice of the gods. But Oba Adejare shows contempt for the due process of divination approved by the goddess and the peoples. He has earlier proposed to marry the votary maiden but she declines. As revenge against this 'insult', he stirs jealousy and hatred against Adetutu so that she can be dropped as Arugba for the year. The plan fails and the wish of the oracle, endorsed by the people is reaffirmed. Adetutu leads the annual procession of worshippers to the river again with pomp and celebration. During the procession, and throughout the celebration, religious tolerance, harmonious coexistence and orderly conduct are stressed through the images.

The film ends amidst ululation and a carnivalesque atmosphere, characteristic of the Osun festival. It affirms the purifying/messianic role of the calabash-bearing maiden priestess of Osun. However, the end also accentuates the communal cleansing objective of the festival as Aigoro, the closest chief to the Oba is accused of diverting funds from the World Health body for private use, when they were meant for building a clinic and improving health facilities in the community. Denied and dethroned by Oba Adejare, Aigoro is promptly arrested by anti-graft agents, and taken into detention. Thus, society rejects another corrupt man of power. The Oba at this moment too is set to abdicate the throne, after arranging for a successor (a metaphor for election manipulation) in a cynical twist of tradition for self-comfort. This will enable him to travel abroad and settle down to quietly enjoy his share of the loot from the public treasury, with plenty of food, drink and women. The scheme will also provide him a convenient distance away from the hands of the law and its agents.

The story of hard politics is however, softened with that of love, between young people, which lends its appeal to younger audiences Makinwa, the theatre-loving student of medicine and an anti-corruption crusader, falls in love with Morenike and later, Adetutu, the Arugba who is also leading a troupe of all-female performing artistes. Makinwa and Adetutu represent a desirable blend of art and science, tradition and modernity, as well as arts and politics. Their union, accentuated through camera manipulation and close-up shots, implies hope for brighter days ahead for the polity under the new leadership of a younger generation.

Through the character of Arugba, the film also seeks to advance the polemics of women's empowerment. Because of her spiritual endowment, Adetutu singlehandedly rescues herself and her friends from two male bullies in school. She fights the boys to the point of surrender and flight. She also sets free about 30 kidnapped children, as she escapes from the dungeon of the abductors. Her name, 'Adetutu', is quite allegorical as it points to her serenity and nobility. She radiates inner peace and carries herself with grace and a royal dignity.

One of the trans-border and cross-cultural devices in the film is the use of music, which serves as the interlude and as part of the plot. The lyrics of a song like '*Afi fila p'erin*' are quite topical, critical of the establishment and well blended with the central themes of the film. The song is sourced in a Yoruba aphorism; '*Afi fila p'erin, ojo kan ni iyi re mo'*. The man who kills an elephant with his cap, will soon earn the reputation of a murderer, if he is not careful. It is a lesson in moderation, a value that is grossly lacking in post-independence politics in different parts of Africa, which has seen the emergence of rulers such as Idi Amin of Uganda, Mobutu Sese Seko of Zaire, Kamuzu Banda of Malawi, Jean-Bedel Bokassa of Central African Republic, Ibrahim Babangida and Sanni Abacha of Nigeria, and so on.

'*Mi o ni Choice*', another song in the film is also worth attention. Rendered in a melodious code-mixing of Yoruba and English, it condemns dictatorship. It expresses the quandary and frustration of African youths who are well educated but have no jobs after graduation, yet, the option of armed robbery and other crimes in general, however lucrative they may seem, is quite unappealing. It traces the source of the social crises to corrupt government, constituted by a powerful, authoritarian clique that misappropriates national resources and is still bent on self-perpetuation in power. According to the song, 'absolute power corrupts absolutely ... excessive love for power courts disgrace.'

A critical close examination would reveal that excesses and democratic aberrations still define contemporary Nigerian politics and the song points to the transient nature of power while giving an assurance of a disgraceful end to those who like Oba Adejare govern recklessly.

Summary and conclusion

Nigerian video films enjoy wide acclaim within and outside Africa. Apart from their exhibition at international film festivals, they are the staple of digital satellite television stations devoted to the presentation of African cinema. However, many critics have observed that the popularity of Nigerian video films has not succeeded in papering over their inadequacies which have been highlighted in this paper. In spite of reservations expressed by critics, there are already in existence representation mechanisms and strategies that can boost video ratings among its consumers. It is against this backdrop that the article describes and analyses what Mainframe, one of Africa's outstanding film production organisations, does in its attempt to extend its audience appeal beyond Nigeria. As illustrations, the article highlights trans-national polemics and trans-cultural aesthetics offered in three selected films produced by the organisation, which include *Abeni* I&II, *Narrow Path*, and *Arugba*. Though grounded in Yoruba culture and Nigerian socio-political realties, in the final articulation, the films have enduring relevance to Africa and indeed, the contemporary world.

In discussing the films, the paper emphasises those artistic designs used to communicate beyond borders of language, culture, gender and generation. These include the trans-border partnership among film practitioners and the use of language in a way that neutralises colonial boundaries signified by English and French. It also includes universal subjects like love and politics. On the issue of love, Mainframe treats it in an archetypal manner that makes the films ever fresh and relevant. Love is sometimes used as a vista to larger issues of politics as seen in *Narrow Path* and *Arugba,* but politics in Mainframe films constitutes another genre with its own manner of representation.

From the foregoing, one can conclude that if the Nigerian home video film tradition is to sustain the local and global interest, judging from the Mainframe examples, it should emphasise themes, plot, characterisation, images and production/consumption mechanisms that ultimately target people across the globe who cultivate an interest in the movie medium.

NOTES

1   Kwah Ansah made this revelation in his key note address delivered at the second Ife International Film Festival held at Obafemi Awolowo University, Ile-Ife, on 27 January 2009. Kwah Ansah is a Ghanaian moviemaker and Chief Executive of TV Africa.
2   Yoruba is one of the three major indigenous languages at the forefront of video industry in Nigeria. But Yoruba speakers are also found in other African countries like Benin Republic, Togo, Sierra Leone and Ghana. There are people of Yoruba descent in Brazil, Trinidad and Tobago, and other parts of the Caribbean world (see Abimbola 2003).
3   English translations are provided for Yoruba film titles, except those films that derive their titles from the names of central characters like *Anikura, Ireke Onibudo* and *Papa Ajasco*, among others.

WORKS CITED

Abimbola, Wande (2003), 'The Yoruba Diaspora or Yoruba Cultural Empire'. Distinguished Guest Lecture, Faculty of Arts, Obafemi Awolowo University, Ile Ife, Nigeria. 18 December.
Adamu, Abdalla Uba, Yusuf M. Ada,u and Umar Faruk Jabil (2004) eds, *Hausa Home Videos: Technology, Economy and Society* (Kano: Centre for Hausa Cultural Studies/Adamu Joji Publishers).
Adeoti, Gbemisola (2008), 'Nollywood and Literary/Performance Studies in Nigerian Universities: A Case for School-Street Connection' in *Africa Through the Eye of the Video Camera* ed. Foluke Ogunleye, (Manzini, Swaziland: Academic Publishers), 198-214.
Adeoti, Gbemisola (2009), 'Home Video Films and the Democratic Imperative in Contemporary Nigeria', *Journal of African Cinemas*, 1.1: 35-56.

Ake, Claude (1994), *Democratisation of Disempowerment in Africa* (Lagos: Malthouse Press).

Armah, Ayi Kwei (1968), *The Beautyful Ones are not yet Born* (London: Heinemann).

Drewal, Thompson (1992), *Yoruba Ritual: Performers, Play, Agency* (Bloomington: Indiana University Press).

Gugler, Josef (2003), 'Between the African Mass Market and International Recognition' in *African Film: Re-Imagining a Continent* (Oxford: James Currey Publishers), 177–91.

Haynes, Jonathan and Okome, Onookome (1997), 'Evolving Popular Media: Nigerian Video Films' in *Nigerian Video Films* ed. Jonathan Haynes (Jos: Nigerian Film Corporation), 21– 44.

Jeyifo, Biodun (2008), 'Will Nollywood Get Better? Did Hollywood and Bollywood Get Better'? (5). *The Guardian Newspaper*, (Lagos) Sunday 28 February, 76.

Kelani, Tunde (2008), 'Give Nollywood A Chance', Interview with Tony Ogaga. Thursday 21 February. Available online at <*http://www.modernghana.com/movie/2003/3-GIVE-NOLLYWOOD-A-CHANCE*>

Kieh, George K. and Agbese Pita O. (2008), eds, *The State in Africa: Issues and Perspectives* (Ibadan: Kraft Books Limited).

Larkin, Brian (1997), 'Hausa Drama and the Rise of Video Culture in Nigeria' in *Nigerian Video Films*, ed. Jonathan Haynes (Jos: Nigerian Film Corporation), 105–25.

Ogunleye, Foluke (2008), ed., *Africa Through the Eye of the Video Camera* (Manzini, Swaziland: Academic Publishers).

Okome, Onookome and Haynes, Jonathan (1996), *Cinema and Social Change in West Africa* (Jos: Nigerian Film Corporation).

Ousmane, Sembene (1970), *Gods Bits of Wood* (London: Heinemann).

Oyono, Ferdinand (1958), *Old Man and the Medal* (London: Heinemann).

Soyinka, Wole (1999), *Open Sore of a Continent: A Personal Narrative of Nigerian Crisis* (Oxford: Oxford University Press).

VIDEOGRAPHY

Arugba (2008), Dir. Tunde Kelani, Prod. Tunde Kelani, Scr. Ade Adeniji.

Abeni I&II (2006). Dir. Tunde Kelani, Prod. Tunde Kelani, Scr. Ade Adeniji.

Narrow Path (2006), Dir. Tunde Kelani, Prod. Tunde Kelani, Scr. Bayo Adebowale and Niji Akanni.

Campus Queen (2003), Dir. Tunde Kelani, Prod. Tunde Kelani, Scr. Akinwumi Isola.

Agogo Eewo (2002), Dir. Tunde Kelani, Prod. Tunde Kelani, Scr. Akinwumi Isola.

Thunder Bolt (2001), Dir. Tunde Kelani, Prod. Tunde Kelani, Scr. Adebayo Faleti and Femi Kayode.

Saworo Ide (1999), Dir. Tunde Kelani, Prod. Tunde Kelani, Scr. Akinwumi Isola.

Tanzanian Films
Between innovation & incompetence

VICENSIA SHULE

Introduction

Video film as a genre has made massive strides in Tanzania during the past decade as in other parts of the world. Technological advancement has played a major role in such transformation which has led to the film industry in Tanzania receiving substantial applause but also criticism from various stake-holders for its lack of professionalism compared to Euro-American and Asian films. The purpose of this article is to explore and analyse the current patterns of video-film production in Tanzania and the challenges it faces. With a focus on current practice, this article deals with some of the compliments and criticisms which film producers face. It briefly reviews the historical background to the film industry in Tanzania, current practice, as well as the level of audience participation in the produced films. The case study examples have been influenced by the author's personal involvement in the film production processes in Tanzania, but also refer to the produced films which can be found in the film shops and among street vendors. For this article, Tanzanian films are broadly conceptualized to include those produced by Tanzanians and/or in collaboration with Tanzanians describing Tanzanian lifestyles, issues and politics. When the phrase video film industry is used it represents what Mwakalinga (2010: 16) defined as 'local, popular, privately funded and commercially based industry that has been criticized for its orientation towards commercialisation and its apolitical stance as compared to African cinema'.

Historically, the film industry in Tanzania can be traced back to the 1930s when British colonial administration used films for literacy, entertainment and propaganda. Most of these films were imported from abroad including America, Britain and India. Later in the 1950s Tanganyika's governor Sir Edward Twinning introduced a project to use Africans in making their own films in Kiswahili. This was done in collaboration with African Film Produc-tion of South Africa. Before the project was abandoned due to independence upheavals, more than ten films were already produced. These included *Chalo Amerudi* (Chalo Has Come Back), *Wageni Wema* (Kind Guests), *Ali Mjanja* (Cunning Ali), *Dawa ya Mapenzi* (Love Portion), *Meli Inakwenda* (The Boat is

Sailing), *Mhogo Mchungu* (Bitter Cassava) and others (Smith 1989: 391). Most of these were based on morality tales and were created to 'civilize' Africans through the practice of good manners.

After independence in 1961, film production was not high on the national agenda until 1968 when the Tanzanian government created Tanzania Film Company (TFC). TFC aimed at producing and distributing films for locals (Smith 1989:392). This coincided with the adoption of *Ujamaa* (African Socialism) through the Arusha Declaration of 1967 that aimed at liberating people from neocolonialism. The produced films were supposed to propagate *Ujamaa* and nation building. Films produced with such an aim include *Fimbo ya Mnyonge* (A Poor Person's Salvation) 1976 and its sequel, *Yombayomba* (1985) and *Wimbo wa Mianzi* (The Song of Bamboo 1983) a Tanzanian/Dutch co-production focusing on irrigation using bamboo conduits.

Other productions and co-productions in the 1980s and 90s were *Arusi ya Mariamu* (Mariamu's Wedding 1984), *Mama Tumaini* (A Woman of Hope 1986) and *Maangamizi* (The Ancient One 1995-2001). These used either 35mm or 16 mm technology and focused on issues of social awareness, education or politics.

After the introduction of Structural Adjustment Programs (SAPs) under World Bank (WB) and International Monetary Fund (IMF) conditions in 1980s, *Ujamaa* ideology began to be replaced by capitalism. Trade liberalisation gave room for more importation of foreign movies from Hollywood (USA), Bollywood (India) and Nollywood (Nigeria). Technological advancement enabled the young, amateurs and people with low budgets to produce films using video cameras. This socio-political transition gave rise to the massive production of commercially motivated video-films in Tanzania. Most of the stories and themes used to produce these video-films are market oriented, targeting audiences with commercially viable topics such as love, witchcraft, modern religions, fashion and to a lesser extent political issues. The choice of such themes can be argued to be in line with constructivist communication theory which describes how humans can develop knowledge and meaning from their experiences. This implies that the audience influences the themes and expectations of video productions.

Most of the films are geared towards creating an avenue for giving audiences a chance to reflect on social issues. To give a personal experience, in November 2010, I was travelling by Dar Express bus from Moshi to Dar es Salaam. In the bus they played a film known as *14 Days* written by Jacob Stephen and directed by Adam Kuambiana. The film describes a confrontation between a couple, Michael and Irene. Out of jealousy towards his wife, Michael insults and beats his wife Irene in what he claims to be a way of disciplining her. Irene, understanding her gender-based oppression resists Michael's violence by demanding a divorce. Michael decides to look for advice so that he can rescue his marriage, upon which a friend gives him fourteen days' activities to win back Irene's heart. In the end, Michael manages to stabilize the relationship.

In one of the scenes in *14 Days*, Michael abuses Irene by saying that Irene's relatives think his responsibility is to take care of her extended family ... Michael uses the phrase 'Kwa Sadala' to mean cheap or easy life in reference to

Irene's relatives. Actually Kwa Sadala is a steep section of the Moshi-Arusha road and the local reference made the whole bus – which was quiet for some time – burst into laughter. This shows how the film appeals to its subaltern target audience through the use of local references.

This reaction from the audience can be explained from different perspectives. First there were some audience members who related the scenario to their relatives who depend on them. Secondly, it can be described as a situation whereby those relatives (amongst the audience) reflect on their dependence. Lastly, those who know the place, Kwa Sadala, managed to relate the literal meaning of the phrase – slope – with their difficult experiences. Such an example from *14 Days* shows clearly that film reflects the norms and traditions of society and to some extent exposes complex situations and scenarios which gives the audience opportunity for self reflection. This audience participation is quite different from the peak of *Ujamaa* in the 1970s where top-down political statements and leaders' speeches were mostly used to create film themes for propaganda purposes.

The use of Kiswahili language has helped to reach a wide audience and to showcase Tanzanian films as unique in the region and abroad. One can argue that Kiswahili as a language used mainly by Tanzanian film makers has created dual functionality. On the one hand the national language has managed to reach more Kiswahili speakers. On the other hand, the films being distributed in neighbouring countries like Rwanda, Burundi, Kenya, Malawi, Uganda, Mozambique, and Democratic Republic of Congo (DRC), have spread the language across borders. Kiswahili being a national identity, Kiswahili films have contributed immensely to the signification of such African identity, a goal which African film-makers have aimed at since the 1960s.

The pattern of film distribution has changed in recent years. Previously Tanzanian films were for domestic consumption or Kiswahili speakers. They were also regarded as poor films in terms of picture and sound, compared to Hollywood and even Bollywood films. With technological advancement and the shared experience from the audience, the perception has changed. Films are now accompanied with English subtitles which imply that the film makers have discovered a potential Anglophone audience which distributors are now targeting. Perhaps in the future they will put French or even Chinese subtitles. It should be noted that due to historical reasons, especially colonialism, English for the majority of Tanzanians is still considered an elite language. Hence, by having English subtitles, code mixing and code switching done by characters in the film, implies that Tanzanian films have now crossed the border to reach neighbouring countries and most importantly to try to fill the gap between the 'elites' and non-elites of Tanzania.

Challenges unfold: *Kasri la Wageni*

On 7 March 2010, I received a call from two colleagues with whom I have worked in various film productions since 2005. This time they wanted to produce the script that I wrote in 2005 known as *Kasri la Wageni,* which literally means visitors' mansion or palace. *Kasri la Wageni* dramatises the story of Tonga, a young girl from Ngagao village who escapes female genital mutilation and forced marriage. She is welcomed in the convent and later she becomes a nun. She experiences a lot of convent politics such as hate, jealousy and even sexual abuse. At last Tonga is chased away from the convent for failing to abide by its rules and principles, an experience that makes her realise that oppression in the village and the convent was almost the same.

Even though it was a 'brilliant' idea to produce the film, I was not really comfortable about accepting the offer. There were many reasons, the major being that perhaps my ideology had shifted from where it was in 2005. I was also faced by the challenge that the industry in Tanzania was 'condemned' for lacking professionalism in film making, resulting in films with weak form and content. But I was comforted by the fact that I would be able to demonstrate my thoughts from the six years prior to writing the script.

After thinking for some time I accepted the 'offer' – as I would call it – under the condition that no changes would be made since I didn't have time for any rewrites, the backers proposed that I should be a producer in the real sense of providing financial support to the production. This was another challenge as I was not ready to invest in such a project. I was not sure how the film would do in terms of marketing and distribution. On the other hand, I believed that it could be a learning experience to see how the industry was performing. The decision was also complemented by the fact that academic studies should contribute to the current practice of film making in Tanzania. So I decided to take the risk. Two colleagues prepared for the production, one as a director and the other as a camera operator, and from there the production began. The process involved casting, script distribution, location identification, recording and finally editing. The recording was scheduled according to the location in the script, i.e. scenes which used similar locations were shot together. Finally, the film was completed in 2011 ready for distribution.

Addressing incompetence to hallmark complements

The production of *Kasri la Wageni* took a route similar to many video films in Tanzania. Such films are often received by an audience with two different opinions: with compliments or with criticisms of incompetence. Taking *Kasri ya Wageni* as a case study, I can argue that there are many multifaceted and underlying factors for what is seen today in the Tanzanian film industry. In order to analyse the production scenario which bring these challenges one has to focus on three major areas: artistic (acting, directing, language, mise en scène), technical (sound, light and editing) and managerial (copyright, marketing and distribution), factors which in totality must complement each other.

The current acting in films shows the maturity of amateurs compared to the video-films produced in the early 2000s. Storylines have begun to acknowledge the existence of artists who 'think outside the box'. Apart from such improvement in the production of *Kasri la Wageni*, acting was not that easy for all actors. Most actors are amateurs or semi professionals, and the director has to find ways of dealing with such actors. For example it was difficult for some actors who were used to improvisation to use scripts and, as a result, they failed to perform to the director's expectations. Since they also possess inadequate acting skills, it became a challenge even to apply such techniques as Stanislavski's 'emotional recall'.

During the production of *Kasri la Wageni* one of the main characters almost decided give up acting as she believed it was too difficult. This happened when she was supposed to deliver several takes in the middle of the night and she complained of being tired. If this was a trained actor, perhaps she would have had a different way of understanding acting as a job in its fullest right. This challenge clearly shows that there is a need to mainstream arts subjects in the Tanzanian education system from primary to secondary schools especially performing arts. This would enable young people who are fond of the industry to understand the dimension not only for film production but also as a creative industry which provides both income and employment opportunities.

The other challenge is the influence of theatre and radio drama acting on film. Most actors are not in a position to differentiate between such 'media'. As a result they overact by enlarging gestures and raising their voices in front of the camera, a style described by some audience members as oracle-speech acting. Regardless of the script directives, actors try to speak as if they are addressing a public rally, whereas they are conversing with other characters in the scene. This clearly shows the influence of community theatre or Theatre for Development (TfD) in film as in most cases actors on the stage have to address the audience through a process of audience participation or involvement. In order to improve acting in Tanzanian films, it is important to provide in-service training for practising actors. Such training, which can be done during the production or in separate sessions, should focus on the differentiation between radio drama, theatre and film acting, and can be used to raise awareness of acting as a viable job, which should be done professionally. Providing such basic knowledge, gives room for improvement, especially for practising actors who cannot fit in the formal Tanzanian education system.

Directing for film is not an easy task as one has to be conversant with both artistic and technical elements of the production. Since directors in Tanzania usually have a theatre background, they are more conversant with community theatre or Theatre for Development techniques and they fail to remember that in addition to having actors on the scene, light and sound need to be directed too. Most of the time, light is used purely for illuminating the scene rather than creatively. This makes many of the films look too bright, with tasteless top-lighting and no atmosphere. Sound is another problematic area. Directors concentrate purely on the audibility of the actors' dialogues, without considering the camera work or editing; as a result, the sound tone and the shot often do not match. For example an actor can be seen in a two-shot but the tone comes out as if s/he is in an open space giving a speech. Thus directors too have to go through training to update themselves with the basics of film production and modern digital techniques.

Another problem is the emergence of some sort of 'djing'. By djing I refer to the situation where in post-production the film is augmented with heavy music which sometimes overrides the characters' dialogue. The music which accompanies film tends not to complement the theme mood or *mise en scène* but merely to prolong the scene. This can be clearly noticed in some films such as *Chanzo ni Mama 1&2* (Mother is the Cause) where there are scenes in which a character is captured walking in a single, long, non-functional take accompanied by music.

The issue of prolonged films points to the phenomenon current in the Tanzanian market: as with Nigerian videos, most films are in parts one, two and even three. These are not sequels but films produced together then separated during editing. This issue of having film in more than one part has been advocated to be a counter solution to piracy. Producers of such films argue that having a film in more than one part makes it easy to solve piracy problems as one work can be sold for the price of two; distributors have a similar argument, though they are also interested in the financial gains. So the use of music 'djing' is one of the easiest ways to prolong the film during editing to get two or three out of one slim script. Even though the language is controlled by the script, in most cases when the director allows actors to add their creativity they prefer to code switch between Kiswahili and English. The motive behind code mixing is unclear, whether it is to show the class of the participants, as English is presumed to be an upper class language, or whether it is a realistic reflection of the way Tanzanians speak nowadays. Another reason could be the influence of English on Tanzanian actors. If the script was in English perhaps they had to understand it first in Kiswahili then act in English, so, due to insufficient English vocabulary, they opt to use code switching. On one occasion I heard one person complaining after seeing actors code mixing. He questioned, "What is the logic of using English in Kiswahili dialogue? Is it to add emphasis?" However, code switching can be also argued to be a strategy to capture both English and Kiswahili speakers within Tanzania and across the borders. On the same language issue, most of the produced films, like *The Cold Wind, 14 Days, Family Disaster, Girlfriend, Dilemma*, and *Uncle JJ*, use English titles while the dialogue is mostly in Kiswahili, probably because an English title upgrades a film's status in the market. The scenery in many Tanzanian films depicts exaggerated wealth, often contradicting the storyline which necessitates a background of poverty. It is clear that these video films are trying to appeal to a realism which does not necessarily reflect the characters' profiles. Characters' clothes used in the film often seem to advertise new fashions in the market rather than plausibly reflecting the class to which characters belong. I recommend that the director, costume and props designer thoroughly analyse the script. Such collaboration would not only complement the mise en scène but also add value to the film's themes.

Since these films often have a pedagogic function, the audience usually debate and compare their lives with those of the actors. Actors as well as producers have been criticised for failing to reflect social reality. At this point the audience has crossed the border of seeing these films as fiction rather considering them as real representation of their lives. The editing of these films is done using available software. The common ones include *Adobe Premiere Pro, Final Cut Pro* and *Avid* which are considered to be professional editing software, while *Pinnacle* and *Imovie* are used by amateur editors as they are for home use. By the use of such software, editing has become a relatively easy job. This software provides various options, and enables editors to do image manipulation, such as through the use of colour filters. In *Mahabuba* (Lover/Darling), for example, the editor has used a yellow colour filter from the beginning to the end of the film. In day scenes it tends to match and bring the sense of coolness. The challenge has been how to balance between day and night scenes versus interior and exterior scenes. It could be possible to select some scenes which would fit within a yellow filter, rather than making the whole film look yellowish. Regardless of such minor challenges of improper use of filters, *Mahabuba*, directed by John Kallage, is considered one of the best films produced in 2008.

Despite the general popularity of Tanzanian films, cover designs and titles have received criticism. From the audience perspective, it is important to see in the film what has been reflected on the cover, since the latter, along with the title is what makes most of the audience buy or watch a film. But what has been observed is the extreme beautification of characters on the cover. The way characters are seen in the films do not match the artwork. For example in *The Cold Wind*, Daniel is seen differently from the way he appears in the film, especially in his skin complexion. On the cover he is seen as a lighter person compared to the reality. Regardless of its position as a selling point and device, a cover should at least be able to reflect the story and characters of the film.

The production process has developed what I can refer to as multiple responsibilities. This is the situation where participants of the film carry out both technical and artistic duties, even managerial in some cases. Although the levels of such multiplicity differ, the highest has been between the directors as the main characters. For example in the film *Kwa Heshima ya Penzi* (In the Respect of Love), the director, Single Mtambalike, also plays Dominic, the main character of the film. Likewise in the *The Cold Wind*, the director, Vincent Kigosi, plays Daniel, also the main character, while in *Chanzo ni Mama 1&2*, the director, Suzan Lewis, doubles up as Mama (mother of the main character). Such multiple responsibilities make films lack directorial focus and the story remains undeveloped. Film actors sometimes seem to be 'jack of all trades', i.e. preaching instead of talking as they assume both the role of the director and the star of the films.

'Starism' is another problem in Tanzanian films as it reduces the motivation which a character can have when cast to play a certain role. The so-called stars/ directors/main characters opt in the film for lifestyles to which they aspire. This means if they adore rich people, they would prefer to act as rich in most of the films they produce. Since it is nearly impossible to convince actors/ directors/ producers to decentralise their powers, it is important to bring to the fore the technical and artistic challenges of multiple roles in the film. This can not only be addressed by film critics but also through workshop training.

There have been complaints from various viewers that Tanzanian films are half cooked. This is supported by the fact that artists produce too many films within a short period of time and fail to provide quality. In responding to such challenge, one of the famous actors in Tanzania, Vincent Kigosi, argued that the film industry does not encourage production of high quality films. Film producers have no capital so they are forced to produce numerous films within a short period of time in order to survive. He emphasised that the film industry in Tanzania is different from Hollywood where famous actors are involved in big budget films, creating profit margins so high they can survive by producing one film in a year (Kigosi, 2010). Kigosi might have a point but still there are issues to query. Most of the produced films are too short and are in one, two or even three parts. This is also cheating customers as they buy one film for the price of two or three. This might also start to motivate buyers to buy pirated cheap films. Perhaps the best solution could be to mobilise film stakeholders to pressurise the Tanzania Revenue Authority (TRA) to provide tax stamps so that they can effectively collect taxes and therefore help to minimise piracy. Collecting taxes from film would allow producers/distributors to know their contribution to the national economy and hence request for the formalisation of the industry.

Some of the managerial challenges include marketing and distribution, whereby there are no defined distribution channels. This means that one cannot trace easily how many films are sold and where. There is no such tracking as most of the distributors buy films, pay a lump sum to the producers and remain with total distribution rights. The other challenge is political neglect, which has left the industry unrecognised for the whole decade. There is no tracking or economic support for the industry. A claim that the industry is in its infancy and has to be nurtured is political propaganda which needs thorough investigation. I would argue that the industry is not at the infant stage because it has survived the political and economic shifts from socialism to capitalism and from nationalism to neoliberalism. It has also survived donor funding and foreign aid interference to some extent as compared to theatre which has arguably been overwhelmed by donors (Shule 2010). Therefore the model which the film industry in Tanzania has pursued needs thorough study to capitalise on the most sustainable and creative practices.

The victory ahead

Regardless of the challenges which face the Tanzanian film industry, there are remarkable improvements. Take for example the film *14 Days* (Stephen 2010). One can realise the improvement in terms of story development, *mise en scène,* sound, acting even editing and distribution of the final piece. The director has managed to centre the whole story between two people, Michael and his wife Irene. This shows clearly that it is possible to have few characters and still produce a gripping film. In terms of acting Jacob Stephen has strikingly presented the character Michael to perfection. The combination of his voice, movements and actions stimulates the story from the beginning to the end. Perhaps this is because he is the one who provided the story and hence is emotionally attached to it and to the character Michael.

With such history and current improvement in the production of films in Tanzania, criticism of film makers should be muted. Most of them are working purely from their own creativity and observation. They have not received professional training and what they produce seems to be above average for amateurs.

The issue of training and education of artists is deeply rooted in the history of Tanzania. The education policies have excluded art training in primary and secondary schools for more than four decades. It was not until 2008 that theatre and other performing arts were included in secondary schools' syllabus as examinable subjects. Therefore acting and film training were regarded as a privilege for the selected few who managed to join a university and college or were trained abroad. On the other hand, these film makers receive no support from the state or foreign donors. Hence what they produce at artistic, technical and managerial levels is individually developed and market supported. Lack of foreign aid and state support could even be seen as a 'blessing' as the producers have artistic freedom as long as their audience is satisfied.

Apart from the challenges, the major success of Tanzanian film industry is to minimise the number of imported films from abroad. Nollywood films were among the first African films to flood the film market in Tanzania in the 1990s, which is not the case today. Since most Tanzanian films are not shown in movie theatres, the major income for film makers has been through social support from the citizens who buy films. Regardless of such achievement, piracy has remained one of the biggest challenges that needs to be addressed from a regulatory perspective. Lack of support from the Tanzania Revenue Authority (TRA), which could discourage counterfeit goods, has contributed much to the under-development of the film industry.

While there are unsolved outcries about piracy and copyright infringement, in August 2010 the National Art Council of Tanzania (BASATA) launched four major umbrella federations to coordinate artistic works and activities in Tanzania. One of them is the Film Federation of Tanzania. The major objective of this federation is to unite and coordinate film productions in Tanzania. The federation is expected to negotiate for artists' rights and also provide useful information on the role and challenges of the industry in Tanzania. To fulfil those objectives, the federation needs more support from various sectors such as business organisations, legal agencies and revenue authorities as most of the film industry challenges require a multifaceted approach to bolster expertise and professionalism.

However, it is very early to comment on the input which the federation will add to the film industry, considering that it is dominated by amateurs. Perhaps the film industries should start by facing challenges from the audiences' perspective rather than the film makers'. These include production improvement, quality assurance, piracy control and adherence to professionalism. As this analysis reflects, film industry in Tanzania beyond the 2000s suggests tremendous progress as compared to the 1980s. This shows that commercialisation, one of the neoliberal policies, has managed to shape the industry to sustain itself based on the market rather than depending on the state or foreign donors. Being free from the state allows Tanzanian film makers to focus on the market and the audience. This situation is quite different from the African cinema movement of the 1960s which was based on the ideology of Pan Africanism (Mwakalinga 2010: 16). Even though there is no reliable inventory of the number of films produced between 2000 and the present, the number of films seen in the streets suggest much progress in quantity and, in a few cases, quality.

BIBLIOGRAPHY

Armes, R. (2006), *African Filmmaking North and South of the Sahara,* (Edinburgh: Edinburgh University Press Ltd).
Ashbury, R., Helsby, W. & O'Brien, M. (1998), *Teaching African Cinema,* (London: British Film Institute [BFI]).
Bakari, I., & Cham, M. eds,. (1996), *African Experiences of Cinema,* (London: BFI).
Billa, K., [Director], (2010), *Kasri la Wageni* [Motion Picture], Tanzania.
Brewster, B., & Jacobs, L. (1997), *Theatre to Cinema,* (New York: Oxford University Press).
Diawara, M. (1992), *African Cinema, Politics and Culture,* (Bloomington & Indianapolis: Indiana University Press).
Diawara, M. (2010), *African Film: New Forms of Aesthetics and Politics,* (London: Prestel).
Fiebach, J. (2006), 'Identity: Openess and Fluidity. From the Popular Travelling Theatre to Home Video Films in West Africa', *Maske und Kothurn* 12: 3 ,
Gabriel, T. H. (1982), *Third Cinema in the Third World: The Aesthetics of Liberation,* (Ann Arbor: UMI Research Press).
Game, M. G. [Director], (2008). *The Cold Wind* [Motion Picture], Tanzania.
Giroux, H. A. (2002), *Breaking into the Movies: Film and the Culture of Politics.* (Massachusetts: Blackwell Publishers Inc.)
Givanni, J. (2000), ed., *Symbolic Narratives/African Cinema,* (London: BFI).
Hungwe, K. (1991), 'Southern Rhodesian Propaganda and Education Film for Peasant Farmers 1948-1955', *Historical Journal of Film, Radio and Television* 3, 229: 13.
Kallage, J. [Director], (2008), *Mahabuba* [Motion Picture], Tanzania.
Kigosi, V. (2010). *Waraka kwa Mashabiki Wangu,* available online at <http://raythegreatest. blogspot.com/search?updated-max=2010-08-10T15%3A14%3A00-07%3A00&max-results= 50>, accessed 10 August 2010.
Leveri, M. (1983), 'Prospects in Developing a Viable Film Industry: A Close Up of a Decade's Production Performance of the Audio Visual Institute of Dar es Salaam and Tanzania Film Company Limited', MA Dissertation: University of Dar es Salaam.
Lewis, S. [Director], (2008b), *Chanzo ni Mama 2* [Motion Picture], Tanzania.
Lewis, S. [Director], (2008a). *Chanzo ni Mama* [Motion Picture], Tanzania.
Mponguliana, J. (1982). 'The Development of Film in Tanzania', MA Dissertation: University of Dar es Salaam.
Mtambalike, S. [Director], (2008) *Kwa Heshima ya Penzi* [Motion Picture], Tanzania.
Mwakalinga, M. (2010), *Shifting Economy, Shifting Cinema: Tanzania and Its Cinema.*
Ngakane, L., & Shiri, K. (1991), *Africa on Film,* (London: BBC2 Publication).
Nicholas, T. (1994), *Egyptian Cinema,* (London: BFI).
Pramaggiore, M., & Wallis, T. (2006), *Film: A Critical Introduction,* (London: Pearson Education, Inc.).
Shaka, F. O. (2004), *Modernity and the African Cinema,* (Trenton: Africa World Press, Inc.).
Shule, V. (2010), 'Beyond Socialism: Tanzanian Theatre, Neoliberalism and Foreign Aid Complexity', (PhD Dissertation, Johannes Gutenberg Universität, Mainz).
Shule, V. (2004). 'Effectiveness of Video Film in Reducing Young Men's Gender Violence and

other HIV Risk Behaviours', (MA Dissertation: University of Dar es Salaam).

Smith, R. (1989), *The Future Film in Tanzania*, available online at <http://afraf.oxfordjournals.org/content/88/352/389.full.pdf>, accessed 28 August 2010.

Stephen, J. [Producer], Stephen, J. [Writer], & Kuambiana, A. [Director], (2010), *14 Days* [Motion Picture], Tanzania: Steps.

Ukadike, N. F. (1994), *Black African Cinema*, (Berkeley: University of California Press).

'Telling our Story'
Conversations with *KinaUganda* home movie directors, Mariam Ndagire & Ashraf Simwogerere

SAM KASULE

Introduction

KinaUganda means 'of Ugandan origin'. It refers to that which is typically Uganda: bearing indigenous cultural characteristics and articulating a Ugandan point of view. It is the prefix *kina-* (of), that invokes the question of cultural identity in the word and expresses the meaning of home movies. Conversely, *EkiNigeriya* is its opposite in that it describes Nollywood home movies in Uganda. The genre rejects the old binary ideologies that divided theatre between indigenous and Western, local languages and English, to create hierarchies of audiences and complexities in its reception. It has emerged as a performance space, benefiting from the peace and economic growth of National Resistance Movement's government, and in addition, displacing theatre as a critical form of cultural entertainment. In this space, Ugandans re-examine perceptions of *katemba* (theatre/performance) as they strive to reconceptualise their traditional understanding of performance and communal entertainment. For this paper, I transcribed and translated interviews with two home movie directors, Mariam Ndagire, working in English, and Ashraf Simwogerere, working in Luganda and other Bantu languages.

A Conversation with Mariam Ndagire

Filmography
Down This Road I Walk (2007)
Strength of a Stranger (2008)
Hearts in Pieces (2009)
Tendo Sisters (2010)

Mariam Ndagire has been producing films since *Down This Road I Walk* (2007). For this study, I wanted to write about her career up to date. In particular, I wanted to hear her story in relation to other developments in the home movie industry. Ndagire is the only successful young female director ever to work in

Fig 1 *Mariam Ndagire, Bat Valley Theatre, Kampala, 15 April 2010 (© Sam Kasule)*

KinaUganda. Because she has been able to attract sponsorships, thanks to her success in the popular music theatre, her films have made money. The interview took place in her office at Bat Valley Theatre (formerly Theatre Excelsior), a converted school hall. Her favourite film, she said, was *Down This Road I Walk*, because '[it] was my first movie so I love it'.

The questions that I wanted her to address are critical ones, which covered issues such as her initial work in theatre, representation of women in her scripts, and the future of *KinaUganda*.

SK: Tell me about your early days in theatre.

MN: I have been in the theatre world since 1987. I started when I was in Senior Three and I don't look back. I took part in school plays but my Mum wasn't happy about my participation in drama so she withdrew me from a day school and took me to Trinity College Nabbingo. But I formed a drama group at that school as well. That is how dedicated I was to theatre.

SK: Which other school did you attend?

MN: I was at Kampala High School for 'A' level.

SK: Were you in the school's production of *The Road*?[1]

MN: In the play called *The Road* by Wole Soyinka…

SK: Yes, directed by Joseph Mpoza…

MN: No, I wasn't but he was my first stage director at Kampala High School.

SK: What set you off on your theatrical career? What made you go into drama?

MN: I can't put a finger on anything because it was a calling for me. I found a passion for theatre.

SK: What brought you into the area of video?

MN: As an amateur, I was working with Omugave Ndugwa in the Black Pearls. From there, a few of us including Kato Lubwama, Ashraf Simwogerere, John Segawa, Abby Mukiibi formed our own group, the Afri Diamonds. After a few years, we thought we had done everything so we decided to try film.

However, I must say that all along I had a crush on the screen, particularly when I was watching movies on the screen. I am a fan of movies. Since I used to do many stage plays, I thought I could give it a go. Before I started, I read a lot of literature about filming.

SK: When did you start video filming?

MN: My first movie, *Down This Road I Walk*, was in 2007. I spent a whole year between 2006 and 2007 writing the script. In 2007, I decided to try it out and called the auditions but of course, until then I wasn't sure whether Ugandan actors were interested in filming. An overwhelming number of people came so I auditioned, cast and started shooting. I got somebody, Chris, who I had met at Wavah Broadcasting Service (WBS) while shooting *Ensitaano*[2] who was a good cameraman (cinematographer). I told him that I had a script I intended to direct, 'Could he do the shooting?' I have been with him ever since.

SK: Under what circumstances did the video film industry start in Uganda?

MN: I think people who first made movies saw a gap because there were many Nigerian films in circulation and our audiences seemed interested in them. Therefore, they asked: 'What if our own people acted something like that?' Remember, what made the Nigerian stories so interesting were stories that were close to our hearts.

SK: Ordinary stories…

MN: Yes. The audience would say, 'I think I have seen that before… I have seen that happen at my neighbour's home.' Therefore, those people who started thought they could have Nigerian movies done in a Ugandan way.

SK: So, is that is how they started?

MN: That is how they started. They were emulating the Nigerians. Basically that is what happened. However, I for one when I came in I didn't want to emulate the Nigerians, I wanted to make films telling our Ugandan stories. I wanted to have a Ugandan style of movie making, telling our Ugandan stories in a better way, better than the Nigerians do.

SK: How do you distribute and market your movies to the public?

MN: Initially when I was writing the script, I got the Nile Breweries to sponsor me. Up to now, they still give me some sponsorship. They introduced me to DSTV, the cable network that shows in several African countries…so that is one of my outlets. A month after the movie premieree I distribute it on DVD. I negotiate with businesspersons with retail/wholesale outlets who sell the movies in their shops in the City and upcountry towns. In addition, I distribute outside the country.

SK: Some Ugandans have said that home videos/DVDs lack artistic merit, that this is a money-making industry that peddles special effects, witchcraft and magic. What are your comments on this?

MN: I would say that there are varieties of filmmakers in the industry … with several intentions. Each person comes in with different aims. Those who first started in the industry looked at making money because they were seeing a gap … there was that demand for movies. They were not looking at the quality of the movie, the stories and all those basics of making a good film, but they were just looking at the [finished] product and getting money out of it. Then there are some others who take their time, put in a lot effort, do the homework and release very good movies.

SK: Would you say that that there have been phases in the development of *KinaUganda*?

MN: There was a phase when they were in it for money although now they are more professional. Nevertheless, I think both professionals and profiteers are here. The good thing is that the modern-day Ugandans are getting to know the difference; they appreciate good movies. People in the second category … the mediocre… are starting to fade out.

SK: How would you describe your work? Is it as video film, home video or home movie?

MN: I wouldn't say it is home video [or video film] because it wouldn't be taken to cable television. They are several Ugandan moviemakers who would like their products to be bought [or sponsored] by these multinational companies but they are struggling because their films are of a basic nature; they are so 'home' … not for the diverse audience. I wouldn't say that mine are very good but they are ok.

SK: Would you categorise yours as home movies?

MN: Yes.

MN: OK.

SK: How do you go about developing film scripts, shooting scenes and bringing the complete work to the consumer's screens?

MN: I first prepare myself. I first come up with the story … what I want to talk about, the log line…

SK: What do you mean by log line?

MN: I don't know what you would call it in UK…but it is the line that governs the story … what the movie is going to be about. Then I come up with my characters, how I want the plot to move, and I come up with the treatment. By this I mean how the story is going to move…which scene comes after the other and how the story develops. Then I put the flesh on the skeleton… At times, I have a scene breakdown; at other times, I don't because when you are writing the story just flows… I just write the script then I go back and look at what I have…

SK: How long does it take you to write a script?

MN: Ah, I wouldn't say…it depends on the strength of the script…the story… *Down this Road I Walk* took me a long time because I didn't know what I was doing. I was transforming from stage to screen so I didn't know the basics … I didn't know anything. *Hearts in Pieces* took me one month to write the draft; one month to come up with the draft, and after that, it took me up to the audition time to make it right. Sometimes you may look at what you have written only to discover that there are not enough conflicts or there isn't enough suspense...

SK: Why did you kill off your characters?

MN: [*Laughs*]... do you mean in *Down This Road I Walk*? [*Laughs*] I didn't want a Part Two [a sequel].

SK: You don't have to have a Part Two.

MN: I didn't want a Part Two so I had to solve the conflict. I had to resolve everything...all the conflicts...

SK: By killing...

MN: [*Laughs*] No, that is how it was flowing in my head. Because if this man stayed around the movie would have ended on a cliffhanger, he wouldn't have anywhere to go.

SK: Do your characters experience (emotional) reactions from the audience when they walk on the street?

MN: Yes they do.

SK: In the past people wanted to relate to us on the street as if we are the stage characters...

MN: This is happening more in the TV series, *Tendo Sisters*[3]. In that script, there is a wicked girl studying at the University who is always disorganising her friends. When the public meets her, they call her names. It doesn't happen to me because I play many roles in various performance events, for instance, I am a musician, film director, and actress so it is very hard to pin me on [identify me with] any character. However, for others they have not seen before they think that the movie character and the individual are the same, therefore, they are treated differently.

SK: Filmmaking is expensive, how you do finance your projects?

MN: As I told you before, I have Nile Breweries who have supported me since I launched my film career. At first they didn't trust the [home movie] industry, they said, 'how are we sure we are going to benefit out of it?' However, with time they started to believe in me and offered me sponsorship. I get some money out of product placement from *The Weekly Observer* [News Co-corporation], and other companies. I also get money when I sell the DVDs of my movies and television serials of my other plays. Finally, my singing [musical performances], an area that is already established, earns me a reasonable income. That is how I finance my film projects.

SK: What are the sources of your stories?

MN: It is just what is around me at the time. They are not from what I have read, heard or recollections of folk stories. Maybe one time I will write a play on [the Baganda myth of] Kintu and Nambi. I am so much into fiction...I love creating stuff. I am not like Ashraf [Simwogerere] who is very good at adapting contemporary events for film. The problem with that style is that people will say, 'That is not how it happened.' I am not good at that.

SK: So, you love fiction not faction.

MN: I love fiction.

SK: Why don't you work with oral tales or folk narratives?

MN: I haven't looked at that angle. It hasn't inspired me yet because I think I still have some good stories in my head.

SK: But you don't travel in commuter taxis so you don't know the stories people tell.

MN: I speak to people who use them and others who live in *mizigos*, two-roomed houses.

SK: Have you ever thought of adapting Ugandan literary work?

MN: Yes. It is just that I don't have a lot of time on me to adapt them. I only do one movie a year. For instance, I would like to adapt Omugave Ndugwa's plays…that would be my starting point.

SK: What about other works, for example, Kawere's *Zinnunula Omunaku*[4] or Kiyingi's *Lozio BbaSsesiriya*?[5]

MN: Well, because I was in *Black Pearls* I know Ndugwa's plays on my fingertips; therefore, it would be easier to work on them.

SK: Why don't you do two movies a year?

MN: Because I have several projects, for example, I have a television serial that runs for two seasons a year. I have another reality show, a talent search show for young musicians - so I don't have a lot of time. On top of that, I have the singing …[*Laughs*]. When I was doing *Hearts in Pieces,* I wrote two scripts and I thought I would be able to produce them but I didn't get the time; therefore, I shall work on the second script this year.

SK: Is that as depressing as *Hearts in Pieces*?

MN: [*Laughs*] I don't know.

SK: What kind of stories do you tell?

MN: [*Silence*]

SK: Have I asked a difficult question?

MN: [*Laughs*] … kind of. I am told that my movies demonstrate that I am fighting for women's rights – that struggling woman. [*Laughs*]

SK: What you have said brings me to the next point. Certain scenes seem to be stable in *KinaUganda* home movies. There are domestic scenes in which cameras zoom on the interior decorations of the houses or on beautiful girls or cars. However, the real people are not there.

MN: It is because Ugandans love beautiful things such as women, property and cars. They aspire to possess them. When they see something beautiful they ask, 'Where did you get that from?' So, the more you put these in your movies the more they watch them.

SK: What you have said brings us to that crucial question concerning your work and women. You have stated that you are committed to women but from your work and that of other artists, women are presented from a male perspective. In addition, they are not assigned leading roles. Is this a fair observation?

MN: Yes, that is a fair comment but this is how we as Ugandans, whether male or female, see women.

SK: Is that how YOU see the woman?

MN: It is not just me but other Ugandan directors as well. That is why I start by presenting the woman as they see her. Nevertheless, I also try to bring her out, as she would like to be seen.

SK: But the role you play in *Down This Road I Walk* is the role of a woman who is malevolent, an evil mother-in-law. No woman is positively portrayed in that movie.

MN: There is. The mother to the young woman is portrayed very positively.

SK: But she is a minor character.

MN: True. Because we want to show these evil women so that people see that these types of women should be eliminated from society.

SK: But there are many strong women in Uganda….

MN: There are very many women who are oppressed. Many of these can't stand up to talk about their problems. Domestic violence is rampant and it directly affects around seventy-eight per cent of the women's population.

SK: But in your film, the mother-in-law inflicts torture on her daughter-in-law and in the end, she does not learn from her mistakes.

MN: She does. She is taken to jail.

SK: But she is removed from the scene of her atrocities…

MN: That is why I didn't want Part Two because then I would have to show the details. However, since she goes to jail, she learns that if you behave like that [in that manner] your end is not going to be very good.

SK: In future, do you intend to portray stronger women on stage?

MN: It is unfortunate you did not watch *Strength of a Stranger* because there is a widow oppressed by the sister-in-law, but in the end, she wins.

SK: Which of your films is your favourite?

MN: That is a hard question. I have a passion for each of them: *Down This Road* was my first movie so I love it. *Strength of a Stranger* has its own style…it has a strong woman who wins. *Hearts in Pieces* is different because it represents culture in a variety of ways.

SK: Do you get a lot of media reviews or feedback from people?

MN: Yes I do. When I wrote *Down This Road,* I had a screen bash where I invited the cast, well-wishers and the media. At the end, everyone had to write their comments on the back of the invitation.

SK: What do you think about theatre reviewers in Uganda?

MN: Some good ones give you a genuine opinion. The genuine ones don't write it for money whereas others demand money before they publish the reviews. So, the latter write impressive reviews for monetary gain. These always come to you asking your opinion about the review even before it is published. I don't like that category of reviewers. I don't want to hear the praises but critical evaluations.

SK: Do your films address themselves to any specific audience?

MN: I am targeting that woman between the ages of fifteen to fifty-five. Their response is good.

SK: What is the age group of your audience?

MN: Fifteen to sixty.

SK: Is the reception the same across the age range?

MN: I think so.

SK: When you observe audiences watching films in *bibanda*[6] or makeshift cinema halls, they tend to interact with the films. Sometimes they denounce actions that they see as unacceptable or [they] confirm actions. Is such audience interaction what *KinaUganda* directors aim for? Is that what you aim for?

MN: I do to a limited extent because it is part of the Ugandan popular culture. That aspect is there because it is the traditional Ugandan way of engaging with a performance. When they watch a play or film, they interact with the actors. Nevertheless, I would like my movie to be screened in a cinema where people will watch quietly just like what happens in modern movie halls. I would like them to receive my films the same way they would receive any other.

SK: What languages do you use?

MN: I use English in the movies but sometimes I drop in some few lines of Luganda that I have to translate. I use subtitles because I am not aiming exclusively at local Ugandan audiences but I want to tell the story to the rest of the world.

SK: So, is the language aspect important?

MN: It wouldn't be very important but the reason why I didn't want to use Luganda was because I was moving from stage to film which meant using the same actors that performed in stage productions. Hence, using the same language [Luganda] would mean having actors who ad lib or replicate live stage styles on screen, which is wrong. You have to remember that actors have been exposed to theatre for a long time and they know how that medium works; so even if they have not learnt their lines they ad lib.

SK: When one watches your movies, there are three variations of English, Ugandan, West African and 'British' English. Do you deliberately use Ugandan English?

MN: Yes because I wouldn't want the story to get lost. In Uganda there are people who 'translate' the movies; I mean they do live voice-over translations. I don't know whether you have watched a Ugandan translation of a foreign movie because there are people in makeshift cinema halls whose occupation is to make these translations. It sounds like a running commentary. Some of my movies are translated as well. However, my aim is to enable people outside Uganda to watch, understand and enjoy the movie.

SK: Does this influence the casting process?

MN: Yes, because in the Ugandan context people will not understand the performer who speaks posh English, moreover, he will appear 'foreign' to the rest of the cast. I have a Nigerian performer in one of my movies who speaks English with a heavy accent that is different from Ugandan English. I intentionally gave her a character that is foreign to the community so that people notice her ethnic or (African) regional origin. Because there is an international Luganda-speaking audience in the diaspora who I would want to who watch my films in the movies I include some few lines of Luganda.

SK: What do you think about the comment that home movies use stage scripts not filmic scripts?

MN: It is because we don't have film schools, and people have no reading culture. I have a large library but when I invite people to borrow books on film no one bothers to come. With theatre, they know how it works so they tend to do what they want.

SK: Is the home movie just a phenomenon or does it have a future?

MN: It will fade into television soaps and serials.

SK: Why?

MN: Because I don't think it has a sense of direction. I don't think home movies will survive.

SK: Won't they fade into full-blown films?

MN: May be if they change the way they are made.

SK: Do you think you will come to a point when you remake your movies into full films?

MN: I don't think so. Maybe directors will do if they want to remake them.

SK: Have you been in touch with the so-called serious committed Ugandan writers from the 70s and 80s?

MN: Not really...I think it is because I don't know where to find them. Mind you, a few of them are outside the country.

SK: Tell me something about your own work as a writer or a director.

MN: I like making quality movies, scriptwriting and casting. I like focusing on the best product; something better than what came before.

SK: What do you see as the important themes that you may pursue in the future, especially if you are to reflect on Uganda after the 1986 grassroots struggle?

MN: I grew up after the Milton Obote regime of the early 1980s. This is the time when ethnic discrimination was widespread particularly concerning people from Northern Uganda. I would like to work on this theme. Another area I want to explore concerns the growing up experience of King Oyo of Toro Kingdom [in Western Uganda]. We don't know what happened during the sixteen-year period from when he was crowned, aged three years, until his eighteenth birthday when he took charge of the kingdom. Finally, I would like to work on a script exploring the world of night dancers (wizards) because I believe that practice or cult only exists in Uganda.

SK: Have you read Nuwa Sentongo's play, *The Invisible Bond*?[7]

MN: No. When I was at Kampala High School, my colleagues, [Benoni] Kibuuka and [Charles] Senkubuge, told me that they had taken part in the production. I may make a filmic adaptation of the play.

SK: Apart from the adaptation of *Tendo Sisters* to a home movie, what else are you working on now?

MN: I am working on a movie about a childless couple.

SK: Why?

MN: Just as I told you, I see these things happening around me; stuff we don't talk about, so if we bring them into the open we may be more accepting about people's situations. If we expose the issues, the process may provide answers or solutions and give the audience a different perspective of the problem.

SK: I have known of people who have had no children but have adapted by adopting children.

MN: But have they been successful in their venture?

SK: I think they have but I know that in Uganda, people will blame…

MN: Blame the woman.

SK: In that case, do you see *KinaUganda* as an instrument to address the problems of modern Uganda?

MN: I look at it as a medium for telling our stories and definitely, when you tell a story you have to have a solution to the problem. To me storytelling is about identifying a problem, telling a story about the problem and finding a solution to the problem. Therefore, I look at *KinaUganda* as a form that is trying to tell OUR stories.

SK: Is there anything you would like to say?

MN: Making a movie in Uganda is very expensive although making money out of it is much more expensive. The government is not helping so much but I wouldn't say they are the problem, so I would just love to call upon filmmakers to get together and try to work to uplift the industry.

SK: Is it possible to work as a cooperative?

MN: May be…if we reach some form of agreement. However, because you are a director in your own entity when you meet with your colleagues you find it difficult to blend. I am not worried whether the government knows that we exist or not but I just want filmmakers to come together.

SK: Do Western film artists inform your work?

MN: Somehow.

SK: How?

MN: I am a fond of Tyler Perry. I like the way he tells the story of how black Americans can live better. Just like him, I am trying to tell Ugandan stories which demonstrate that people can change their lives.

SK: Thank very much.

(*Interview conducted on 7 April 2010*)

An Interview with Ashraf Simwogerere

Filmography

Films/Home movies:

Mukajanga(2009) script, director, actor.

Feelings Struggle (2005)script, director, actor.

Murder in the City (2006) script, director, actor

Honourable(date?) script, director, actor.

Hope/Suubi(2009) script, director.

Documentaries:

Voice of Men on Domestic Violence (2009) Commissioned by Mentoring Programmes for the Young Girls & UNDP.

Television Soaps:

London Shock (1999) (aired on Uganda Television) script, director, actor.

*Hope/Suubi (*2010) (aired on Bukedde Television) script, director.

It is evident from his filmography that Simwogerere, reputed to be the most successful *KinaUganda* director, has expanded his movie portfolio since *Feelings of Struggle*. For this interview, I wanted to underline key aspects of his career in film. In particular, I wanted to explore the socio-political context informing his work, including movies such as *Murder in the City* and *Mukajanga*. In addition, I wanted to discuss the absence of strong women characters in his movies.

We talked in the Green Room at the Uganda National Theatre, Kampala, which is the meeting point for many Ugandan artists. At the start of our conversation I asked him which language he would prefer for the interview. Not surprisingly, while he indicated that he was comfortable speaking in English and Luganda, most of his responses were in the latter.

SK: How did you start in theatre and *KinaUganda*?

IS: I spent twenty-four years working in theatre as a playwright, actor and director. I started acting in dramas when I was in primary school but when I joined Kampala High School I met Joy Matovu who introduced me to Kampala Dramactors. This group later broke up and they formed the present day Bakayimbira Dramactors. During that period we staged Shaw's *Androcles and the Lion*, Soyinka's *The Lion and the Jewel* and *The Road*. However, at that time I was acting like a parrot because I did not even understand the plays. Although I went to Makerere University to study dentistry I continued acting with another group, The Black Pearls. In 1994, I wrote my first play, *Omuyaga mu Makoola* that won the prize for the best production. In 1994, we formed our performance company, The Diamond Ensemble. Our most successful project was *London Shock*, staged both in Kampala and London, in 1999. The implication in the play is [that] refugees should not look at London as a solution for all their problems. Following the live productions, we filmed the selected scenes on locations in London and Kampala. Uganda Television (UTV) serialised the play but it only lasted six weeks, therefore they asked us to make more episodes. This was very demanding especially because we were filming on location every week. UTV would give us a camera for three hours, which meant we would shoot on Tuesdays, edit on Thursdays and these would air on the weekend. The play became very popular with the audience and within four years, we aired thirty-eight episodes over four years. Nevertheless, local productions were not popular with sponsors so we were always competing with these for up to four years. When Nigerian films came on the scene in 2004 it gave me an idea to make my own full-length movie. I bought my own camera, a Sony DSR-PD170. I had a young man, Kimera, who had trained in Nairobi, Kenya. I know how to tell a story, so I was determined to venture into the industry. We filmed, edited, and premiered a movie on a young man's struggle through life. The story was a feeling struggle. Some professional cameramen, for example, Faustin Misanvu and George Sengendo formerly of Uganda Television (UTV), who attended the premiere screening of the movie were impressed. Some other people had started making local movies but they had problems marketing and distributing them; however, our marketing was

Fig 2 *Ashraf Simwogerere, Bat Valley Theatre, Kampala, 15 April 2010 (© Sam Kasule)*

effective. The film craft was not the best but the audience liked the story, and I have never looked back. The movie premiered in Britain where it was a hit with the African diaspora community. A company called Urban bought the distribution rights. Up to now, this film has been the most profitable. My other profitable film is *Mukajanga*.

SK: Say something about your work.

AS: First of all, my work is affected by the shortage of money to fund large projects. Secondly, I experience problems with the professional attitude of people working in the industry. Ugandan performers lack professionalism and this is affected by the culture attitude to theatre. They use the concept, '*ngendakuzanya*', which loosely translated means, 'I am going to play.' This connoted a lack of seriousness or commitment, for instance, they don't always keep time. It is disappointing that the good ones do not keep time. For this reason, I always kick them off the production. Cinematographers do not always do that and worst of all, they hate directors who impose their authority. Even though we don't have movie stars (only stage stars), there are no stars cast in major roles in my films because they give me headaches. When I am casting I avoid them unless that person gives me the commitment. If you dock their pay, because of undisciplined behaviour, they don't turn up; a situation that may arise after you have shot half of the script.

SK: Under what circumstances did *KinaUganda* start?

AS: To begin with Ugandans had started making films on a small scale, but the arrival of *EkiNigeriya* (Nollywood) on the scene demonstrated that our stories were similar to the Nigerians so they expanded their activities. I realised that if people like Nigerian stories they will be more excited by well-made local movies. The key issue is that all of us have learnt through experience, by trial and error. The truth is, *KinaUganda* is very popular with Ugandans in the diaspora.

During the initial period, there were many writers, producers and stage scripts but very few screenplay scriptwriters and actors; hence, people who formerly worked in theatre joined film production. As a result, when popular theatre actors, for instance, Kato Lubwama and Abby Mukiibi, are in a movie, it sells a lot. Most Ugandans buy the movies because 'their' favourite actors are the stars of the show. Nevertheless, there are people such as Maisha (a training organisation for filmmaking) who, apart from training people, bring into the country professional directors and producers to conduct workshops. That said, we are still in a transition stage moving from stage to screen.

SK: How has the transition from stage to screen impacted on the way you make films?

AS: Stories are the same but the delivery differs. The way you present a play on stage is different from the way you produce it for the screen. Mind you, my initial training was rooted in live theatre performances and on stage, you engage with eyes and ears but for the screen, you are solely focusing on the visual. You have to imagine that you are producing a movie for the Chinese to watch and understand. For example, we buy Chinese films in which characters speak Mandarin, but the housemaid (semi-illiterate in English) at home will watch it and narrate the story. Now there lies the difference; before venturing into movie making, we were focusing on the dialogue at the expense of the visual images but now we are trying to strike a balance.

SK: Some people say home movies lack artistic merit, and that the industry is just moneymaking, merely showing effects, magic or witchcraft….

AS: The percentage of *KinaUganda* films that focus on magic is very small. However, in Nigeria, the situation may be different, because from my experience – I have been to the country several times – witchcraft is common and acceptable in some ethnic groups. I disagree with the allegation that there is plenty of witchcraft in our movies. Nevertheless, while there will be a few producers who want to copy *EkiNigeriya* styles, most of us have made a conscious effort to avoid presenting scenes of magic and witchcraft. On the issue of labelling home movie producers as moneymakers one has to draw a line between stage and filmic productions. In the Ugandan theatre context, if you have a working script, you may gather some people together, cast, rehearse, advertise and stage the play. In fact, you may premiere your play without investing any money. However, in filmmaking you need a lot of capital before you start. When I started I thought I would mint money but I realised that it would be difficult, therefore, after filming the movie I had to hawk it, screening it in small places around the country – for instance in Jinja, Mbarara, Masaka and Entebbe. Surprisingly, most people thought I had made a lot of money so they jumped on the bandwagon. However, as I said earlier, there are few scriptwriters and skilled directors of photography, therefore, their film scripts were underdeveloped; in addition their artistic work and photography were poor. Unlike Kenya where there are many film schools, Uganda has none. Nevertheless, I don't discourage anyone from venturing into the industry, all I say is that we should get together and start training. Although the university has a section in the literature department that focuses on critical cinematography, there are hardly any local films to critique.

SK: There was a German national who ran a film school during the early eighties...

AS: Those were Germans who came in during Obote's political regime but they left soon after his government was overthrown. Our colonial masters (the British) did not encourage this craft, whereas if you look at Kenya, where they developed the industry, the local people are skilled. In the current economic climate you can start to make a film on a limited budget. People with limited funds come to me wanting to start filming a movie. Maybe this is better because my view is that artistic content will follow after we have launched ourselves into the trade.

SK: How do you go about developing your scripts? How long does it take you?

AS: It depends on the project. I got training at the Makerere University Department of Music, Dance and Drama. I also attended a summer residence at the Royal Court. Therefore, I have developed script-writing skills. I have learnt other skills through correspondence studies or e-materials downloaded from the Internet. The script takes me up to a month to write the draft, but if it needs researching, it may take longer. My handicap is English. If I am working on a commissioned project where the person wants it in English I have to look for a translator. After writing the script, I give it to various people to read it, both ordinary people and academics at the MakerereUniversity. After their feedback, I write the final scripts. Nevertheless, if it is in Luganda, it takes a short time. For instance, since *Mukajanga* was a historical play, I did not want to write it in foreign languages other than Luganda, so it took a short time. The only other languages were Runyankore and Rutooro because I wanted characters from other ethnic groups to speak in their languages.

SK: How long did you take to write *Mukajanga*?

AS: It took six months to research. The advantage was that everything was in Buganda, the central region, and I did not need to go up country.

SK: Did you interview many people?

AS: Wakayima, my grandfather, who died in 1979, was a great resource. At the time, he was over one hundred years of age. When they killed the martyrs, he was about six years old. He lived in Kira village, a suburb of Namugongo, one of the main sites of the massacres. One day in 1977, when he was hospitalised in MengoHospital, they played *Bewaayo*, the Church of Uganda martyrs' anthem. However, when he heard the chorus, 'bewaayo...*battibwangabayimba*' (they died singing...) his response was that those reports had been falsified. He said that they cried a lot. In addition, he told me about Kyaliwajjala, which is on the outskirts of Namugongo.

SK: Why do they call it Kyaliwajjala?

AS: The boys thought that King Mwanga was joking and he wouldn't massacre them because they were his friends. They expected him to send a messenger to instruct Mukajanga to stay the execution; therefore, they resisted the guards' commands to move them at a fast speed. Unfortunately, the guards in a streak of violence hit them and threw their bodies in the King's gardens, looked after by Kyaliwajjala. Hence the saying, 'What happened at Kyaliwajja's garden's is shocking.'

SK: I want to know about King Mwanga as a young man.What are the possible sources of information?

AS: You may go to Mackay's archives at Mackay's Church in Nateete [five miles from Kampala City Centre] or his contemporary the Roman Catholic Mapera's archives [Fr. Loudel] at Mapera Church Place in Kasubi [just three miles from Kampala]. Mackay was the leader of the CMS [Church Missionary Society] missionaries while Mapera [Fr. Loudel] lead the White Father missionaries. The problem is that their records are biased because the narratives are told from a European perspective. But there is a man called Bulwadda whose archives are kept by his great grandchildren. He used to be Mwanga's Arabic translator. Unfortunately, many of the diaries have not been fully translated from Arabic into English.

SK: How do you go about shooting the screenplay?

AS: I don't do auditions. Many people who come to auditions are not good actors; they are after jobs. Out of three hundred who come, you may only need twenty. I like people who have a passion for the acting. Sometimes I approach people who I have seen in films or on stage. It might take me a month before I finalise casting and start filming. I try to change cameramen [cinematographers] or directors of photography [DPOs] depending on their work portfolio. I avoid people who film documentaries or news reports. They are not as artistic as those who film music videos. For example, Bashir, the cameraman for *Mukajanga* had previously worked with music video producers. Because the budgets are limited, I try not to spend a long time shooting; at the same time, I avoid using numerous locations.

SK: How do you finance your productions?

AS: I use my own resources. From the start, I inform the cast that since I have limited resources I will pay them per hour or day spent on location. They are not paid if they don't turn up. Sometimes I make part payments and the rest is paid following the completion of the project. These days it is easy to talk to distributors because they like my work. They pay you an advance; therefore, they fund part of the projects. Therefore, they have funded all my recent film projects.

SK: How do you distribute the movies?

AS: That is a big challenge. Apart from my first film, I have not distributed any of my movies. We start our distribution at the Kampala movie premiere by auctioning the DVDs, but after that, the distributors take over. They usually advertise on radio and television channels. Initially, I give them rights for three years but after that, I regain the copyright. Although the new establishments of new cable television companies has been an exciting positive development for the moviemaker, most of them are more interested in soaps which cost them up to a hundred and fifty pounds as opposed to films/movies that cost three hundred pounds a week in sponsorship.

SK: In the late seventies, we used to do Sentongo's *The City Game* for Uganda Television (UTV), we would record four episodes a day. How many episodes do you record at a time?

AS: You used to have one location, The National Theatre or Nommo Gallery. In our case there are several locations, therefore, on a given day we may film two episodes on different locations.

SK: What are the sources of your stories?

AS: Most of my stories are from local news. I read local newspapers, watch and listen to television news but I do not read [source] stories from books. The last book I read was Apollo Lawoko's *The Dungeons of Nakasero*.

SK: Tell us about your home movies, *Murder in the City*.

AS: *The Daily Monitor* was the first to publish the story. After it was alleged that Dr Kiyingi killed his wife, the ensuing court case was widely reported in the local newspapers. I used the opportunity to write a script with a [fictional] story with characters that had resonant experiences. One journalist who interviewed me asked whether I had based my film on that particular court case but my response was that these were similar, not the same characters. At that point, I was already scheduled to attend the London premiere of my movie, *Feelings Struggle*; in addition, I had arranged to shoot some scenes at London locations for a new play. The presiding judge's reaction to the movie's reviews was to summon me to court to explain why I was prejudicing the case of the defendant (Dr Kiyingi). I got the court summons and notice of a court date on my return to Kampala. The Ugandan Citizens Rescue Organisation (CITRO) sponsored a lawyer to represent me in court. The judge concluded that although the story was similar there was no evidence that I had based it on the case.

SK: Do you base your narratives on oral folk stories?

AS: Sometimes I do. But apart from the folk stories I base some on Ugandan contemporary socio-political experiences. My new film is based on the Yoeri Museveni's Luweero triangle liberation struggle. I have called it *Museveni the Wild Cat*.[8] When Museveni was in the bush [waging a guerrilla war against the Uganda government] many people, particularly members of the armed forces, believed in the fallacy that he used special powers to turn himself into a cat or other forms of wild animals. For instance, one day a man was travelling along Gayaza Road, northeast of Kampala, when at Magigye road block [an army checkpoint] a cat escaped from his bag. The army men panicked, shot at the cat but it disappeared. The man was accused of collaborating with the bandits [guerrillas] and we all suspected that he was killed afterwards.

Other movies in this category include a movie based on the Baganda myth, *Kintu and Nambi*. However, I use it for demonstrations at film festivals. You know it is impossible to market a fifteen-minute movie DVD in Uganda.

SK: Have you thought about adapting Ugandan literary works?

AS: In Uganda, the reading culture is very poor. A large percentage of

Ugandans like watching films but they do not buy or read books. For example, apart from secondary school students, how many people have read Soyinka's play, *The Lion and the Jewel*? Alex Mukulu's *Wounds of Africa* is a published play but I don't know whether many people have read it, whereas hundreds watched it at the National Theatre. So, if he made it into a movie it would help him reach a wider audience.

SK: What stories do you tell?

AS: Melodramatic stories, especially those that narrate events or reflect on people's urban experiences. However, my interest is in faction.

SK: What is your favourite film?

AS: *Feelings Struggle,* my first film, set me up and gave me a reputation as a good movie director. Because of this film, people call me the pioneer. *Murder in the City* made me a household name; *Honourable* introduced me to multinational sponsors and partnerships work with non-government organisations [NGOs], and *Mukajanga* put me on the international market. I like *Mukajanga* because of the professional work I invested in it. However, although people call me the pioneer of Ugandan movies I was not the first one on the scene.

SK: Wasn't Jimmy Katumba, the late popular music theatre artist, the first person to make a local Ugandan movie?

AS: No, it is Ngoma Players when you made *The City Game* television episodes in the late seventies. *The City Game* reminds of Katende Lutwama because he played a key role both as a star and in influencing me to think about the moving image as an option to stage plays. The only problem is that you never marketed your films.

SK: Unlike today, at the time very few people owned TV sets.

AS: In Uganda people who buy films are very few, maybe not more than 10,000, however, in Nigerian there is a large market. In Ugandan village communities there are very few people who own video players but quite a few will have television sets. Those who own DVDs have to hide them because they fear being robbed.

SK: In *KinaUganda* home movies, cameras zoom in on beautiful women, cars, good décor? Why?

AS: That is a Nigerian influence but it is not evident in my films. It is not a Ugandan culture, nevertheless, it is encouraged by the distributors who push this practice, and therefore, cars used in filming may include SUVs or other front-wheel drive vehicles, Mercedes Benz and other expensive cars. Most times, they forget that the story cannot accommodate these things. Concerning houses, I watched a film where someone used a hotel as the main character's home. Nonetheless, this is not true of Ugandan society but the directors are using stereotypes.

SK: Why don't we have strong women in these stories?

AS: Well, if you look at the Holy Scriptures or the Koran, women are the sinners. We tend to present stereotypes of our society that takes women as bad people. Arguably, the directors are men who are products of these ideologies, so they project weak women. However, Mariam Ndagire as a female director is trying to project positive female characters.

SK: How are you going to change these representations of stereotypes?

AS: I have tried in some of my films, for instance, in *Honourable* I have positive female characters. I am aware that films play a role in changing people's attitudes and perceptions but you will note that women, who control homes and make up a large percentage of our audiences, like films with evil women characters. By extension, in Uganda where most people employ house girls to look after their homes and care for the children; surprisingly, what house girls (housemaids) enjoy is what the men enjoy.

SK: In the Luweero triangle movie, are you going to present the strong female liberators [fighters]?

AS: Yes, fighters like Lieutenant Colonel Nalweyiso and Captain Zizinga, but the problem is that the leaders of the uprising also leave them out of the narrative of the struggle. These were the first ever women to join the army in Uganda...

SK: Nobody has told their stories...

AS: Not yet...even in Museveni's *Mustard Seed*, they are not mentioned. But I shall try to project those women who were at the frontline. I shall be exploring Hajati Mukwaya's [another brave female liberator] experiences in the bush.

SK: Do you receive feedback from the audience?

AS: Yes, I try to talk to the audience after the screening of my movies. The problem with Uganda is that because of insecurities during Milton Obote's second presidency [1980–1985], live theatre performances would last up to four hours. Contrary to this, movies are two hours in length. Since people remain seated, I take the opportunity to ask them for their views.

Journalists are a problem because they try to compare you with international filmmakers such as Kevin MacDonald, the director of the *Last King of Scotland*; but we try to respond to their interviews by informing them that the *KinaUganda* industry is still in its infancy. There are major problems of sound for our films because on many occasions we use camera mikes [microphones].

SK: Can you comment on the fact that in live performances people tend to talk to the actors and interact with the audience?

AS: I am happy with it because when it happens I know my message has been delivered. My problem is when they react negatively to a sad scene.

SK: Do you have a policy of encouraging upcoming directors?

AS: I am organising a clinic that will last for a month. I will be taking on twenty people. I will not charge them a lot.

SK: When will this film be ready?

AS: June this year.

SK: Thank you.

(Interview conducted on 9 April 2010)

NOTES (TO BOTH INTERVIEWS)

1   For this production, Wole Soyinka's *The Road* (1965) was adapted and acted both in Luganda and English.

2   Afri Talent's television serial, *Ensitaano* aired on WBS between 2003 and 2005.

3   Mariam Ndagire's *Tendo Sisters* (2009) originally ran as a television serial but has now been made into a film

4   Edward Kawere's *Zinnunula Omunaku* (1961) was the first full-length book of fiction written in Luganda.

5   Wycliff Kiyingi's *Lozio BbaSsesiriya* (1972) focuses on poverty and political unrest in Amin's Uganda.

6   Shelters whose walls constructed using bamboo or *mabanda* in Luganda.

7   Nuwa Sentongo was one of the early Ugandan playwrights writing in English. His play, *The Invisible Bond* (1999) has been widely performed in East and West Africa.

8   In a recent discussion with the playwright – on 4 November 2010 – he informed me that government agents have ordered him to drop this title and replace it with 'A Night in a Day' otherwise they would withdraw their cooperation on the project. He explained that they were concerned that the title would be negatively interpreted.

Zimbabwe's Studio 263
Navigating between entertainment & health messaging

SAMUEL RAVENGAI

Background and context

My focus in this article is a Zimbabwean television soap opera, *Studio 263*, concentrating on the period 2002 to 2006, even though it is still running on ZBCTV, albeit with intermittent stops and resumptions. *Studio 263* has also been screened in Tanzania, Zambia and South Africa (from the Mnet Africa Magic channel). The *Studio 263* sponsor, PSI-Z, is a Non-Governmental Organisation that originates from (and arguably represents the interests of) the United States of America. During the period 2002–6, PSI-Z was funded by the United States Agency for International Development (USAID) and the British Department of International Development. The funding of *Studio 263* by western development aid agencies is generally seen as bringing about development which I will argue places the developing world in a dependent relationship with the West, making it a prisoner of history. During the same period PSI also sponsored a television talk show called *This is Life*, co-produced by PSI-Z and ZBCTV. The talk show offered a platform to discuss issues of sexuality, health, HIV/AIDS prevention, treatment and mitigation, stigmatization, condom use and safe sex.

The United States government was also involved in fighting HIV/AIDS through a radio soap opera called *Mopani Junction*[1] which was launched in February 2003 for a planned broadcast of two years and was broadcast at 18:30, three days a week, in three languages – Shona (Monday), Ndebele (Wednesday) and English (Thursday) with repeats in Shona and Ndebele on Saturday and Sunday at 19:30 hours (US Embassy 2003: *The Daily News on Sunday*). This was also the first soap opera in Shona and Ndebele on Zimbabwean radio. *Malikopo*, which began in 1947 and was broadcast in Tonga by the Central African Broadcasting Services (CABS) could be considered the first radio soap opera in a central African language (Kerr 1998: 127). Samatha Nyakabau (2004) recounts the dramatised reading of Shona novels on Rhodesia Broadcasting Corporation–African Service from 1971 and the popular dramas of Safiro Madzikatire (*Mhuri yavaMukadota*). Radio dramas and songs during the Zimbabwean struggle were beamed from the Voice of

Zimbabwe in Mozambique, but none of them can be classified as soap operas. David Kerr (1998: 121-6) enumerates various CABS radio dramatic serials like Masiye's *The Lands of Kazembe*, broadcast in English in 1957 as well *Mumba and His Bicycle* broadcast in Shona in the late 1940s, but none of these fit into the soap opera genre. After Zimbabwean independence in 1980, there was a great outburst of articulation on both radio and television. Samatha Nyakabau (2004) traces this artistic development, but argues that the plays were merely dramatic serials rather than soap operas.[2] This seems to suggest that both *Studio 263* and *Mopani Junction* were the first soap operas to be created and broadcast in Zimbabwe.

According to a US Embassy Press Release (2003) the money for financing *Mopani Junction* was channelled through the United States Centres for Disease Control and Prevention-Zimbabwe. *Mopani Junction* targeted the rural youth while *Studio 263* targeted the urban youth. I will argue that American aid agencies were setting the agenda for debate in Zimbabwe through the various media products that they were funding. The Technical Advisor of PSI-Z between 2002 and 2003, Soumitro Ghosh, read and approved all *Studio 263* scripts before shoots then was replaced by Yasmin Madan in 2004 when Ghosh left for Botswana. During the same year I joined *Studio 263* first as a Story Consultant (replacing Aaron Chiundura Moyo, the then story creator and head writer) and then as Associate Director until my departure at the end of 2006. Godwin Mawuru has been the *Studio 263* Executive Producer since its inception in September 2002. The evidence that I rely on in this article is therefore empirical, based on ethnographic participation and observation of the production process at first hand.[3]

Studio 263's original working title was *MuHarare Hamurarwe (People Work all Night in Harare)* which was abandoned for the former title as it brought a national identity to the show (263 is the national telephone code for Zimbabwe) as opposed to a city identity. Aaron Chiundura Moyo (2002-4) headed the creative department and was assisted by Leonard Matsa and Tawanda Gunda who worked as Associate Writers. Right from the beginning, the PSI-Z Technical Advisor, Soumitro Ghosh, was involved in the conception of characters. As PSI-Z is preoccupied with issues of health and HIV/AIDS, the creative department was asked to create ten characters who represented the various HIV/AIDS messages that PSI-Z wanted to put across to the viewers. The characters at conception level are symbols of a poetic vision, who represent various ideas and symbols on the Aids epidemic, but they evolved into three dimensional fictional human characters, as the script writers pursued clearly defined goals for each character with various obstacles involved in meeting that objective. Each character was given a plan of action, will power expressed in dialogue and action, a clear value system, personality traits and complexity. The character, Vimbai Jari stands for the ideal business woman who goes through the rigours of education, achieves her professional goals, and resolves to abstain from sex until she meets a suitable marriage partner. To test her resolve, the character of Tom Mbambo is created to be charming and lustful, a rapacious businessman with predatory ways of creating wealth. Tom together with another male character, James, use various ploys to seduce Vimbai. Although she is emotionally bruised by their advances, she remains steadfast in abstaining from sex before marriage. The character Wellington Shereni is the binary opposite of Vimbai in the sense that he represents risky behaviour, sleeping around with women, living fast and having unprotected sex. Beverly, while in every way like Wellington Shereni in terms of having multiple sex partners, is projected as a consistent condom user.

Muvengwa and his wife Siphilisiwe represent a discordant couple. Muvengwa sleeps around and fathers a child with Eve outside marriage. He contracts HIV, but his wife Siphilisiwe tests HIV-negative. The couple is meant to teach a typical family how to live in a healthy way, even in discord. Tendai Jari becomes pregnant by her high school teacher Kenge, who infects her with HIV. The child that is born is, however, HIV negative. Tendai, therefore represents people who are stigmatised because of their positivity. After Kenge is imprisoned for statutory rape, Tendai, who is now a single mother, falls in love with Bruce, who is HIV negative. She does not know how to tell Bruce about her HIV status. The community and the church who know about Tendai's status stigmatise her and she has to carry the burden of all the pressures that come from the society. While all other families in the soap opera are scandal-ridden, the Jari family – Chenai, Jari and later Shereni (who falls in love with Chenai when Jari dies) – represent the ideal family that the average urban dweller should emulate. In the Jari family, Jabu represents African patriarchal authority as he assumes the headship of the family when his father dies. Even though he is younger than Vimbai, he takes charge of the family and tries to deal with the pressures that emanate from the girl child's resistance to masculine authority. Even though Jabu is not a virgin, he marries Sibo whom the clan and Jabu himself ostracise for not being a virgin.

When Yasmin Madan took over as PSI-Z Technical Advisor, she insisted that the story revolve around these characters. Although initially Soumitro Ghosh had accepted some subplots – for example about JH Construction, Jacob Syndicate and Tom Mbambo Holdings, – for entertainment purposes, these were not given prominence as compared to subplots with a health message potential. This also became the source of conflict between the *Studio 263* Creative department and the new PSI-Z Technical Advisor, Yasmin Madan. In her feedback comments on the 2005 master story Madan stated:

- I sincerely believe that no effort has been made to integrate the health messages within the main storyline or even build subplots around health messages
- We are diluting our focus due to too many subplots and shallow entertainment
- I am not at all comfortable with this (Jacob Syndicate subplot). Please remove this from the plot. This seems to be bordering on ridiculous things and needs to be changed right away. ... Please stop making this a 'police show!' (Cited in a letter, Ravengai 2005: 1)

What is clear from the conception of characters and the focus that the story should take is that there is a strong belief that television can influence the attitudes, behaviour and choices of the viewers. This is indeed a positivist approach to the power of television or the media in general. I am using the positivist theory in the same way it is defined and used by Pieter Fourie as an approach that 'places the accent on film and television as commercial products exercising a certain influence on human behaviour and circumstances, and on the functions of the media' (1988: 1). *Studio 263* can, therefore be located within the corpus of pro-development soap operas.

Theorising development and pro-development soap operas

Development is a multi-dimensional process which, when it has taken place, results in major changes in social structure, popular attitudes and the national condition of life from unpleasant to satisfactory. If, for example, patriarchal authority in a country such as Zimbabwe takes away the power from women to decide how and when they can have sex, that can be challenged through informational programmes like *Studio 263* where characters like Muvengwa and Siphilisiwe will engage in a duel which results in Muvengwa's resolve becoming softened. Siphilisiwe is empowered in *Studio 263* through attending post-test counselling sessions to challenge the masculine authority that Muvengwa used to disempower his sex partners. In this case a cultural institution – the patriarchal home – is targeted for change. The crisis of this sociological approach is that third world countries are asked to emulate western stages of development, which audiences view not as a creative process, but as aping western models. Development can also be understood through human-istic approaches. An alternative Afro-centric model is that of *unhu/ubuntu*. If individuals have the spirit of being human, they will not be malicious to others, and change can easily take place in a community where people with such a disposition reside. This approach seeks to liberate the human being and where there are liberties there is creativity in all sectors of life. If oppressive individuals and institutions are changed for the better, there will be creativity and development in that society.

Development can also be understood in terms of underdevelopment/ dependency theories. This refers to the relationship that exists between Europe and its former colonies where the former processes raw materials (into finished products) supplied by the latter. Developing countries such as Zimbabwe are seen as prisoners of history where they cannot disentangle themselves from this unequal relationship. This seems applicable even to the *Studio 263* case where western funds are channelled to Zimbabwe through NGOs to generate and package information that would be used to effect change in Zimbabwean society on the subject of HIV/AIDS. What is clear in all these approaches to development is that the end result is change of attitude, social structure and the national condition of a given country from unsatisfactory conditions to a satis-factory one. What is at the centre of this development is information that is dis-seminated through *Studio 263* to improve people's lifestyles. A pro-develop-ment soap opera like *Studio 263* operates like any other generic soap opera but above all, as Florence Mukanga notes:

... a pro-development soap opera [is] an ongoing episodic work of fiction which contains messages concerning national issues like family planning and HIV and AIDS. [It is] designed to promote development and [its] structure is in such a way that there is a balance between entertainment and developmental messages being communicated. [It] is aimed at overcoming specific ignorance or prejudice on the part of the public. (2005: 6)

Studio 263 during the period under review was an intervention strategy providing persuasive messages of empowering individuals to protect themselves against HIV. The message revolved around prevention, mitigation and treatment of HIV/AIDS. In 2005, 24 *per cent* of sexually active adults in Zimbabwe were HIV infected and 3,209 people died weekly due to HIV/ AIDS-related illnesses (Mukanga 2005: 7).

As I stated above, PSI-Z's approach to information dissemination through *Studio 263* is positivist, a theory which assumes that media products can influence human behaviour to bring about development. The positivist approach can be explained in five different but related ways all of which, except one, imply that the information channelled to viewers must be captivating before it can be consumed by the target audience. PSI-Z seemed to negate the aspect of entertainment and dwelt on the health content of the programme. The weaknesses of that approach will soon be clear.

The first positivist approach to media use is the hypodermic needle theory which 'equates the influence of the media with the effect of an intravenous injection: certain values, ideas and attitudes are injected in the individual media user resulting in particular behaviour' (Fourie 1988: 8). This approach seems to have been driving the choices of PSI-Z as they seemed to subscribe to the view that once information is conveyed through television and therefore reached out to many people at once, other variables did not matter. The viewer is seen as passive and helpless object of reception. The other four positivist theories deviate from this position and I apply them in the analysis of *Studio 263* to underscore the fact that a balance needs to be struck between health messages and entertainment in order for the objectives of development to be realised. The remaining four positivist theories underscore the importance of other variables in order to make message reception effective.

The two-step flow theory developed by Klapper (1958) concludes that 'as a rule media communication in itself is not a necessary or sufficient cause for behavioural change. At most it operates in conjunction with and via certain mediating factors and influences' (cited in Fourie 1988: 10). These factors may include the level of education of individual viewers, religion, aesthetic taste, traditional authority and other factors. Since *Studio 263* was aimed at urban young people, it needed to capture the flavour and tone of urban youth popular culture and one of the best ways of reaching out to them was to offer entertainment through other subplots while health messages were then grafted onto a captivating programme. Neither of the two PSI-Z technical advisors – Ghosh and Madan – had stayed in Zimbabwe long enough to know adequately the urban youth popular culture. The *Studio 263* creative department had the advantage of having five Zimbabwean associate writers who had recently graduated with theatre arts degrees. This natural advantage that the creative department had was not fully exploited as the preoccupation was to present factual information on HIV/AIDS. Listed below are examples of scenes and episodes with health messages:

> Episode 329, Scene 2 – A hospital Matron highlights that a baby is tested [for HIV) when she/he is one year, eight months old.
> Episode 340, Scene 3 – Amai Chiko and Tendai discuss the possibility of Chiko[4] contracting HIV. Tendai explains that she breastfed exclusively.
> Episode 359, Scene 2 – Amai Chiko approaches a doctor to get information on Chiko contracting HIV from Tendai. The doctor gives her professional advice.
> Episode 475 – Muvengwa goes for post-test counselling on marital discordance.
> (Ravengai 2004/5, Studio 263 Step outlines)

The scenes for these particular episodes were written after a thorough research which involved interviews with *Studio 263* health consultants, Doctors Karen and Chivaura. The scripts would be sent to Yasmin Madan for approval before shoots. Madan demanded that timelines be set for the screening of health messages as evidenced for instance by the following messages:

> Early September [2004] – Jabu will continue pressing for sex and Sibo will refuse.
> Mid-September – Muvengwa collects results. The issue of discordance between him and Siphilisiwe comes into play.
> End of September – Tendai develops TB symptoms. The message is opportunistic infections. Tendai is diagnosed as having TB [and] at the same time stigmatisation on Tazvitya by Muvengwa's children begins.
> Early October [2004] – Siphilisiwe and Muvengwa go for post-test counselling on discordance. (Ravengai 2004-5: Studio 263 Step Outlines)

Apart from the health messages in the story, PSI-Z had advertising time on the show. The structure of each twenty-five- minute episode was such that there was a thirty-second opening billboard, three eight- minute segments and a thirty-second closing billboard with credits. After every eight minutes PSI-Z ran at least three advertisements encouraging men to use condoms, encouraging viewers to go for HIV testing at New Start Centres and encouraging mothers to prevent transferring the HIV virus to their new born babies by taking appropriate drugs. While the intention of conveying information was noble, the method of presentation created schisms and conflicts between the sponsor and the creative department. In a letter to Yasmin Madan as the Story Consultant I raised the following objection regarding health messages and advertisements:

> In some cases sponsored soap operas can have little or nothing to do with the sale of a sponsor's product. The soap will have been sponsored for entertaining viewers while the mileage for the sponsor comes from putting its name and products before viewers who are watching a good soap opera and the message in the advertisement will remain in the minds of the viewers who see

the soap opera with a friendly and likeable connotation... The problem with this show [*Studio 263*] is that the sponsor is trying to put everything, interfere with the entertainment value of the story, put large quantities of health stuff in the story and at the same time advertises on health issues in the same show! It waters down the whole episode as the best way to instruct viewers is to appeal to them at a subconscious level (Ravengai 2005: 3, letter to Yasmin Madan, 21 January).

The third positivist theory – the uses and gratification theory – demonstrates the importance of packaging health messages in an entertaining story. The theory proceeds from the needs of viewers and the gratification that they derive from a programme like *Studio 263*. Fourie (1988: 12) argues that viewers watch television essentially for three reasons – diversion, personal relations and personal identity. From the perspective of the first reason, viewers watch television for entertainment to temporarily escape from reality, getting some king of therapy through emotional relaxation. If a television programme like *Studio 263* does not offer this aspect of entertainment viewers may choose to ignore it. This is analogous to Albert Bandura's social learning theory, who is cited by Florence Mukanga as saying that 'individuals, especially children, imitate or copy modelled behaviour from personally observing others and the mass media. However, there are three conditions governing the operation of observational learning, that is attention, retention and motivation' (quoted in Mukanga 2005: 21). For the behaviour to be imitated and retained, it must hook the attention of the person viewing it. The implication is that viewers should focus on the behaviour first before they can successfully imitate it and the question is, how can this be possible if the image is not captivating or worthy of catching the attention of the viewer? The second dimension of personal relations is established between the viewer and the character who may eventually be experienced as a friend. Somewhat related to this is the third dimension of personal identity where personal traits of a television character may affirm the personal identity of a viewer. The viewer then gets gratification of self-knowledge through the character who behaves or has the same condition as the viewer. As I have demonstrated above, the message carrying characters in *Studio 263* in one way or another reflect the health conditions of some Zimbabwean viewers. There are those who are HIV positive like Tazvitya, Tendai and Muvengwa, there are discordant couples like Muvengwa and Siphilisiwe and those who choose to abstain from sex like Vimbai. Viewers who share the same identity will develop a strong connection with these characters, persuading them to watch *Studio 263* when it is on air. However, the storyline must also be captivating in order for the viewers to establish a personal relationship and personal identity with the characters. The press indeed had unkind words for the *Studio 263* story of 2004. Garikai Mazara of *The Sunday Mail* wrote, 'how many viewers out there could stand those scenes, endless indeed they were when Jabu was at the New Start Centre? ... Those scenes of Jabu answering HIV and AIDS questions can at best suit a documentary' (2004: *Sunday Mail Entertainment*).

The last two positivist theories – the cultural indicators theory and the agenda setting theory – are somewhat related. Like all other positivist theories the cultural indicators theory assumes that 'the values, knowledge and attitudes of all individuals are constructed, sustained, adapted and changed through the exchange of symbols' (like television images) (Fourie 1988: 12). Since television and the media in general are important in influencing values of viewers it is therefore important to determine three areas of television content:

- On what television focuses attention
- On what it places the emphasis
- The value-judgements it passes. (Fourie 1988: 13)

When such questions are posed, the answers resonate with the fifth positivist theory – the agenda setting theory – which Fourie (1988: 17) explains as the tendency of the media to release a list of topics similar to the agenda of a meeting which it sees as the most important. The practice of the theory rests on amnesia in the sense that it consciously or unconsciously omits other events as unimportant and projects those it has chosen as the most important ones. For PSI-Z, HIV/AIDS was the most important topic which it had chosen to put on the agenda for Zimbabweans. The approach was comprehensive and multi-sectoral. During the 2002-6 period, there were a number of billboards and images on municipality bins in all cities and towns sponsored by PSI-Z on HIV/AIDS. When *Studio 263* took a four-week break in August 2003, it came back screening five episodes per week at 7.30pm from Monday to Friday. Much of the content dwelled on HIV/AIDS issues and PSI-Z also ran advertisements on the same subject on the show and other television and radio programmes. The radio soap opera *Mopani Junction* did the same thing on three working days and weekends. There was a media blitz on the issue of HIV/AIDS. While no doubt this approach helped to bring awareness of the HIV pandemic, it collaterally created an image of a sick country which constitutes a western preferred reading – the presentation of Africa as a disease-ridden continent that needs the intervention of the West to save it. This reinforces the underdevelopment/dependency theory that I have discussed above.

If this theorisation can be accepted, it may help us to understand the bigger issues in *Studio 263* where PSI-Z hardly allowed positive images of Zimbabweans to see the light of day. Apparently-preferred images on *Studio 263* were mostly negative. Some Zimbabweans working with PSI-Z shared the creative department's concerns about positive images. For instance the Marketing Officer of PSI-Z David Chikonde wrote an email to Yasmin Madan which was copied to the *Studio 263* Story Consultant suggesting that:

> The idea of an ideal business concept has to be developed [in *Studio 263*]. In the soap we are having 'indigenously' run businesses and there is absence of a sound and professional business empire benchmarking with other soaps like *Kabanana*. Focus should be on JH Construction improving the level of managerial skill because we are having a group of family members who most of them do not have business back-

ground and are good at boardroom squabbles. This is artificial because the business is still kicking yet there is no expertise. Let's have a turnaround like the route where Vimbai is going for evening studies, doing a professional course (Chikonde 2004: email to Madan 21 September 2004, 8:12am).

However, Yasmin Madan accepted the JH Construction subplot only if 'HIV/AIDS issues in the workplace – at JH Construction' (ibid) were given prominence. All other subplots that did not talk about HIV/AIDS were supposed to be scrapped as I have demonstrated above. When the creative department resisted the dictations of PSI-Z, the sponsor threatened to withdraw funding and in February 2004, PSI-Z held a meeting with the national broadcaster ZBCTV where the threat to withdraw funding was discussed, although Soumitro Ghosh publicly refuted the fact (Mazara 2004: *Sunday Mail Entertainment*). Subsequent to these events, the creative department held several meetings with the new Technical Advisor, Yasman Madan, and also attended by the new PSI Country Director Mr Chomey and the Executive Producer of *Studio 263* Godwin Mawuru at both *Studio 263* (43 Churchill Road) and PSI-Z (30 The Chase, Emerald Hill) offices. Some of the meetings were abrasive and emotional, but the creative department stood its ground as evidenced by the letter sent to Yasmin Madan:

> You refer to some of the stories as 'shallow entertainment'. We believe that health messages become more effective if they are engraved in an entertaining story... Film art is not a school. It is an art form which is able to project the image of human nature which delights and instructs mankind through splendid actors speaking splendid dialogue and involved in typical human problems, lovely settings, brilliant lighting effects that dazzle and overwhelm viewers, music and other things that arouse, agitate and stimulate our nerves more and more. If you employ professionals to write a script for film art, their preoccupation will be on those things that will give the show a cutting edge. And that is what we have done with the master story... We believe that a soap opera must not only be a purveyor of moralistic and factual issues especially if the story has to revolve around the ten AIDS characters you have singled out. Its lessons must be pleasurable, entertaining and enjoyable, and this can be achieved in other subplots that are intriguing. (Ravengai 2005: 2, letter to Yasmin Madan 21 January)

After these meetings and letter writings, PSI-Z adopted a quiet diplomacy approach. When the contract between Afro-Eye and PSI-Z expired during the first quarter of 2005, it was never renewed and *Studio 263* was alone, but continued to enjoy technical support (scaled down to equipment) from ZBCTV. Because of the potential that *Studio 263* had demonstrated during its troubled three-year run, Doves Funeral Services took over the sponsorship of the project and was later followed by Zimbabwe Allied Banking Group (ZABG). The creative department maintained the characters and subplots inherited from PSI-Z and sharpened other subplots that PSI-Z had rejected. Viewership shot up from 2.6 million to nearly three million by the end of 2005 taking the show to first position ahead of the traditional favourite ZBCTV News Hour as the most watched television programme in Zimbabwe (Mazara

2004; Select Research). It won National Arts Merit Awards (NAMA) in virtually all soap opera categories – acting, directing and production between 2005 and 2006. However, a combination of weak administration and exogenous factors caused by the collapse of the economy during the crisis period in Zimbabwe negatively affected *Studio 263* and it faced new challenges that could be investigated in another study.

Conclusion

I hope to have demonstrated the difficulty experienced by the scriptwriter where the sponsor's objectives seem to negate fundamentals of television techniques and aesthetics. I suggest that the scriptwriter must decide in his/her professional conscience whether the sponsor has made a good decision or there are some aspects of the decision that would prove to be ineffective as in the case with *Studio 263*. The creative collective took a position that its artistic integrity was not going to be compromised by financial considerations.

Through recourse to the five positivist theories, I hope to have clarified that health messages that are located in a non-captivating story are not as effective as those that are part of a story that is entertaining. While making sure not to project all foreign NGOs as inherently evil (some of them are doing a splendid job in Zimbabwe and other Third World countries) I have highlighted that the *Studio 263* project through the 'agenda setting approach' did not proffer positive images of Zimbabwean cultural, political and business institutions (such as a good police force, a soundly run business empire or the value of traditional practices) opting to project the image of a sick country in public imagery. While the Zimbabwean crisis remains one of the worst crises in Africa, at least there were also good things that were worth including as part of the public imaginary. Theorisation on the influence of NGOs or sponsors in general on art works have tended to project the power of the sponsor as absolute, making artistic demands that are carried out to the letter by the creative collective. Throughout this discussion, I hope to have shown that the *Studio 263* creative collective had a level of agency that made it difficult for PSI-Z to carry out some of its negative objectives with impunity.

NOTES

1   The Zimbabwe Broadcasting Corporation (ZBC) issued a notice of intent to terminate this soap opera on 30 July 2003 after six months. It was eventually taken off the air for political reasons. Its target audience of the rural youth was considered a traditional ZANU PF stronghold and some of the themes in the soap ruffled the feathers of politicians. The soap opera was also used as an excuse by NGOs to distribute free shortwave radios that were able to receive signals from the so-called pirate radio stations such as SW Radio and Studio 7 of the Voice of America.

2   For more detail about the generic codes of a soap opera see Ravengai (2004a, 2004b) and Allen (1985).

3   I did not join *Studio 263* for purposes of research, but for purely economic reasons. It is only now that I look in retrospect and take advantage of the knowledge that I shared and gained during the process.

4   After Tendai gave birth to her son, Kenge (the coloured boyfriend teacher) sneaked into hospital and stole the baby and replaced it with a black child (in order to escape responsibility on the basis of lack of biological similarities with the father); Tendai looked after the child.

REFERENCES

Allen, Roberts (1985), *Speaking of Soap Operas* (London and Chapel Hill: The University of Carolina Press).

Chikonde, David (2004), <dchikonde@psi-zim.co.zw>, email to Yasmin Madan <ymadan@psizim.co.zw> Harare: PSI-Z, 21 September, 8:21 a.m.

Chiundura Moyo, Aaron (2002–4), Studio 263, Harare: PSI-Z and Afro-Eye Film and Video Productions.

Fourie, Pieter J. (1988), *Aspects of Film and Television Communication* (Cape Town and Johannesburg: Juta Press).

Kerr, David (1998), *Dance, Media Entertainment and Popular Theatre in South East Africa* (Bayreuth: Bayreuth University Press).

Mazara, Garika. (2004), 'Studio 263, PSI Parting Ways?' *The Sunday Mail Entertainment*, 15 February.

Mukanga, Florence (2005), 'An Investigation into the Treatment of the Theme of HIV and AIDS in the Soap Opera Studio 263', unpublished BA Hons Dissertation, Harare: Department of Theatre Arts, University of Zimbabwe.

Muonwa, Ngonidzashe (2006), Studio 263, Harare: Afro-Eye Film and Video Productions.

Nyakabau, Samatha (2004). 'The Emergence and Development of Soap Operas in Zimbabwe', unpublished BA Hons Dissertation, Harare: Department of Theatre Arts, University of Zimbabwe.

Ravengai, Samuel (2005), Letter to Yasmin Madan, Harare: Afro-Eye Film and Video Productions

Ravengai, Samuel (2004/5a), Studio 263 Master Story, Harare: PSI-Z and Afro-Eye Film and Video Productions

Ravengai, Samuel (2004/5b), Studio 263 Step Outlines, Harare: PSI-Z and Afro-Eye Film and Video Productions

Ravengai, Samuel (2004a), 'ZTV is Still to Make a Soap', *Sunday Mirror Review*, 7 March.

Ravengai, Samuel (2004b), 'Not Everything Called a Soap on ZTV is a Soap', *Daily Mirror*, 26 February.

United States Embassy (2003), Press Release: 'US Embassy Regrets Decision to Terminate Broadcast of Mopani Junction', *The Daily News on Sunday*.

Wallace, Pamela (2000), *You Can Write a Movie* (Ohio: Writer's Digest Books).

Vele Abantu Sinjalo[1]
Nationhood & ethno-linguistic dissent
in Zimbabwean television drama

NEHEMIAH CHIVANDIKWA &
NGONIDZASHE MUWONWA

Introduction

In Africa and elsewhere television programmes normally advance and promote
state ideology as they are usually exploited as an instrument to construct and
protect the values and institutions of the ruling elite or the interests of those in
control of capital (Bramlet and Farwell 1996, Strinati 1996). However, the
overall social and ideological objective function of television programmes can
only be fully comprehended within the complex interrelation of their texts,
audiences and producers (Abercrombie 1996). Television is a medium of
power and significance in and for everyday life, However, this power cannot
be understood without attending to the complex over- and under-determining
inter-relationships of the medium and the various levels of social and political
reality with which it engages (Silverstone 1994:12). This article examines the
way in which dramatic performance styles have been incorporated in the construction of and engagement with national and ethnic identities in Zimbabwe.
Focus is on the construction and 'performance' of dialogue as ethno-linguistic
dissent with reference to *Sinjalo*[2] (2002), a popular drama series aired on
Zimbabwe Television (ZTV). Considerable attention is paid to the function
and limitations of ethno-linguistic dissent in the construction of nationhood in
a multi-lingual and democratic society. The overriding thesis guiding the
investigation is the recognition that language is not merely a form of domination but is also a 'terrain' of dissent (Bleiker 2000:215).

The choice of the drama series *Sinjalo* derives from the huge popularity of
the programme among viewers across the ethnic divides. The apparent contro-
versy when it was removed from the schedule under suspicious political
circumstances and the attempt made by its makers to represent a variety of
ethno-linguistic categories makes the drama series worthy of ideological and
intellectual investigation in a continent where local and western cultural
imperialism on national television is rife (Chivandikwa 2010, Furusa 2000,
Kerr 1998, Mashiri 1998).

Zimbabwe's ethno-linguistic context

Zimbabwe is characterised by ethno-linguistic diversity. Officially all ethnic groups are recognised although the minority languages have not yet been practically afforded the same status as Shona and Ndebele which are the 'major' languages in the country (Ndlovu: 2010). Considerable friction and animosity has characterised the interaction between speakers of Shona and Ndebele in Zimbabwe. Ethno-linguistic tensions that began in pre-colonial days and were further 'manufactured' by colonial regimes have not eased in the Zimbabwean context notwithstanding the fact that the official imagination generally glosses over them. Accusations and suspicions of marginalisation, hatred, and threats of 'extinction' still hold considerable sway in Zimbabwe. For example, Ndebele people frequently complain against Shona domination in political, social and economic spheres. Sachikonye succinctly sums up this disgruntlement: 'Popular opinion in Matabeleland is that the Ndebele should take to the streets in their thousands and stage demonstrations against Shona domination and non-Ndebele speakers should not be awarded jobs in Matabeleland' (1996:118).

These conflicts are replete with political innuendoes and aspirations (Bond and Manyanya 2003, Sachikonye 1996). Political identities are inseparable from the language question. Before independence, the Zimbabwe African People's Union (ZAPU) was generally associated with Ndebele speakers while Shona speakers were linked to the Zimbabwe African National Union Patriotic Front (ZANU PF) (Bond and Manyanya 2003). After the merging of the two parties,[3] the Movement for Democratic Change (MDC) has become generally popular with the Ndebele much more than is the case with ZANU PF.

Language is an important aspect of Ndebele consciousness. The people of Matabeleland have had to choose isiNdebele against isiZulu in order to protect and perpetuate Ndebele consciousness (Msindo 2005:79). Thus, the grassroots Ndebele ethno-linguistic consciousness robustly resents Shona linguistic hegemony. Of course, this consciousness tends to homogenise all Shona speakers, overlooking the fact that Shona has more than five dialects with their own tensions (Chimhundu 2002, Hachipola 1998), each competing for supremacy.

This article highlights that in a context where popular opinion and practices are not necessarily in harmony with official ideology, the mere fact of repeating and giving prominence to popular ethno-linguistic and cultural constructions provides tremendous opportunities for various forms of dissent. These possibilities become much more enhanced if popular constructions are articulated in a mass electronic medium such as television. The potential subversive reception of television fictional narratives (Chivandikwa 2010, Tullock 2005) cannot be underestimated in such a context. Subsequent sections of this article discuss specific textual and contextual elements which inform the observation that *Sinjalo* simultaneously embraces the political elite's discourse of nationhood and significantly transcends it using various language structures and forms.

Background and synopsis of *Sinjalo*

Sinjalo (*We are like that*), is an Amakhosi Theatre Production (ATP) of 2002. ATP is a township-based theatre production house which from 1985 has produced many plays, musicals and television productions under the guardianship of its founder, Cont Mhlanga. It is situated in Bulawayo, part of a culturally assertive region of Zimbabwe that has developed into a political community semi-detached from the main and predominantly Shona-speaking greater Zimbabwe (Msindo 2005:79). Cont Mhlanga, both a television producer and a writer, has a long tradition of writing social and political satires since 1985. *Workshop Negative* (1985) was one of his most successful plays and launched him as a serious socio-political writer and artist. *Workshop Negative* tackles the racial and ethnic integration of whites, Shona and Ndebele people following independence in 1980. Mhlanga uses *Sinjalo* to continue to advance his political aspirations which centre on ethnic and regional consciousness.[4] One of the factors that caused *Sinjalo* to be broadcast in a generally restrictive media environment is the fact that the then Minister of Information and Publicity, Jonathan Moyo who was sympathetic to the 'Ndebele cause', encouraged productions from the Matebeleland region.[5]

Sinjalo is a comedy series that features two friends, Sakhamuzi, who is Ndebele and Foromani, who is Shona. The two live in separate rooms in the same premises while their wives remain in the rural areas but occasionally come to visit. The inciting incident of the series is when Sakhamuzi invites his girlfriend to his house. Unfortunately, Sakhamuzi's wife, Mai Sponono makes an unexpected visit from the rural areas. Sakhamuzi's housemate, co-lodger and friend, Foromani is called in to help and hides the girlfriend in his room in order to prevent Mai Sponono from discovering her husband's infidelity. All seems well until a few minutes later when Foromani's wife, Mai Shupi also arrives unannounced. Mai Shupi finds her husband with a woman in her house and she erupts in a violent frenzy. He is cornered to a point of confessing that it is Sakhamuzi's girlfriend. Sakhamuzi denies this confession. Mai Shupi and Mai Sponono pack their bags and leave the two men.

The comic episodes revolve around the two men trying to mend the damage to their marriages. They realise that the best way of to do this is to work together rather than against each other. However, this unity is engineered by Foromani who incites Maurine, who has a son with Sakhamuzi called Fanyana, to dump the teenager on Sakhamuzi as he is not paying maintenance for the boy's upkeep. Therefore, their unity is engineered out of a need to save their marriages or home *(musha)* which can further be interpreted to mean the nation. From then on, the two resist any attempt to divide them, and prevent any ethno-based discrimination that outside forces try to instigate against them. Consequently, *Sinjalo* reflects and engages with forms of ethno-regional and ethno-linguistic consciousness.

'Border to Border One Nation Jive':
Metaphors and symbols of nationhood

The two protagonists, Sakhamuzi and Foromani are the major vehicles for expressing the need to construct Zimbabwe as a country where ethnic differences should be a source of celebration, not of conflict and political animosity. In fact the relationship between the two can be read as a metaphor for an ideal Zimbabwean society where once in a while personal tensions between 'family' members might arise, but such tensions should not be allowed to develop into socio-political conflicts.

The two protagonists and other characters deploy soccer images, song, dance and chants to construct and engage in ideas on nationhood. Sakhamuzi and Foromani are associated with the dominant soccer teams, Dynamos and Highlanders, who are linked to Shona and Ndebele speakers respectively. Foromani warmly refers to Sakhamuzi as *Mfana kamantengwana* (the nickname for Highlanders) and Sakhamuzi affectionately calls Foromani *Mfana weDembare* (Dembare boy – Dembare being the nickname for the Dynamos). From the above soccer metaphor, the 'imagined' community is one in which ethno-linguistic differences should be constructed in friendly, harmless competition and rivalry – which is characterised by deep tolerance or playfulness, and which also detests segregation and exclusionism. Sakhamuzi's out-of-wedlock son presents them with a challenge. He says he does not want to play soccer with Shona boys because *'IShona ngiyalizonda lile wala'* (I hate a Shona person. Shona people are presumptuous). At this point his father and Foromani engage in 'sermonising' speeches on national unity in diversity:

> **Sakhamuzi:** *Abantu bonke kumele sihlale sonke. Khule mihlobo eminengi. Sonke singa bantu beZimbabwe ukhuthi uyasapotha iteam kumbe iparty hakula ndaba.*

We should all unite. We have many ethnic groups in Zimbabwe. All of us are Zimbabweans. It does not matter which soccer team or political party you support.

Clearly, the dominant Zimbabwean teams in *Sinjalo* represent the major ethno-linguistic categories in Zimbabwe. The social, cultural and political identities of the teams cannot be divorced from the ethno-linguistic constructions of the two languages. For example, in the same episode Fanyana tells his father:

> *Iboyfriend kamama yathi abantu beDembare kabadli amacimbi.*
> My mother's boyfriend told me that Dynamos supporters do not eat caterpillars.

This is another linguistic stereotype based on culturally-based food practices. At this level, *Sinjalo* functions to challenge ethno-linguistic stereotypes that produce 'negative popular attitudes towards certain languages and [the] people who speak them' (Kamwendo 2000:142).

The picture of Dr Joshua Nkomo, the late Ndebele nationalist, is also deployed to construct and reinforce a sense of nationhood beyond ethnic divides. In Episode 13, Godogodo, Sakhamuzi's anti-Shona elder brother is overwhelmed with nostalgia and pride. He compliments his brother for having the 'correct' and authentic historical and national perspective. Godogodo and Sakhamuzi gleefully agree that Joshua Nkomo was 'The Father of the Nation', a metaphor which has become a regular if not monotonous feature of official nationalistic discourses. In fact the Ministry of Information and Publicity introduced an annual musical gala which celebrates the life of the 'Father of the Nation'. While this metaphor of nationhood is clearly different from the 'homogeneous and homeostatic society' (Kerr 1998:207), that was imagined in Malawian and Zambian television programmes, the same ideology is expressed, one that aspires to a unified nation-state against western imperialism under the stewardship of the 'Fathers of the Nation'. However, in official discourse, this idealised image of the 'Fathers of the Nation' does not accurately reflect historical or contemporary ethnic conflicts in the country. Refreshingly, *Sinjalo* does not gloss over these ethnic fissures, thus transcending the official discourse in nationhood which has tended to manipulate 'patriotic' history while it forgets the cultural and political sins of the nation's real past.

Dance, song and chants are appropriated as symbols and metaphors of cultural and national integration, tolerance, and peaceful coexistence. One of the rare occasions where English is used is in Episode 8 where Sakhamuzi and Foromani chant the English cliché: 'United we stand. Divided we fall!' While the immediate context and motivation of the chant is their desire to co-operate and assist each other in disguising their extra-marital affairs, the chant also symbolically functions to remind viewers of their obligation to the unity of the country. The other Ndebele cliché from Sakhamuzi is: '*Vhaliumukhenke*' (cover the cracks) advice by way of metaphor for his friend to distort or manipulate any information which might lead to the exposure of their romantic and sexual escapades. Symbolically this chant can be read as advice to Zimbabweans to cover any information that could lead to national embarrassment and humiliation.

In Episode 11, several songs are performed 'theatrically'[6] as symbols of nationhood and pan-African identities. The song '*Nkosi Sikhelela iAfrica/Ishe Komborera Africa*' (God bless Africa) is performed in a comic scenario where Sakhamuzi and Foromani sing enthusiastically out of tune as a tactic to divert attention from the urgent issue in which they are failing to sufficiently account for the presence of feminine paraphernalia such as a wrapper, a basket, perfume and some keys. Realising that the comically amusing song is doing the trick, as it were, the two mischievous friends and neighbours sing another popular song, '*Samanyemba*' accompanied by an apparently improvised exhilarating dance christened: 'Border to Border − One Nation'. The songs as well as the harmonious chants and dances in the episode clearly articulate the need to have one 'national rhythm' inspite of specific ethnic differences.

Soon after the above scene, Mafufu, an energetic woman with a legendary appetite for money comes to claim what she is owed by Foromani. Mafufu notes that the '*Zimkwacha*' (Zimbabwean dollar) would rapidly lose value in each minute that Foromani delays in giving her money back. Sakhamuzi remonstrates against Mafufu at her apparent 'denigration of the national currency':

Wena Mafufu. Zwana! Tshiyana lento yakho leyo ungasoli into ophila ngayo.
Hey Mafufu! Listen to me! Please desist from this bad habit. Do not criticise your very source of livelihood.

Clearly this is an attempt to instil national pride at a time when the Zimbabwean economy had taken a 'plunge' (Bond and Manyanya 2003) as inflation severely reduced the power of the national currency.

The deployment of the above symbols, metaphors and linguistic codes was part of a commendable process to use the electronic space to instil national pride. Many local languages are still faced with extinction (Ndlovu 2010). The electronic space is currently one of the best sites to make sure that local languages enter the 'modern' era (Banda 2010). This means television drama can clearly legitimise and curate local languages for national pride and effective communication. *Sinjalo* thus gives prominence and vitality to national languages and provides space for informed democracy in the overall human rights discourse, which includes the right to one's heritage such as language, in articulating cultural and political aspirations. The drama series was not simply providing a 'conduit in which dominant elite values and ideology were transmitted to viewers' (Bramlet and Farwell 1996:188), but rather it was a complex narrative on nationhood which had discursive space for working class people, peasants, 'minority' and 'majority' language speakers. This reading of the ideological function of *Sinjalo* should be linked to the recognition that the 'social role of television can only be satisfactorily tackled by considering the interrelationship of text, producer and audiences' (Abercrombie 1996, Tullock 2005).

Counter hegemony and Ndebele consciousness

Dialogue-construction is largely based on Ndebele ethno-linguistic identities. For example, all Shona characters except Mai Shupi can easily switch from their languages into Ndebele or they can code mix in one word, phrase or sentence. The following are some of the many typical examples cited from Episodes 3, 8, 11 and 13:

Character	Code-mixed word	Meaning	Episode
Foromani (Shona speaker)	Mari **yelembu** rangu **lembu** is Ndebele word	Money for my cloth	3
Foromani	Tiri pakati **penkinga** **nkinga** is Ndebele word for deep trouble	We are in deep trouble	8
Foromani	Itai **masinyane** tiende. **masinyane** is Ndebele word for fast	Do it fast we want to go	13
Mai Shupi (Shona speaker)	Ndipei **ntsaru** yangu. **ntsaru is** Ndebele word for wrapper	Give me my wrapper	11

The above are some of the many examples where Shona speakers code-switch and in some cases they use whole Ndebele sentences without necessarily translating them for Shona speakers. Within its context, this is subtle and symbolic resistance against Shona hegemony and arrogance. A popular sentiment in Bulawayo is that since Ndebele is the *lingua franca* of the Matebeleland region, all Shona speakers should learn the language and speak it well. In fact, radical Ndebele consciousness can be demonstrated by the fact that if a Shona speaker addresses a Ndebele speaker in Shona, the Ndebele speaker will insist that the Shona speaker address him/her in Ndebele notwithstanding that the Ndebele speaker might be conversant with Shona.

Radical anti-Shona sentiments are given linguistic space in *Sinjalo* with very limited 'censure'. In Episode 3, Mafufu mocks Foromani for being perpetually broke:

Mafufu: *Hey bakhithi lijombe izezuru lidla amathemba* (My goodness the Zezuru man is typically broke. He is eating dried kapenta fish).

In Episode 13, Godogodo who prides himself as a 'pure' Ndebele comes home from his rural home in Gwelutshene to sort out: *Imihlolo yemaZezuru* (Zezuru abomination) by coming to report to his brother Sakhamuzi that he had beaten a Zezuru woman with a donkey whip ostensibly for daring to contaminate Ndebele space by wanting to settle in Gweluthsena.

Curiously both Sakhamuzi and Foromani find Godogodo's logic at least merely amusing and they do not challenge it as is the case in previous episodes. What they challenge is the physical violence but they subtly sympathise with Godogodo's aspirations. This is the producer's acknowledgement and endorsement of popular Ndebele sentiments that the Shona people unfairly dominate educational, cultural, economic and political spaces in Matabeleland. The beating and chasing away of Mai Shupi can therefore be constructed symbolically as a way of suggesting that this should be rectified though radical action of removing Shona people from the spaces in which they dominate. This discourse resonates with the suggestion from the region that the country's constitution should adopt federalism in order to realise fair and equal development opportunities in all Zimbabwean regions.

In Episode 13, *Sinjalo* provides a new construction which if read within the broader socio-political historical trajectory of the country is a challenge to official Shona politico-spiritual hegemony. In the public media, the late Kaguvi and Nehanda (both Shona anti-colonial heroes) have been consistently projected as the national ancestors of Zimbabwe and apparently no Ndebele ancestor is given national status. It is therefore curious that after singing a liberation song in praise of the late Joshua Nkomo's national leadership qualities, Foromani, Godogodo and Sakhamuzi in a rare moment of agreement rhythmically chant 'Joshua Nyongolo Nkomo! *Idlozi leZimbabwe*' (Joshua Nyongolo Nkomo! The Ancestor of Zimbabwe).

Evidently, this is a new title and metaphor which has not been projected in official politico-spiritual discourses. This counter hegemony is further extended in the same episode where Highlanders, the 'Ndebele' soccer team is elevated to the status of a team that belongs to the whole Zimbabwean society. Yet the same status is not given to Dynamos. These then are covert forms of counter-hegemony.

Ethno-linguistic parody and transgression

Shona ethno-linguistic codes and structures are mocked and parodied as a form of dissent. In Episode 10, Foromani and Sakhamuzi have a small quarrel arising from a misunderstanding over the way the former is perceived by the latter to jeopardise family stability through his lack of tact in handling his extra-marital affairs. Before the argument, Sakhamuzi is seen singing a common Highlanders song which pokes fun at an imaginary Shona speaker who sits at the Soweto Stand of Barbourfields stadium. This, in real life, is not only sacrilegious but also a dangerous move:

> *Wakhe walibona nini izezuru elihlale eSoweto.x3* (When did you ever see a Zezuru seating at the Soweto stand)
> *Lihlale eSoweto x 3* (seating at the Soweto Stand x 3)

The Soweto stand is infamous for soccer hooliganism where Dynamos or Shona speaking supporters are usually subjected to different forms of physical and verbal violence. This song mocks Shona speakers for lack of tact by risking their lives and limbs through sitting at the Soweto end.

In addition, Shona linguistic codes and structures are transgressed. The few times that one or two Ndebele speakers speak in Shona are characterised by apparent exaggeration not necessarily arising from lack of competency in the language. Take Sakhamuzi for instance; who refers to Mai Shupi as *nakaTshupi* thus replacing the Shona syntax with Ndebele syntax and the pronunciation is deliberately exaggerated in making Shona sound like a 'funny' and 'strange' language. All this mundane humour demystifies the hegemonic Shona 'royal' language.

Another interesting lampooning of Shona political culture is provided by Mafufu in Episode 3, when she comes to claim her money from Foromani:

> Mafufu: *Zwana ke wena Zezuru. Hangilandanga konke lokho. Kumbe ufuna ukhungiman-galela kuma war vets. Into elizenzayo ngezejambanja khuphela.*
> (Listen you Zezuru. I did not come here for all that nonsense. Perhaps you want to report me to the war veterans. You people have such a violent disposition.)

The above is the only direct reference to broader political issues which was cleverly placed in just one sentence. War veterans have been the foot soldiers and enforcers of the left – nationalistic discourse which culminated in the invasion of white owned farms in 2000 in the name of addressing colonial imbalance. These acts were usually accompanied by violence (Bond and Manyanya 2003). What is curious in the above dialogue is that Mafufu casually attributes this violence to Shona people, and is thus an implicit exoneration of Ndebele people from the alleged violence of war veterans since 2000.

What is clear is that the ethno-linguistic space of the minority Ndebele language is symbolically expanded at the expense of a hegemonic Shona language. This symbolic representation goes beyond the cultural realms. It provides tacit negative criticism on practices that are engineered by political elites.

The limits of dissent in *Sinjalo*

We briefly examine some of the limits of dissent within the broader context of the televisual narrative. First, the use of stereotypes to provide humour or as counter discussion has its own limits. It is problematic to subvert stereotypes with counter forms of stereotypes. For example, Ndebele characters such as Sakhamuzi and Godogodo exhibit disturbing tendencies towards physical violence. Whilst we have argued that the beating of Mai Shupi could be read symbolically, the event could be easily read literally, thus reinforcing the stereotype that Ndebele people are violent. The risk of reinforcing stereotypes becomes even greater if one considers the possibility of overstretching the potential meanings of the linguistic metaphors in the narrative such as the nickname for the Matebeleland based football team, Highlanders which is called '*Mantengwane*'. '*Mantengwane*' is a bird of prey which terrorises other birds which resonates well with the stereotype of the Ndebele as violent and imperialists bent on destroying and destabilizing Shona peace. Mhlanga's recourse to such stereotypes increases the risk of producing unintended meanings.

The second stereotype is related to gender identity portrayals. For example, both Mai Shupi and Sakhamuzi's wife, NakaSiponono are easily manipulated and deprived by their husbands, projecting an image of intellectually and socially weak characters. In addition, Siponono and Shupi, although socially and intellectually far sharper than their mothers are also manipulated by their fathers. It is problematic to subvert one form of hegemony while reinforcing another one in the same text.

Further, while it has been noted that *Sinjalo* is progressive and subversive through its consistent and immensely effective appropriation of working-class and peasant ethno-linguistic forms and sensibilities in combining and engaging discourses of nationhood, it nevertheless lacks direct linguistically communicated forms of resistance against targeted elite institutions and practices. For example, we have noted that criticism on the conduct of war veterans was directed at Shona grassroots people. However, it has been consistently argued that in fact the operations of war veterans were sanctioned by the military and political elites of the country (Bond and Manyanya 2003).

Of course, the major reasons for such an 'omission' are tactical. It would be wishful thinking and authorial suicide to expect to have direct linguistically communicated criticism of the ruling elite in a general context where candid discussions on sensitive issues or 'radical critiques of the political establishment' (Kerr 1998:208) are almost non-existent.

Conclusion

This article has examined the ideological and cultural functions of *Sinjalo*, a television drama programme that is much more socially engaged than the average television drama in Zimbabwe. The central observation made in the chapter is that *Sinjalo* functions dialectically in terms of 'serving' the interests of official discourse as well as the needs of marginalised groups, thus confirming the contention that the margins are not just sites of deprivation but are also sites of resistance (Peterson 2000:222). *Sinjalo* demonstrates the capacity of using electronic spaces as sites for enhancing the project of nationhood such as in the popularisation and revitalisation of local languages for the promotion of informed democracy, and in particular providing opportunities for resistance. Popular language forms have tremendous dissent possibilities which is conceptualised as mundane, less spectacular resistance that can slowly and gradually transform values and attitudes (Bleiker 2000:270). However, it is not easy for the ruling elite to allow subversive programmes to be aired on national television. The success of *Sinjalo* derives chiefly from the fact that popular dissent was subtly disguised in official nationalist rhetoric but in such a way that it transcended and sometimes subverted that discourse.

A second reason for the success of *Sinjalo* is the strategy of weaving and integrating theatrical performance styles on the electronic space thus indicating immense possibilities for incorporating theatrical performance aesthetics into television dramatic texts in constructing dissent with its potency and limitations.

Sinjalo can therefore be identified as a programme that represents a counter-narrative to create dissonance against homogenised unity, identity, and politics as constructed and projected by other television narratives of the nation. The drama represents a voice for people who are not able to identify with the narratives offered through official sources but seek the value of their own expressions and experiences. The textual evidence provided in this chapter reveals that linguistic expressions can be viewed as media for the creation of identity, as conditions for both sustaining, challenging and subverting power and control to open spaces for differences. This is especially potent in a context of intense struggle over definitions of national identity and unity.

NOTES

1   *Vele Abantu Sinjalo* means 'we people are like that' or 'that's who we are'. It is derived from the programme's theme song.
2   *Sinjalo* features at least five indigenous languages including Shona, Ndebele, Venda, Kalanga and Zulu. However, current focus is on Shona-Ndebele ethno-linguistic relations.
3   In the 1980s Zapu and Zanu, the former liberation parties fought each other and thousands of

people were killed. The conflict between the two parties had ethnic dimensions. In 1987, the two parties reconciled and merged into one party, Zanu PF.

4   Mhlanga is also a political activist who is currently an independent councillor in his rural Lupane District and a former secretary of Zapu2000, a party with strong roots in the Matebeleland region.

5   Cont Mhlanga actually publicly acknowledges Jonathan Moyo's role in the continued production of *Sinjalo*. When the Minister left, the production was controversially removed from the screen. Available online at <www.newzimbabwe.com>, accessed 10/01/11

6   A distinguishing feature in *Sinjalo* is the deployment of indigenous theatrical performance and aesthetics, such as direct address to the audience (camera), in order to enrich the televisual product. The actors, directors and producers have a strong theatre background, particularly in political protest aesthetics.

BIBLIOGRAPHY

Abercrombie, W. (1996), *Television and Society* (Cambridge: Polity Press & Blackwell Publishers).

Bleiker, R. (2000), *Popular Dissent; Human Agency and Global Politics* (Cambridge: Cambridge University Press).

Banda, F. (2010), 'The Political Economy of Space and Multilingualism: Exploration of Linguistic Landscape at Three Universities' (unpublished paper).

Bond, P. and Manyanya, M. (2003), *Zimbabwe's Plunge: Exhausted Nationalism, Neoliberalism and the Search for Social Justice* (Harare: Weaver Press).

Bramlet S. and Farwell, T. M. (1996), 'Sex on the Soaps: An analysis of Black, White and Interracial Couples' Intimacy' in *Berry T (ed) Mediated Messages and African American Culture. Contemporary Issues* (London: Sage Publications).

Chimhundu, H (2002). *Adoption and Adaptation in Shona* (Oslo: Unipub AS).

Chivandikwa, N. (2010) 'Okay let's make soaps real: Women , Soaps and Cultural Imperialism with special reference to Sunset Beach' *NAWA Journal of Communication* 1, 4[Nov.]: 116-133.

Furusa, M (2000) 'Culture and Development in Zimbabwe', in Chiwome E (ed) *Indigenous Knowledge and Technology in African Diasporian Communities* (Harare: Mond Books).

Hachipola, S.J (1998) *A Survey of Minority Languages of Zimbabwe* (Harare: University of Zimbabwe Publishers).

Kamwendo, G.M. (2001). 'Ethnic Revival and Language Associations in the New Malawi: The Case of Chitumbuka' in Englund, T. (ed) *A Democracy of Chameleons: Politics and Culture in the New Malawi* (Blantyre: Christian Malawi Literature Association).

Kerr, D. (1988) *Dance, Media Entertainment and Popular Theatre in South East Africa* (Bayreuth, Bayreuth University Press).

Mashiri, P (1998) 'The Impact of American Soap Operas on Zimbabwean Sensibilities' in Chiwome, E. and Gambahaya, Z. (eds) *Culture and Development. Perspectives from the South* (Harare: Mond Books).

Msindo E (2005) 'Language and Ethnicity in Matebeleland: Ndebele–Kalanga Relations in Southern Zimbabwe, 1930-1960', *International Journal of African Historical Studies,* 38: 1: 79-103

Ndlovu, E. (2010) 'Mother Tongue Education in Official Minority Languages in Zimbabwe' (unpublished paper).

Peterson, R. (2000) *African Theatre and the Unmaking of Colonial Marginality* (Johannesburg: Witwatersrand University Press).

Sachikonye, S. (1996) 'The Nation-State Project in Zimbabwe' in Adebayo, S. (ed) *Challenges for the Nation-State in Africa* (Uppsala:, Nordiska Afrikainstitut).

Silverstone, R. (1994) *Television and Everyday Life* (London, New York Routledge).

Tullock, J. (2005) *Watching Television Audiences. Cultural theories and Methods* (London: Oxford University Press).

Tullock, J. (1990) *Television Drama: Agency, Audience and Myth* (London, New York: Routledge).

Within Between
Engaging communities in contemporary dance practice in East Africa

CHRISTY ADAIR

Introduction

Western perspectives of dance in Africa frequently focus on spectacle and ritual. Contemporary dance in East Africa challenges such perceptions. This article discusses the emerging dance practices, specifically in Kenya, which offer insights into the art form. Many contemporary dance works in Nairobi exemplify dance engaging communities without spectacle, focusing on the embodied experience of the dance practice. Lailah Masiga, one of the few female performers in an art form dominated by men in East Africa, created a solo, *Within Between*, which addresses issues of female genital mutilation (FGM).[1] Masiga performed the work in Nairobi, Kenya and Canberra, Australia receiving very different responses to the solo in each location. Whereas in Nairobi the audience positively responded to the work, in Canberra the African officials in the audience were concerned about any negative portrayal of African culture as this has been a continuing legacy of the colonial heritage. She also toured the work to rural areas in Kenya where it was met with both gratitude and hostility. This article locates *Within Between* in the specific contexts for contemporary dance in East Africa and the wider context of dance studies.

African dance/contexts/performances

For western audiences and performance students, notions of dance in Africa are formulated through a range of sources including watching national dance companies, participating in classes and written texts. Within both dance and performance scholarship and in critical responses to African dance, there has been a tendency to equate artistic practices from the continent with spectacle. The focus of such writing often discusses traditional dance practices. There has, however, been a gradual shift in dance and performance writing as cultural studies methods have been applied to dance. Texts which acknowledge the creative work of artists in a global context provide the means to acknowledge

91

the specificities of dance in Africa.² Such an approach is in contrast to the many examples of texts which focus on work from Europe and America ignoring the rich cultural sources from other continents. Joann Kealiinhomoku, in her well-known essay 'An Anthropologist Looks at Ballet as a Form of Ethnic Dance' (1970, 1983) criticises the evolutionist approach and eurocentricism of a number of dance texts. Such texts tend to make generalised statements about 'primitive man' and the role of dance in early history. Dance from Africa is usually included without specific information about the dances, context or location in which they are performed. These texts offer such information as a context for the history of western theatre dance.³

The contexts in which African dance forms are practised in Europe and the States are significantly different to that of the African content. As Nicholls states, 'Historically, dance is embedded in the ritual activities of specific communities … arts are not specialist pursuits set aside from everyday life' (Asante 1994: 53). In western countries, however, when African dance is practised it is separate from the contexts which gave birth to it.

The images of spectacle which are often associated with African dance come from the touring national dance companies from Africa such as, Les Ballets Africains de Guinée and the National Dance Company of Ghana and to some extent companies such as Adizido Pan African Dance Company, based in London until its demise in 2005. Such works celebrate traditional dance forms which usually would have been performed in rural settings for particular events.

As Asante points out,

> In Africa, dance is part of a process that is ongoing and connected in such a way that it is inseparable from other phenomena in society. Therefore, one means something entirely different when describing dance in Africa (2000: 7). …it must always be viewed as an integral part of a larger system rather than as a self-standing, independent entity. (2001: 13-14)

Another aspect of dance viewed as spectacle is the dance work offered for visitors to African countries who want to see the dance of the continent. In such a context traditionalists are keen to preserve this heritage even though urban existence threatens the conditions for traditional dance practice and governments use the art form to generate goodwill both at home and abroad (Asante 2000).

Indeed as Fleming points out, 'most international art exchanges are political and economic investments' (Gere 1995: 37). Certainly, touring companies from Africa play both a political and economic role as Edmondson (2007) writing about Tanzania and Castaldi (2006) writing about Senegal make clear. Such company performances also reaffirm audience's expectation of dance from Africa providing a spectacle for their entertainment as does the recent show *Afrika! Afrika!* which toured in Europe (Heller 2005).

Such commercial shows and the dance provided for tourists contribute to the images of spectacle which have entered the popular imagination. Both contexts are driven by economics rather than aesthetic development. Nicholls suggests that '…under the corrosive effect of tourism, the culture of the host country is commercially exploited and becomes devalued, and consequently the local inhabitants lose dignity performing for the benefit of giggling strangers' (Asante 1994: 52).

It is not only tourism which distorts dance performance. Edmondson discusses the complex development of dances which received official approval in Tanzania, highlighting the process of invented traditions. The procedures of official sanction led to dance associations being refused permission to perform certain dances and specific dance styles being associated with one ethnic group when previously they had been performed by a range of groups. This process was undertaken to strengthen notions of national identity and unity.

Despite issues of dance legacies and the negative effects of tourism, dance continues to play an important role within the tourist industry specifically in East Africa. As Lange points out, within the tourist industry, dance is used as 'a symbol to the outside world' (Edmondson 2007: 74). Further she suggests that since the Tanzanian government attempted to compete with Kenya for East African tourists, the need for a symbol to the international community has significantly increased (Edmondson 2007). Despite the limitations of the provisions for popular audiences, such performances also offer the opportunity for viewers to gain some insights and information about specific aesthetic qualities found in African dance. Asante reports that, 'some characteristics are: polyrhythms, polycentrism, angularity, asymmetry, soft knee … and isolations' (Asante 2000: 11). These characteristics can also be identified in the work of some contemporary dancers. For such dancers, the focus on traditional dance, particularly in Kenya, can be problematic. Contemporary dance receives very little coverage in the national press and when it does writers are frequently ill-informed about the art form accusing artists of making work which is not authentic or relevant to African culture (Micheni 2010: 18).

There is another perspective to consider, however, which is articulated by Ngũgĩ wa Thiong'o. 'Writers, artists, musicians, intellectuals, and workers in ideas are the keepers of memory of a community' (Ngũgĩ 2009: 114). Whilst Ngũgĩ is arguing against the restrictions of linguistic practices after colonisation, his comment is relevant to consider in relation to Masiga's work. Memories are not static and evolve in relation to time and location. Within communities which carry out FGM there will be many significant memories attached to the rituals which surround the practice. FGM is viewed by certain communities as being an important cultural practice which affirms the community and women's identities within it (Walker and Parmar 1993). The World Health Organization defines female genital mutilation as 'the partial or total removal of the external female genitalia or other injury to the female genital organs whether for cultural or other non-therapeutic reasons' (Estabrooks 2000).

It could be argued that Masiga is resisting rather than keeping such memories and current practices. At the same time she is also embodying traces of traditional dance which is steeped in memories from specific communities.

The role of FGM in communities is a topic in literature, for example in Ngũgĩ wa Thiongo's *The River Between,* which is on Kenya's national syllabus for secondary schools. In this book one of the characters reports, 'Circumcision was an important ritual to the tribe. It kept people together, bound the tribe. It was at the core of the social structure. ... End the custom and the tribe's cohesion and integration would be no more (1965: 66).

Such description gives insight into the power of the ritual of FGM and its role within some communities. Ngũgĩ's character comments on the lyrics of the songs which were part of the ceremonial activities before circumcision, 'uncircumcised girls were the objects of cutting attacks. Everything dirty and impure was heaped upon them. They were the impure things of the tribe' (Ngũgĩ 1965: 117).

Communities

The significance of the roles of communities in relation to African dance is frequently mentioned in dance texts. A distinctive feature which is noted of much performance throughout the African continent is the role of participation of the audience. David Kerr draws attention to an instance of an audience in which there was 'active and sometimes acrimonious participation' and where the vigorous input of 'the traders' and villagers' viewpoints [were] being debated with a frankness unimaginable outside the context of theatrical role-play (Harding 2002: 4).

It is such animated debate which was evident in the response to Lailah Masiga's performance of *Within Between.* Whilst her intention was that her work would have political impact, as yet there has not been resistance to it from those in power. Harding suggests that there is a 'safety valve' system which operates in African performance, which, I suggest, may have influenced the response to *Within Between.* She comments that 'It is possible to ... state that it is because of the opportunities *permitted* by authorities and *tolerated* by them for populist expression that the social order favouring the politically and economically dominant group is sustained. This is the 'safety valve' syndrome in action' (Harding 2002: 10).

Whilst *Within Between* cannot be categorised as populist expression, it was tolerated, and to some extent supported by the authorities, particularly when the work was being toured as will be discussed later. Not only was the topic of Masiga's performance controversial but also her role as a female performer. Whilst women have had significant roles in traditional dance there are a number of restrictions which affect their participation in contemporary performance. As Kenyan activist and founder of the Green Belt Movement Wangari Maathai (2007) points out, traditionally more value has been placed on boys than on girls within Kenyan society. Boys are expected to achieve more than girls and often have more access to education. The roles females are expected to play in the family in relation to caring for children or sick parents and carrying out household chores do not combine well with the requirements of

Fig 1 *Lailah Masiga performing in the premier of* Within Between, *at the Nairobi Festival of Solos and Duets, GoDown Arts Centre, 2007 (© Justus Kyalo)*

performance. Edmundson (2007) in her study of the National Dance Troupe of Tanzania noted that there was a high turnover of staff but retention of female performers was particularly complicated. In such a context it is not surprising, therefore, to find that females are in the minority in this art form. Masiga is one of the few women contributing to an emerging body of contemporary dance practice in East Africa.

Dance training

An important catalyst for the contemporary work in East Africa is Opyio Okach with whom Masiga trained. Together with Faustin Linyekula from Congo and Afrah Tenambergen from Germany/Ethiopia he formed La Compagnie Gàara. Their performance of *Cleansing* 'a piece in which the mundane gestures of everyday cleansing evoke sometimes violent purification' (Okach 2009a) won an award at the Rencontres Chorégraphiques Africaines in 1998 and brought them invitations to festivals in France and to tour in Africa. The artists gained the support of choreographer Régine Chopinot and her company Ballet Atlantique, who invited them for residencies in France and choreographic exchanges.

Prior to this Okach had established an interest in contemporary dance work whilst studying at the Desmond Jones Mime School in London on a British Council scholarship following his studies at the University of Nairobi. He participated in a range of dance workshops including one with dance artist Russell

Maliphant and enjoyed the released-based style. This style informs his work today[4] and he is also inspired by a range of arts available in the city (Okach 2009b).

When Okach began making work in Nairobi on his return from London the context was, as he describes it, something of a vacuum. Traditional dance had always been part of the context but contemporary creation did not exist. There was an established theatre group, the Phoenix Players, which still performs today. Their repertoire in the 1990s was based on English plays such as those of Alan Ayckbourn and also musicals. The Little Theatre in Mombasa still has this focus and a company was rehearsing a version of *Ipi Tombi* when I visited in 2009. Clearly such a focus from the theatres does not encourage experimentation nor develop an audience for such work. Few writers were doing original work in the 1990s whereas Okach wanted to develop work from an African Heritage (ibid.). As producer Eckhard Thiemann comments, Okach's work is being created in a context where

> ... more people in Africa live in large cities than rurally. The cities have become melting pots of diverse communities harbouring all kinds of different cultures, religions, languages and tribal backgrounds. This bracing socio-cultural multiplicity puts paid to many European stereotypes of dance in Africa .' (Thiemann in Hutera 2009). Perceptions of African Dance being collectively created and performed in rural locations to live drumming and offering authentic experiences of African culture are challenged by the developments of those artists in Africa whose work is driven by concepts and is politically questioning. (in Hutera 2009)

Traditional dance and African heritage is an important aspect of most con- temporary dance artists' practice. Training for contemporary dancers lacks infrastructure and relies mainly on workshops organised by cultural exchange centres in the region. In the Report of Pre-Summit Arts Meeting for Contemporary Dancers and Choreographers in East Africa (Bantu 2006) it was noted that there were no trained instructors of contemporary dance, rather training was through workshops and artist-led work. The responsibility for follow ups from workshops is with artists and many of these artists take work into the poorer communities where they have been well received. It was suggested in the above report that such dissemination is key to the develop- ment of contemporary dance in the region. Masiga is one of the artists who has disseminated her work and has been part of a training programme for young people at the Go Down Arts Centre, Nairobi. She has created a number of solos including *Within Between*.

Within Between (2007)

Within Between premiered in Nairobi as part of the Solos and Duets Dance Festival 2007 (I attended the 2009 Festival). The work was toured in rural Kenya and also performed twice for Africa Day in Canberra, Australia where Masiga now lives.

The work is significant for a number of reasons:

- the political content of *Within Between* is highly contentious in a country in which women's viewpoints are often ignored and where corruption is endemic (Maathai 2007)
- women are in the minority in dance both as dancers and as choreographers (Bantu 2006)
- the work was taken to rural communities where people were invited to discuss the issues which it raised (Masiga 2009).

Masiga has chosen to play a film from the United Nations and the United Nations Children's Fund for the duration of the performance which shows the preparation and event of a female circumcision in graphic detail together with scenes from everyday life. The projection is screened at the side of the performance space and engages the viewers in consideration of the politics of this practice. As Masiga says, the projection allows the audience to engage with the dance and she works with images which enhance the content of the film. As she turns towards the screen, the image of children and adults standing in a circle becomes part of her audience. Later, the projected image of elders debating FGM hovers over Masiga as she turns slowly on the ground, on her side, legs bent and parted. She embodies the experience of FGM whilst the elders who might stop the practice continue to talk. As preparations for the ritual cutting are projected on to a screen behind her, Masiga embodies flight from the event as she slices through the air with her propelling arms and fast-moving feet. She said that she made a specific choice not to edit the film as most of the time there is a taboo about showing what actually happens. For example, men know that women are circumcised but they do not necessarily know the exact process and she was interested in some of the shock reactions to the performance and the projection. Women in the audience appreciated what she was doing as they acknowledged that they did not have a forum to discuss the issue (Masiga 2009).

Wearing a long white dress with loose long sleeves and a hood, Masiga powerfully draws the audience into reflecting on her chosen topic. Her choice to have a hood was to represent the way in which women are cocooned and not allowed to speak freely but audiences often assumed that she was trying to 'attack' Islam because of the white gown and hood. Music from Kenyan musicians, Idi Aziz, Shutu and The Neck accompanies her dance and was chosen specifically in order to relate to a range of communities who were likely to respond to such music and to 'give more substance to the work' (ibid.).

The movement vocabulary is drawn from both traditional and contemporary dance. The percussive foot stamps and vigorous whole body vibrations echo movements from her traditional dance background. Masiga works with images drawn directly from the practice of FGM as, for example, when she crosses and re-crosses her legs, referencing the way in which girls legs are tied together after the operation. She draws attention to both the process of FGM and the vulnerability, pain and shock of those undergoing what is frequently termed 'the cut'. There is also a stitching motif which Masiga creates. The most invasive form of FGM entails the genitalia being stitched together after being cut.

In Alice Walker's novel *Possessing the Secret of Joy* one of the women who undergoes this procedure describes her experience of circumcision which

> joined her, she felt, to these women, whom she envisioned as strong, invincible. Completely woman. Completely African… In her imagination, on her long journey to the camp, they had seemed terribly bold, terribly revolutionary and free…It was only when she at last…unbound her legs, that, she noticed her own proud walk had become a shuffle. (1992: 61)

Masiga received funding for the piece to go to various communities who practice FGM. There was a recognition that dance could be a powerful medium through which to relay a message to those in Northern and Central Kenyan communities who use traditional dance. It was also an opportunity to introduce contemporary dance and other mediums including projection and song to specific rural communities.

Her starting point for this work was her mother's best friend who is a Kenyan Somali. In such communities FGM is a common practice and the friend would say 'it is painful' and termed it the 'difficult fashion of FGM'. Masiga says, 'I don't understand what it feels like to go through this' (2009) but recognised that through other female experiences such as menstruation or giving birth it is possible for women to identify with the pain of FGM. As a dancer she wanted to engage a wide community of audiences in consideration of this topic. Her choice of the title, *Within Between* was an acknowledgement that whilst she did not accept the practice she did not feel she had the right to condemn it as communities have their own reasons for FGM. She felt, however, that it is a political issue which she wanted to communicate through her dance work. When she was touring the work she was clear that the issue was not about censoring communities which practise FGM but to offer a forum where it was acknowledged and could be discussed. She also thought that the term female circumcision suggests that the practice can be equated with male circumcision when in fact both the physical and psychological damage is not comparable. Her approach is in line with the most successful models for elimination of the process which focus on education and the recognition that ultimately it is the communities themselves that make the decision to stop FGM rather than legislation which is difficult to implement (Estabrooks 2000)

The tour of *Within Between* was to three distinct communities and areas. Masiga and the technicians, who also acted as security, chose a suitable performance space when they arrived in each location and began to set up. They were offering, from the audience's point of view, an impromptu performance with no pre-advertising or booking.

Isiolo
Isiolo is in the pastoral North East of Kenya where cattle rustling and violence has been an issue. Community policing projects have had some impact on

security in the region. Islamic culture is dominant and many of the men in the audience watching *Within Between* were booing and attempting to intimidate the performer and her crew. They asked her who gave permission for the performance.

At the end of each performance Masiga explained that she was presenting a dance project and that the costume was not intended to represent Islam. She suggested that white symbolises that women need peace of mind and freedom to speak about the practice of FGM. She stated that she persisted with audiences and refused to acknowledge negative reactions. Eventually people who were resistant calmed down. She asked the audience about their perceptions of the performance and its content and noted that women said that they felt aided by it and that men seemed to deny the issue (Masiga 2009).

Nyeri

In Nyeri, a bustling town in fertile Central Province, people thought that the performance was like a political stunt and that a political party supported Masiga. She had to explain that she was not with the government. Initially, men found the issue of women's reproductive organs funny but as the performance progressed they considered the images and began to change their attitudes. Masiga said that she appreciated the offer of help from the local police but that there was no trouble as people were interested in the dance and treated the event 'like a day out' (Masiga 2009).

Kajiado

When Masiga performed in Kajiado, a small town south of Nairobi, populated mostly by Maasai pastoralists, she said that people went quiet and stood in the middle of the road watching and concentrating. After the event one man said that he thought that it was right for people to speak about the issue and reported that his sister had died through FGM. The topic of death through FGM has featured in a number of novels including, Ngũgĩ's *The River Between* (1965) and Alice Walker's *Possessing the Secret of Joy* (1992). After Masiga's performance one woman asked which side Masiga was on and she said, 'I am on the side of women' (Masiga 2009).

In speaking about her views Masiga said that for many older women the practice of FGM was all they knew but many younger educated women have the information now to resist the practice. She was surprised to be asked to return to Kajiado by the District Commissioner. He wanted her to take the performance to the interior to the Maasai where FGM is a common practice and said that she would be escorted by police. Clearly, he could see the potential of dance as a powerful tool for communication and education.

Masiga contrasted the open, positive response she received in Kajiado to the one she received when she performed in Canberra for African dignitaries. She said that she felt sad that some people asked her why she was projecting a negative image of Africa. She thought that there was a sense of denial in their response (Masiga 2009). It is understandable, however, that the African officials were concerned about any negative portrayal of African culture as this has been a continuing legacy of the colonial heritage.

Conclusion

Clearly, Masiga is providing a forum for discussion about FGM with her solo. She drew on the many stories and images she found in news cuttings, books and DVDs as well as personal testimonies for source material for the choreography. She tends to work on social issues, frequently collaborating with other artists and is interested in both developing dance as an art and its potential as an effective means to communicate. Her decision to integrate film with dance in *Within Between* increased the potential for communication with audiences, particularly those unfamiliar with contemporary dance.

Lailah Masiga and other women dancers are working within a context in Kenya in which quite restrictive views of women's roles are the norm. There is a view that women should not 'throw themselves about' (Masiga 2009) unless it is for a particular ceremonial occasion when they are expected to perform. Generally, dance and movement is considered a male province and, for females, sometimes participation can be linked to sexual promiscuity and prostitution much as it was in Europe in the nineteenth century (Moturi 2009, Adair 1992). Masiga came from an athletic family with liberal views which did not specify women's roles. Masiga says that, 'Having worked a lot with men in Kenya I feel very comfortable and very challenged/inspired with men making a mark and believe woman can also do this' (2009).

Masiga's work, as does the practice of other contemporary dancers in East Africa, offers dance which resists spectacle and the popular notion of dance in Africa as exotic entertainment. The work engages communities and addresses current issues within an emerging dance practice.

NOTES

1   'The terminology from "female circumcision" to "female genital mutilation" was changed by the United Nations upon recommendation by WHO [World Health Organisation] in 1991...While numbers vary, UNICEF [United Nations Children's Fund] estimates that over 130 million women in African countries alone have been mutilated ...Commonly, when we think of FGM, we think only of African countries. Certainly the highest number of victims are in African countries, but FGM historically occurs or has occurred in many countries, including the Arabian Peninsula, Asia, Australia, France, England and the United States' (Estabrooks 2000)

2   *Movinghistory/dancing cultures: A Dance History Reader* (Ann Cooper Albright and Ann Dils 2001) and *Dance in a World of Change* (Sherry Shapiro 2008) and *Worlding Dance* (Susan Foster's 2009) all offer examples from a global perspective.

3   These include *World History of the Dance* (Sachs 1937), *The Dance Through the Ages* (Sorell 1967), *The Book of the Dance* (Kirstein 1942) and *The Book of the Dance* (DeMille 1963). Kealiinhomoku's argument makes clear that dance from specific cultures needs to be assessed appropriately rather than by European values. A number of writers including Suzanne Youngerman

(1974) Drid Williams (1974 and 1991) and Andree Grau (1993) have critiqued dance writing from an evolutionist perspective. See also www.munfw.org/archive/ 50th/ agenda.htm, accessed 3 June 2010)

4   The term released-base style is an umbrella term for a range of corporeal practices which focus on efficiency of movement. In such styles emphasis is given to use of the breath, skeletal alignment, lack of muscular tension and the use of gravity and momentum to assist movement.

BIBLIOGRAPHY

Adair, C. (1992) *Women and Dance: Sylphs and Sirens* (Basingstoke: Macmillan).

Adair, C. (2007) *Dancing the Black Question: the Phoenix Dance Company Phenomenon* (Alton: Dance Books).

Asante, K. W. (1994), *African Dance: An Artistic, Historical and Philosophical Inquiry* (New Jersey and Eritrea: Africa World Press, Inc.).

Asante, K. W. (2000), *Zimbabwe Dance: Rhythmic Forces, Ancestral Voices – An Aesthetic Analysis* (New Jersey and Eritrea: Africa World Press, Inc.)

Bantu, S. K. (2006), *Report of Pre-Arts Summit Meeting For Contemporary Dancers and Choreographers in East Africa*, unpublished, hosted by Kunja Dance Theatre at the Go Down Arts Centre, Nairobi, Kenya, sponsored by the Ford Foundation

Castaldi, F. (2006), *Choreographies of African Identities; Négritude, Dance, and the National Ballet of Senegal* (Urbana and Chicago: University of Illinois Press).

Cass, J. (1993), *Dancing Through History* (New Jersey: Prentice Hall).

Clarke, M. and C. Crisp (1981), *The History of Dance* (London: Orbis)

Cooper Albright, A. and A. Dils eds. (2001) *Moving history/dancing cultures: A Dance History Reader.* Hanover: Wesleyan University Press

DeMille, A. (1963) *The Book of the Dance.* (London: Bookplan)

Edmondson, L. (2007) *Performance and Politics in Tanzania: The Nation on Stage* (Bloomington and Indianapolis: Indiana University Press).

Estabrooks, E. A. (2000) 'Female Genital Mutilation', Model United Nation of the Far West, 50th Session, Equality and Justice in 21st Century, available online at <www.munfw.org/ archive/50th/agenda.htm>, accessed 3 June 2010.

Fleming, B. (1995) 'Looking out: critical imperatives in writing about world dance' in D. Gere (ed.), *Looking Out: Perspectives on Dance and Criticism in a Multicultural World* (New York: Schirmer): 10-39.

Foster, S. (ed.), (2009) *Worlding Dance* (Basingstoke: Palgrave)

Glean, B. and R. Lehan. (2005) *Dance and Diversity: Taking Stock and Making it Happen* (London: Irie! Dance Theatre).

Harding. F. (ed.), (2002) *The Performance Arts in Africa: A Reader* (London and New York: Routledge).

Heard, M.E., and M.K. Mussa (2002) 'African Dance in New York City' in T.F. DeFrantz (ed.), *Dancing Many Drums: Excavations in African American Dance* (Madison: The University of Wisconsin Press), pp.143-153.

Heller, A. (2005) Afrika! Akrica! Programme Vienna: Brandstätter

Hutera, D. (2009) 'Dancing Out of Africa: Eckhard Thiemann interviewed by Donald Hutera' *Dance Umbrella*, available on line at <www.danceumbrella.co.uk/pagve3127/SoloDuo>, accessed I Nov 2009

Kealiinohomoku, J (1983) 'An anthropologist looks at ballet as a form of ethnic dance', in R. Copeland and M. Cohen (eds), *What is Dance?* (Oxford: Oxford University Press) 533-49.

Kirstein, L. (1942), *The Book of the Dance: A Short History of Classical Theatrical Dancing* (New York: Garden City Pub. Co.).

Krauss, R. (1969) *History of Dance in Art and Education* (New Jersey: Prentice Hall).

Maathai, W. (2007) *Unbowed: My Autobiography* (New York: Anchor Books).

Micheni, M. W. (2010) 'The meaning of a new crazy African dance' *The Daily Nation* Nairobi, 12 February, p. 18

Ngũgĩ wa Thiong'o (1965) *The River Between* (Nairobi, Kampala, Dar es Salaam: East African Educational Publishers Ltd).

Ngũgĩ wa Thiong'o (2009) *Something Torn and New: An African Resistance* (New York: Basic Civitas Books).

Opiyo Okach (2009a) available online at <www.Gàaraprojects.com>.

Sachs, C. (1937) *World History of the Dance* (New York: W. W. Norton & Company)

Shapiro, S.B. (2008) *Dance in a World of Change* (Champain Ill.: Human Kinetics).

Sorrell, W. (1967) *Dance Through the Ages* (London: Thames and Hudson).

Walker, A. (1992) *Possessing the Secret of Joy* (London: Vintage).

Walker, A. and Parmar, P. (1993) *Warrior Marks: Female Genital Mutilation and the Sexual Blinding of Women* (San Diego, New York, London: Harcourt Brace and Co.).

Williams, D. (1974) 'Review of Frances Rust, *Dance in Society: An analysis of the relationship between the social dance and society of England from the Middle Ages to the present day* (London: Routledge and Kegan Paul, 1969) in CORD News 6, 2: 29-31.

Youngerman, S. (1974) 'Curt Sachs and his heritage: A critical review of world history of dance with a survey of recent studies that perpetuate his ideas', CORD News, 6:2: 6-19.

INTERVIEWS

Kabaya Moturi, Nairobi, 19 January 2009
Lailah Masiga, London, 20 October 2009
Opiyo Okach, 2009b 7 June 2009; 23 October 2009, London

Water Feels
Layering time in a
contemporary multi-media performance

MORATIWA MOLEMA

This article gives an account of a multi-media production, *Water Feels,* which I created as a part requirement of the Master of Fine Arts in Film and Television programme at the University of Cape Town, South Africa, in 2008. 'Layering time' seemed to me the best way to deal with the importance of unity in diversity and of continuity and representations of traditional culture in a contemporary world. As a multi-media production, *Water Feels* was also an exploration of conceptual relationships between different art forms and the potential, in this use of mixed media, for notions of time present and past existing simultaneously.

All stages of the production were an invaluable experience that contributed towards my discovering a particular visual style. This style involves the heightening of the event of screening a projection by adding live performance to it. A live performance is unique because, unlike film, it can never be repeated the same way twice. Each moment during the duration of the performance thus acquired added value because of the resonances, echoes, reflections, and self-reflections resulting from the interplay of live performance and screening.

The size of the surface area for the performance and its relation to the space required for the projected image was a crucial problem that had to be solved quite early in the process. The successful interplay of the media depended on addressing the tension between the spatial necessities of projection and the practical and aesthetic spatial demands of performance. I used three projectors to project from the rear three video frames next to one another that functioned as a single composition on a vertically erected white cloth. This strategy allowed for sufficient space for performance and projection; it allowed me to develop a measure of complexity in representation by using multiple projections; and it allowed me space to project with and without shadow. The space behind the screen, the screen itself, and the space in front of it were all equally important and were all three integral to the production (see Figure 1).

The spatial layout of the performance area then set the site for the interplay of media as a way to concretise the notions of layering and unity in diversity, and to represent aspects of traditional culture within a contemporary context.

In this article I first discuss what motivated the narrative from which the

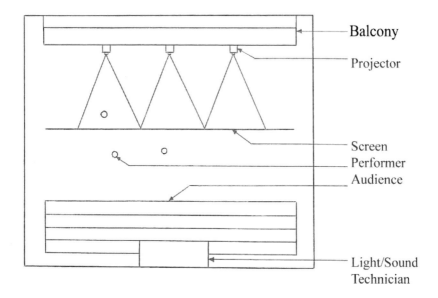

Fig 1 *Floor plan of* Water Feels

performance and the production drew. This narrative did not necessarily resort to plot as a structuring device, but depended on a modicum of prior knowledge of the region's history on the part of the audience to provide such structure. This leads into a discussion of conceptual relationships between the various art forms, the layering of time, and finally an explanation of the techniques I used to realise *Water Feels* on stage.

Motivation

In the plotless narrative that informed *Water Feels*, I intended to counteract the stereotype which has degraded the very foundations and wisdoms of conquered southern African people and their cultures by calling them savage, primitive, backward, and other derogatory names. Concepts such as 'botho' [1] which highlight the ideal of sharing resources equally and sparingly are neither savage nor primitive nor backward because in them lies healing that, to my mind, can reverse the wounds that imperial, colonial and capitalist systems, particularly in southern Africa, inflicted upon the natural and human environment. The ideal of 'botho' obviously also functions as a touchstone by which to hold latter-day African governments and other formations to account. Herein lay my first impulse to create *Water Feels*.

A second motivation arose from the realisation that in the course of resisting colonial conquest and struggling against apartheid, the people of southern

Africa, often in close collaboration with one another, developed a culture of resistance.[2] An aspect of this culture in these trying times was that the very act of daily living for blacks and for many whites, was often simultaneously an act of defiance and resistance against the devastation wrought in personal lives by colonialism and apartheid; a corollary is the temptation to 'do to them as they did to us' and land in the same predatory, rapacious rut. The post-apartheid era is of necessity very dynamic involving as it does the continual redefinition of old and existing identities and the creation of new ones, not only in South Africa, but across the entire southern African region. The region at large is grappling with the imperatives of becoming the kind of region that respects human rights along the lines of 'botho' and its hopes.

A third motivation arose from the above concerns and was of a practical, technical nature – *Water Feels* must not pontificate. To achieve this I used different aspects of traditional and modern culture as a way of representing unity in diversity. I also used a wide range of dance styles, texts, sounds and costumes: Tswana traditional dances found their place alongside ballet and con-temporary dance and gesture; traditional chants rubbed backs with English text; a live band (culled from the night clubs of Cape Town) played strains of Tswana/ San traditional music, Indian classical music, R&B, Jazz, and so on. The cast of mostly white students was made available to me by the University of Cape Town drama school. The fact that the production relied on a white cast dressed in traditional Tswana costume, having been taught the songs and clapping rhythms, and appearing alongside the black Tswana traditional-dance troupe that also appeared in the production, enhanced the sense of unity in diversity. The Tswana dance troupe was made up of Botswana students studying in various institutions in Cape Town and was brought together with the help of the Botswana High Commission. The process of producing *Water Feels* created an exhilarating feeling of giving direction right at the forefront of transition, where we met in our several varieties and capacities and practised reciprocity with real understanding, thus realising the ideal of 'botho' briefly.

Fourthly, the idea to use water as a major symbol in the production was motivated by three things: a United Nations (UN) report released on BBC news, an awareness of the different qualities of water as water; and water as an archetypal symbol of renewal. The UN report on the BBC news states that

> More than 2.7 billion people will face severe water shortages by the year 2025 if the world continues consuming water at the same rate. The looming crisis is being blamed on the mismanagement of existing water resources, population growth and changing weather patterns. The areas most at risk from the growing water scarcity are in semi-arid regions of sub-Saharan Africa and Asia.[3]

I wanted to produce a work that would encourage the wise use of this scarce natural resource.

Literal water has infinite, intricate textures and infinite sound possibilities when it is massed in lakes and oceans or flows in rivers and brooks or falls as raindrops. I projected these lakes, oceans, rivers and brooks onto the screen accompanied by appropriate sound effects some of which were produced by the cast and live band with their musical instruments. Water has a soothing, healing and calming effect on the human body. An initial intention was to facilitate a platform on which all involved in the production could send out intentions to water in an effort to make the audience aware that sounds, thoughts and intentions have an impact on the body.

Water also features in the nexus of archetypal metaphors of renewal. In Ngũgĩ wa Thiongo's novel, *The River Between* (1965), for example, Kikuyu boys undergoing circumcision do so on the bank of the Honia River. The blood (a symbol of life) from their sexual organs (another symbol of life) drips into the earth (yet another symbol of life). Later in the ceremony, the initiates are bathed in the river, thus symbolically leaving their childhood behind, only to emerge from the river symbolically reborn into the men that they are expected to become. Christian baptism also falls in this category of symbolic death and resurrection by water. The focus on water allowed the unstated converse of water to come into play also: If water itself is essential for life, and stands for growth and renewal, then what is drought itself, and what can it stand for'?

Conceptual relationships between different art genres

One is able to manipulate perception to varying degrees when using video. The shapes and figures of a video projection have an intriguing phenomenon; they appear to have form, including depth. The image itself, of course, is actually flat when it lands on the surface it is projected on to. What causes this illusion are the tints and shades of colours or the tones of grey, in the case of black and white film and video, that make a two dimensional property look as if it is three dimensional. Form is an optical illusion in video, photography and painting. The proportions in relation to perspective and depth of field make the images look life-like. In *Water Feels* the 'real'-looking video and the realness of actual live performance were stylistically attractive because they looked similar but had a range of differing properties which made the combination of these forms a rich site for layered meanings. Video and live performance are both time-based media. The performance on screen or on stage lasts for a specific period from the beginning to the end (i.e. before the members of the audience become restive because of loss of concentration and aching backs). Both thrive on movement and action. I used these similarities in *Water Feels* as a visual and metaphorical bridge to build conceptual relationships between the two art forms. I feel the conceptual relationship worked best when I found ways to create optical illusions in which the images appeared to transcend the limitations of the media. The two dimensional property of the projected image became self-reflective when it was connected to the three dimensional live figure with a string attached to the vertical screen or was associated with smoke from the machine.

For example: During the performance one end of a string was tied to the hair of the performer and the other was attached with a needle to the screen.

The point where the string touched the screen was exactly where the projected image, a woman painted in red, had her hand stretched out pretending to be holding the string. It looked as if the projected image was holding on to the performer by a string. The two separate media each carrying a possible meaning, became physically connected. The connection sparked a new meaning. The woman in the projected image represented a nonphysical dimension. The fact that a projected image is something that cannot be touched became more emphasised when contrasted with a live figure. The woman in the projected image looked like she was holding the tangible figure who acted in this scene as if her movements were restricted. A possible meaning of the visual metaphor was that the intangible dimension exists and has effects on the physical world.

Another example of how an optical illusion worked successfully was after a hole had been cut in the vertically erected cloth that served as screen. The hole was big enough for a person to climb through. Smoke coming out of a smoke machine that was placed behind the screen crept through the hole. The projected image on the screen was of a cloud. The smoke, which held some of the digital information in the light from the projector, looked like a cloud. It looked as if the flat image was spilling into a third dimension.

In this particular scene the space behind the vertically erected cloth had a metaphoric meaning in the plotless narrative of *Water Feels*. It represented the 'unseen', or the subconscious mind, or an altered state of consciousness, or what can also be described as the world of departed ancestors. There was interplay between the various components such as projected image, live actor, smoke, space, and the plotless narrative with its key symbol of water together with the unstated, inverse symbols relating to it. The overall result was that the coming together of all these elements, 'resisted', to quote Martin Rieser and Andrea Zapp, 'the inner nature of language and linear representation of history by creating an abundance of possible meanings' (2002: 36). Soeke Dinkla calls this a 'network of associations' (ibid.: 56). I understand 'network of associations' to refer to the conceptual relationships that create an integrated whole when one combines more than one art form. Soeke Dinkla explains further that 'a floating intellectual space emerges, a space of the unsaid, of what is on the tip of the tongue' (ibid.).

It is this 'floating intellectual space' that I continually strove towards in the conceptualisation and execution of *Water Feels*. I wanted the audience to become creatively engaged in the show by finding meaning for themselves. In the particular style that I am discovering and exploring, ambiguity is a deliberate feature. It is my antidote to pontificating. The style of ambiguity resonated with the fact that in the realities of shifting identities, cultural perceptions, and representation not everything can be explained in its entirety. In the show, the unsaid (as in the case of water and its unstated converse, drought, mentioned above) acted as a negative space of the said. But the unsaid also has a second aspect: I wanted the unsaid to be felt by using as little speech as possible, foregrounding the visual metaphors and, thereby, achieving a feeling of upliftment of the type that is present at the end of rituals, which, in my experience, produces a sense of an encounter with something intangible. I hoped the unsaid

Fig 2 *Performers' shadows against projected image in* Water Feels *(© Moratiwa Molema)*

or the mystery spoke for itself in the minds and hearts of the viewers.

The conceptual relationships between video and performance worked as well when no optical illusion was involved. In the case of Figure 2, the relationship was between the projected image and a shadow that was cast onto the vertically erected screen by rear projection. The shadows of the live human figures interacted with the projected image in ways that were meant to elicit direct and indirect interpretations. The proportions of the projected image in comparison to the live human figures did not match and gave the overall image an abstract/contemporary feel (Figure 2).

Layering time and an explanation of techniques

As video projection and live performance are both time-based media, I paid attention to how time operated in the production with a view to taking maximum advantage of opportunities that arose to represent traditional culture within a contemporary context. It was important to develop coherence in this simultaneous representation of different kinds of time.

The media, video and film, permit time to be represented as a succession of still images (frames). Time can be mapped onto a two-dimensional space and be available for manipulation by the editor, who can rearrange time by using shot changes–as happens, for example, in flashbacks and flash-forwards. In film and video, compressions of time are made possible with conventional shot changes such as elliptical editing or cutaways,[4] where actions are presented in ways that consume less time on screen than they do in real life (Bordwell and Thompson 2001: 260). I spanned several hundreds of years in half an hour in both the filmed and staged representation of a traditional ritual.

Live time is the experience felt when moving from moment to moment in the present. It appears to be a 'non-spatial linear continuum where events occur in an apparently irreversible order'.[5] Live performances are experienced in that way. In the moving-image industry, features such as live broadcasts, web cams, and real-time videos on the internet, time moves at the same pace as live time. New Media artists, for example, have used virtual space on the internet to exhibit on one web page performances happening in different locations at the same time as they are happening. Artists have used live-feeds during performances where the act of filming becomes part of the performance and a comment on the process of viewing. Such a technique was used to profound effect and social comment in a Magnet Theatre production, *Rain in a Dead Man's Footprint.*[6]

In *Water Feels* I used a live-feed to foreground the act of viewing and representation but also went on to foreground consumerism. In one scene, a performer dressed in a traditional Tswana costume filmed an actress who held a picture frame in such a way that it framed her whilst she was doing a monologue. She emphasised the word 'I' whenever she said it. The scene expressed individualism and the mentality of consumerism. The effect of the live-feed, as both the actress as well as her double, back projected images were being filmed and projected, was a bombardment of infinite reflections of her projected image. This brought an acute sense of both consumer culture as well as layering in time.

Actions that have been recorded on film or video occurred in the past. The projecting of a recorded image is a replaying of what happened in the past. That, however, does not necessarily mean that the recorded action represents a past action. The actor, for example, could have pretended to be a character in the year 3002 or whatever. I want to expand further the notion that the moment in performance I have described above is an example of layers of time. Live time in the form of the performance was layered with recorded time, which was represented by the two images, facing each other, of the woman. Projecting a recorded image is replaying what happened in the past. The action portrayed may be a representation of the past, present or future, which adds yet another representation of time.

The plotless narrative of the entire show took place metaphorically during one cycle of the moon, but in reality it lasted only thirty minutes, which implies a sense of compressed time. In the instance above, the performer, dressed in traditional Tswana costume and holding the camera, represented historical time. The actress performing the monologue about herself was dressed in contemporary clothes. The contrast of the two figures had the effect of foregrounding the compression of time while showing its metaphorical layering of epochs.

Before cinema was invented, the Zoetrope and its many relatives moved images in a cycle or 'loop', rather than in a linear progression implying narrative structured around plot.(Bordwell and Thompson 2001: 32) Installation artists use video loops to keep the same images projected for long periods of time during the period of an exhibition without having to start them manually from the beginning. This type of representation of time, sometimes appropriately termed cyclic time, is also apparent in ritual, most of which in essence is structured around bringing the past to the present for a better future. In *Water Feels* cyclic time was apparent in two ways. The beginning scene and the closing scene were almost identical in terms of lighting, costume, cast, and the visibility of the symbolic 'moon'. The two scenes tied the beginning to the end and represented a cycle. The second way cyclic time occurred in the plotless narrative of *Water Feels* was in the way ancient rituals were repeatedly brought into the consciousness of the contemporary audience.

In the conceptualisation of the production I considered the time after the performance, the 'future' during the performance. In the final moments of the performance, performers spray-painted outlines of their shadows on the vertically erected screen. Spray-painting onto the screen changed the function of the screen from a light catching contraption into a canvas for paint. As a result of the performers' outlining their shadows with paint, these final moments appeared to be 'frozen', but time of course moved on and the painting that remained after the show acted as a kind of residue of the performance and a marker of a moment in time. The image (Figure 3) was taken whilst the spray-painting took place.

The transformation of the function of the screen was reminiscent of the use of masks that are carved for the purpose of ritual. The purpose of the mask is not entirely aesthetic. A mask also acts as a representation of access to, or a meeting point in another dimension, the world of the ancestors. When the ritual is over, the mask changes its function from a symbol of mediation to a sculpture, a piece of art that can be exhibited in museums or one's living room.

The vertically erected screen in *Water Feels* became an object of metaphorical mediation, because during the scene when the projected image beckoned the performer to walk through the hole that had been cut into the screen, the projected image represented an altered state of consciousness, through a healer or ancestor. The hole was a metaphoric gateway to the altered state of consciousness or world of the unseen and unspoken. In the plotless narrative, this is followed by the coming of rain, a climactic moment in the performance and the outcome of the contact. Similarly there was metaphorical mediation when after the moment of contact and the coming of rain, a representation of permanence (spray-paint on the vertically erected cloth) was added to the ephemeral moment (performance).

After the performance, when the house lights went on, it could be posited that the audience had some kind of a relationship with the painted images on the screen. They had witnessed the making of them and the circumstances of the transformation the screen had undergone. But in the same way that a mask loses a great deal out of its context, so too someone who had not witnessed the performance but walked into the theatre afterwards, might have found the drawings empty and reduced.

Fig 3 *Spray painting of shadows in* Water Feels *(© Moratiwa Molema)*

That the concept of time was important after the performance was further elaborated when all the performers after the curtain call and the house lights were on, crossed the stage line to distribute bottles of water (purchased by me) to the audience. The crossing of the stage line symbolised a spilling over of the message of *Water Feels*, from the theatrical or fantastical plotless narrative, into the real world.

Further explanation of techniques I used

The style of presenting video in *Water Feels* called for a different approach from shooting and then projecting for cinema, or broadcasting for television. Composition for cinema or television occurs in a single frame, with the rectangle of a television set or cinema screen. My own technique, in contrast, required the three separate frames to function as a single composition.

I shot similar and identical objects and people from different angles and projected them at the same time (Figure 4). I called this approach to presenting video 'video cubism'. In futurism or cubism, multiple points of view or stages of motion are depicted in a single image in an attempt to represent the dynamism and complexity of human vision by imaging simultaneously from multiple perspectives.[7] The projections lined up next to each other worked as a single frame. The video projection in the image below is an example of how 'video cubism' worked in *Water Feels*.

Fig 4 *Projected images and perfonnaers in* Water Feels (© *Moratiwa Molema*)

I used three separate video tracks in the editing programme Final Cut Pro for each perspective of the object or person that had been recorded on mini DV tape. Editing the footage in one sequence enabled me to synchronise the clips. When I needed to see what was occurring on the other video tracks I lowered the opacity level line graph in the clip and viewed the images superimposed on the canvas. Once the edit was complete, I copied each video track and pasted it onto a separate sequence and burnt it onto DVD. The soundtrack was burnt onto only one DVD.

I avoided developing an elaborate narrative in the projected images because the video had to have 'spaces' within it for interaction with performance. The video provided hints that invited the audience in and enhanced the plotless narrative performed by the performers. The moments of unexpected, direct interaction between video and performance created a tension which I left to the audience to interpret in the light of their understanding of the historical events of southern Africa. An example of this occurred in the scene where the character that had been 'healed' during the Tswana/San traditional ritual dance walked through the hole in the vertically erected screen. The hole had been cut by one of the performers whose character was that of a healer. The hole was big enough for the audience to see her behind the erected cloth. At the same time part of her body cast a shadow on the screen. The image in the video projection was of a single red hand. The hand moved from the top of the frame until the finger tips reached the shadow of the head of the performer. The hand appeared to be first pointing at her and then caressing her as she danced to the clapping hands of the cast behind the erected cloth. The metaphoric meaning was that the world that was represented by the video projection and the space behind it had made contact with that of the living in yet another, 'third' space which was available to the audience only as shadow. How the interaction of video and performance cohered or clashed became an important means of focusing content, form and, though plotless, narrative progression.

Conclusion

In this valuable exercise of reflecting on the making of *Water Feels*, three major questions have emerged. The first question was, simply, 'what was I presenting in *Water Feels*'? Literally, I was presenting a semblance of a rain-making ritual, but, through it, I was also presenting an instance in post-apartheid southern Africa of the emergence of changing, new identities. A subsidiary question was: if identities were being redefined and were changing and becoming new, what were they before and what did they become after that? These impossible questions I could only answer through the ambiguity afforded by my 'layering of time', which is well suited to the overall nebulousness of identity formation.

The second question was whether *Water Feels* should, as it was presented, be assessed by the authenticity of its representation? The answer here could be both yes and no. Yes, because the old African, Asian and European slave-holding empires did exist; so too slavery in the Americas; so too colonialism; so too the Herero genocide; and so too apartheid and its demise. All of these are facts of history. The accompanying power-entrenching stereotypes are, in addition, facts of history too, as was the opposition to them. This opposition is itself enshrined and exemplified in the Tswana and Sotho proverb, 'motho ke motho ka batho' (a human being is a human being because of other human beings), which indicates that the notion of reciprocity and sharing is neither uncivilised, primitive, nor backward, but is an ethos that can go a long way towards not only exposing and opposing brutal, rapacious regimes, but also healing the social and personal wounds that they have caused. In so far as *Water Feels* found narrative context in all of these, then its content was authentic. Yes, again, with reference to the UNESCO definition of culture as having a 'set of distinctive spiritual, material, intellectual and emotional features of a society or a social group',[8] I suggest that the old lives on in new forms – an argument which assumes that the old is in some measure authentic and constant, and is in some measure identifiable in the new. But no, because the very notion of change, of shedding skin and transforming shape, paradoxically both validates and challenges authenticity. Certainly the representation of water and of the rainmaking ritual in *Water Feels* is not the ritual itself, nor would it be the ritual even if *Water Feels* had been a documentary or a photograph. Furthermore, layering time by creating illusions is a manipulation that speaks against authenticity even as it seeks to present it. Not least, the choices that I made, a Tswana/San ritual rather than a Christian baptismal one and the sequences that I decided upon, invented even, impinge on authenticity as well.

The third question arose from the recognition that *Water Feels* is a construct, and that whatever meaning it has was only one of several that are floating around in the region and abroad in performance, policy documents and social discourses. Did *Water Feels* reflect the truth about contemporary southern Africa, the empirical facts of its history, as spoken of earlier? The answer is, yes, one truth amongst many others. Given this history, it follows that there are also many true ways of being a southern African, not just one. In relation to questions of representation and its forms, and who did it, how and when, the situation became very complex, pointing to the tenuousness of the very idea of 'truth', unless we define it not as accuracy but as the kind of meaning that reaches significance in the context of other meanings.

These questions have been proffered as a result of the work and this explication will continue to inform my art-making process as will my continued work with mixed media. Coming from a background of video production as I do, mixing media in *Water Feels* made it possible for me to explore conceptual relationships between media in a complex and personally enriching way. In the course of this exploration I discovered my own particular visual style of intensifying the screening of projected images by increasing projection surface and using multiple projections, and then adding live performance.

The said conceptual relationships arose largely from the interplay of video and live performance. A highlight for me was that with the aid of various objects it was possible to create illusions in which the projected images seemed to transcend the limitations of the medium and became self-reflexive, thus seeming to be more than just the two dimensional properties that they actually were. Even more rewarding were the points of connection with post-colonial and post-modern art and discourse that reflected the necessary ambiguity for portraying the emerging identities attendant upon the historical changes that continue to affect the southern African region.

Most exhilarating of all was that I have begun to develop a visual metaphor for expressing the cultural transition that is taking place in the region, and have begun developing the metaphor (that of 'layering time') which can, in some measure, mediate its complexity. This layering was possible because of the video editing techniques that allowed me to map time in a two-dimensional space and to manipulate it. The use of live performance helped to create a third dimension. And finally the re-representation of ritual with all its paradoxes and ambiguity facilitated the necessary transitions and discourses through and amongst past, present and future.

NOTES

1   'Botho', in Setswana and Sesotho, means 'being humane' and characterises the reciprocity that ought to be at the heart of the relationships of the extended families and clans that people southern Africa.

2   In 1970, for example, Radio Botswana carried out interviews with 70-80 year-old Herero men and women who were born in the 19th century, and who crossed the Namib and Kalahari deserts into Botswana, fleeing the German genocide with their families. The interviewers, Margaret Motlatshiping and Leloba Molema, reported in the programme called 'Go Tla Ga

Baherero Mo Botswana' (the coming of the Herero to Botswana) that a Mr Stephanus Mbingana (80) of Sehitwa near Maun in Ngamiland pulled out from the rafters of his hut General von Trotha's signed genocide order promising, in the Herero language, to kill 'every man, woman, and child' if the Herero did not submit to German rule.

3   Available online at <http://www.bbc.co.uk/1/hi/world/1887451.stm>

4   Elliptical editing includes punctuation shot changes such as wipes and dissolves or a cutaway which is a shot of another event elsewhere that will not last as long as the elided event.

5   Found on internet. I am unable to find original source. Available at: <http://enwikipedia.org/wiki/Time>.

6   Magnet Theatre. 2003. Rain in a Dead Man's Footprint, performed by Jazzart Dance Thither, directed by Mark Fleishman, Cape Town.

7   Cubism is an early twentieth-century art movement that was part of the French avant-garde. It began with a collaboration between George Braque and Pablo Picasso. See Sturken and Cartwright (2000).

8   http://www.unesco.org/education/imld2002/universal_decla.html (10/5/ 2007).

BIBLIOGRAPHY

Barnouw, Erik (1993), *Documentary: A History of the Non-fiction Film* (New York: Oxford University Press).
Batten, T.E. Amsterdam Jan/Jul/Aug 1996 available online at <http://www.dma.nl/batten/what.htm>.
Bhabha, Homi (1994), *The Location of Culture* (London and New York: Routledge).
Blom, Lynne A., and Chaplin, L.Tarin, (1982) *The Intimate Act of Choreography* (London: Pittsburgh Publishers).
Bordwell, David and Thompson, Kristin (2001), *Film Art: An Introduction* (New York: McGraw-Hill), 6th edn.
Cartwright, Lisa and Sturken, Marita (2001), *Practices of Looking: An Introduction to Visual Culture* (New York: Oxford University Press).
Davis, Miles, (1991), *Doo-Bop*. Warner Brothers (Film).
Erlewine Michael; Bogdanov Vladimir; Woodstra Chris; and Yanow, Scott (1998), *All Music Guide to Jazz* (San Francisco: Miller Freeman Books) 3rd edn.
'Water scarcity', available online at <http://www.bbc.co.uk/1/hi/world/1887451.stm>, accessed 3 March 2007.
Unesco: http://www.unesco.org/education/imld2002/universal_decla.html (Accessed 10/5/ 2007)
http://enwikipedia.org/wiki/Time (Accessed 10/5/2007)
http://en.wikipedia.org/wiki/Transculturation (Accessed 29 /1/2008)
http://www.life-enthusiast.com/twilight/research_emoto.htm (Accessed 1/4/2008)
Hall, Stuart. 1997. *Representation: Cultural Representations and Signifying Practices*. London: Sage Publications.
Magnet Theater. 2003. *Rain in a Dead Man's Footprint*. Jazzart Dance Theater. Directed by Mark Fleishman.
Maswanganyi, Collen. 2003. *Business Man*. Cape Town: Spier Collection.
Mirzoeff, Nicholas. 2002. *The Visual Culture Reader*. Second Edition. NewYork: Routledge.
Ngugi wa Thiong'o. 1965.*The River Between*. London: Heinemann.
Oliver, Roland and Fage, J.D. 1988. *A Short History of Africa*. Sixth Edition. Harmondsworth: Penguin Books.
Radio Botswana. 1970. "Go Tla Ga Baherero Mo Botswana" (The Coming of the Herero to Botswana). Filed as: 'Feature Programmes -1970 (Audiotape and Transcript)'.
Rieser Martin, Zapp, Andrea. 2002. *New Screen Media: Cinema/ Art/ Narrative*. London: Bfi Publishing.
Schapera, Isaac.1971. *Rainmaking Rites of Tswana Tribes*. Vol 3. African Social Research Documents. Cambridge: African Studies Centre.
Sturken, Marita and Cartwright. Lisa. 2000. *Practices of Looking: An Introduction to Visual Culture*. New York: Oxford University Press. p. 352.

The Campus Queen

AKINWUMI ISOLA

Akinwumi Isola's original script of *The Campus Queen* was directed by Tunde Kelani in 2003 for Mainframe films and premiered at the New York Film Festival of the same year. It became a very popular release in 2004. Isola is keen to write an improved version of the script for possible later adaptation to the stage, and the play below is an attempt to improve the film script version as part of that refining process.

Cast List

Banke	Tokunbo (Toks)	Governor
Tolu	Tika	Farayola
Bisi	Tiku	Governor's Secretary
Obente	President S.U.	Rolake
Goroso	Secretary S.U.	Dada (driver)
Ladele	Treasurer	Kendy
Martins	Dean	Bongo
Simbi	Professor	Mrs Bamidele
Ike	Nso	
T.K.		
Olu Ala		
Dr Damisa		

1. Int. decorated stage with huge lighting effects

EVENING
Opens with a huge hip/hop musical concert by THE SILVER LINES CLUB (with selected artistes, SULTAN etc) in full swing. A crowded energetic audience responding to the thrills on stage. This is often a multilayered, musical performance, and in the background, well-dressed beautiful women stride on stage in the manner of a beauty pageant without interfering with the musical which is stylishly embedded with appropriate effects in a pulsating performance.

Cut to:

Martins (MC): See what we have here! It is the whole world! This is the real life! But you know, life comes in all shapes and forms! – in nice nuggets and in crude crabs! Life has curious combinations in ever-changing forms, like the brain and beauty; some are contradictions like the long and lazy. There is the fair and foolish, the little and loud. Fine faces should have smooth hearts and mind! But sometimes you find a very good mind lodged in a mis-shapen body! Brain and brawn should be an escort to brain and beauty. But there are good clothes on bad bodies and bad bodies in good clothes! What are we looking for? Good clothes, good bodies and a sense of occasion! Our cities are full of mansions and mud-houses and the roads welcome bare legs and limousines. We eat everything! Every mouth is an abattoir, every belly a mortuary!

(*Applause*)

Martins (*cont.*): Now we have two great artists who are going to sing in Yoruba! The First artist is called Etiyeri and His song is titled, 'Èèmò Pẹlẹbẹ'.

(*Applause as Etiyeri mounts the stage.*)

Etiyeri: You know, in African Music, there's a lot of audience participation. So chorus – 'Èèmò Pẹlẹbẹ' Ó yá!

Audience: Èèmò Pẹlẹbẹ	Serious matter! [Intractable problem!]
Etiyeri: Ìyá pè mí kalẹ̀ pé kín ni ó maa ṣe?	Mother wanted to know what job I would choose.
Audience: Èèmò Pẹlẹbẹ	Serious matter!
Etiyeri: Mo sì dá wọn lóhùn mo lórin ni n ó máa kọ	I said I would be a singer
Audience: Èèmò Pẹlẹbẹ	Serious matter!
Etiyeri: Wọ́n lọ́mọ líle ni mí, kí n wáá ṣiṣẹ́	She said as a difficult child, I should be a civil servant.
Audience: Èèmò Pẹlẹbẹ	Serious matter!
Etiyeri: Mo níṣẹ́ẹ kín ni, wọ́n láṣọ́já ni!	I asked for the type she said 'a soldier'
Audience: Èèmò Pẹlẹbẹ	Serious matter!
Etiyeri: Ha! Nítorí Olúwa a wa! Ìyá rán mi nílé ìwé, mo yára sá roko Wọ́n rán mi nílée kéwú, mo yára sá roko Mo kọ́kọ́, mo kádàá mo yáa sá roko	For God's sake! I was sent to school, I ran to the farm I was sent to the Arabic School, I ran to the farm With cutlass and hoe, I ran to the farm

Òtítọ́ lokó dún kó jubii ka jẹun lọ	But only food is cheap in the farm
Èlúbọ́ onísísí ó yómi yáyaà mi	A sixpence worth of flour will feed me and my wife
Àmọ́ ká toó ṣiṣẹ́ kọ́bọ́, ojú a pọ́n kankan	But earning just a penny makes you sweat.
Kàkà kín ṣe sójà, nítorí Olúwa wa!	Rather than become a soldier for God's sake
Hà, nítorí Olúwa wa	Ha, for God's sake!
Bó ṣeṣé akọ́dà, mo le bá wọn ṣe	I don't mind being a court-messenger
Bó sí ṣe wolé-wolé mo lé bá wọn ṣe	or a sanitary inspector
Bẹ́hìnkùlé wọn kún, ma maa mú wọn lọ	I'll arrest them for an overgrown backyard
Kàkà kín ṣe sójà nítorí Olúwa wa	Rather than become a soldier for God's sake
Hà, nítorí Olúwa wa	Ha, for God's sake!
Bó ṣeṣẹ́ẹ mọ́tò, ìwọ le bá wọn ṣe	You don't mind learning to be a driver
Kó o faláikọ́ṣẹ́, o máa gbérin lọ	But without proper training you get into a car
Bó o sáré wọ kọ́nà, o forí sọgi	You speed into a bend and run into a tree.
Bí mọ́tò dá ọ lẹ́ṣẹ́, o dẹlẹ́ṣẹ́ kan	You break a leg and have one leg left
Mùnùsín, mùnùsín, ò máalọ bí arọ!	You walk about crookedly
Kàkà kí n ṣe sójà nítorí Olúwa wa	Rather than become a soldier for God's sake

2.   Interior. Hotel lobby. Day

Goroso and Obente confer.

Obente: Goroso, I am worried about that Banke girl. She looks difficult. She is not going to stay!

Goroso: Don't worry she will have no choice. It's getting late already.

Goroso's secretary approaches, holding two keys.

Secretary: We got two rooms sir.

He hands over the keys to GOROSO who gives one to OBENTE.

Goroso: (*to secretary*) Tell the accountant to bring the envelopes here.

Secretary: (*leaving*) Yes, Sir.

Obente: I am rather nervous, she is such a beautiful girl! This is going to be a unique experience.

Goroso: Make the best of it.

They go back to the restaurant.

3. Interior. Hotel room. Evening

A luxurious double room. Obente is overjoyed. He quickly locks the door, throws his coat on one of the beds and pulls off his tie. Banke sits on the cushioned chair still holding her bag. She is calm but scared. Obente also sits on the chair beside Banke.

Obente: Well Banke, cheer up! I know you are rather disappointed, but it may be a blessing. I can assure you that this association will be more rewarding that you can ever imagine. I shall take good care of you. Here… (*taking an envelope from his coat pocket*). Take this…(*giving Banke the thin envelope*). That is the bank draft for your club, N100,000! and…(*giving her the fat envelope*). This is for you. N50,000 cash from me to you!

Banke collects the two envelopes, puts them in her bag.

Banke: Thank you sir.

Obente: (*overjoyed*) Oh, that is nothing! I don't want to brag but I'm very comfortable. You are such a beautiful girl!

Obente stand up, pulls Banke up, holds her very tightly and tries to kiss her, clumsily. Banke manages to struggle free.

Banke: Why? Why are you in such a hurry? We are going to be here all night! We have to plan our time and settle down comfortably.

Obente: (*clumsily moving back*) I am sorry. You are so beautiful!

Banke: Now listen, Mr...

Obente: Call me Fred! Or Oben for short.

Banke: All right, Oben, it's been a long day. We'll first cool down by having a shower together, then the normal things will follow.

Obente: (*laughing clumsily*) Oh! Fine, fine, fine! I am relieved. You know, I thought you were not properly briefed about our normal practice...

Banke: I was! But I don't like rushing over things like that... So, we'll remove our clothes and have a shower!

Banke starts undoing the buttons of her jackets. Obente laughs hysterically as he removes all his clothes.

Obente: Oh! You are my girl! Come on, let's go!

Banke: (*removing her jacket*) I am sorry... I am rather shy. Stop looking at me! Ok... Why don't you go in and I'll join you. But you must close your eyes when I come in.

Obente: (*laughing*) OK., I concur!

Obente rushed into the bathroom and soon the shower starts hissing. Banke quickly puts on her jacket, grabs her bag, tiptoes to the door, unlocks the door, opens it, gets out and closes it noiselessly behind her.

4. Exterior. Front of prestigious hotel. Night

Night-life activities. Banke walks out of the hotel, goes to the car hire stand, enters a cab which drives off.

5. *Interior. Banke's room in the university. Day*

Tolu, Banke's roommate is packing a bag, ready to go out, Banke rushes in, crashes into her bed and starts to cry.

Tolu: (*rushing to hold Banke*) Banke! Banke! What's the matter? What happened to you? You went to Lagos?

Banke gets up suddenly and prepares to go out leaving a lot of money on the bed.

Banke: I'll tell you everything when I come back.

Tolu: But where are you going?

Banke: I am going to give that stupid Toks, the rough side of my tongue.

Tolu: Well, I cannot allow you to go out in this state. Look at your hair, your clothes... and ... no shoes!

Banke relaxes a little, looks at Tolu and asks:

Banke: Tolu, tell me, do I look like a girl who would sell her body?

Tolu: (*rather embarrassed*) Well.. no.. I mean I don't think so... I mean ..

Banke: But Toks arranged that I should sleep with a filthy money-bag in Lagos, to bring some money back for the club!

Tolu: (*looking at the money*) Preposterous! But why did you do it?

Banke: I did not do anything!

Tolu: (*not believing her*) Well, it's one of those things. Be more careful next time. After all you were not a virgin.

Banke: Tolu! But I am a virgin!

Tolu: You were? Oh I am sorry. I know how painful it can be. And what a waste a mean money bag.

Banke: Nothing was wasted, Tolu, I am still a virgin. I still am!

Tolu: Are you writing a novel? The money?

Banke: It's a long story. I did not know that Toks was regularly recruiting girls for some Business Executives in Lagos. How can my own boyfriend do that to me? But I escaped! Now I must ask Toks a few questions.

Tolu: All right, please keep this money in your bag or box before you go. Let me follow you.

Banke collects the money on her bed and locks it up in her wardrobe. She is keeping the key in her bag.

6. *Interior. Decorated stage with huge lighting effects. Evening*

The Silver Lines Club's concert in full swing. The beauty pageant queens in new costumes flank MC who comments appropriately and launches us into the next number.

7. *Interior. A room off campus. Night*

The Silver Lines meet. Ladele, Ike, Martins, Simbi, Banke, Tolu and others are present.

Ladele: I welcome you all. The first item on our agenda is the admission of new members. Banke and Tolu have scaled through our interview and I recommend them for admission.

Simbi: I support the recommendation.

Martins: (*jokingly*) Women solidarity ! You are still in the minority.

Simbi: Not in quality. A woman is always greater.

Ike: How?

Simbi: "Man" has only three letters "Woman" has five!
They all laugh.
Ladele: Do we all support?
Members, Silver Lines: Yes!
Ladele: So, Banke and Tolu, I welcome you into the Silver Lines Movement, SLM. Initiation will follow.
Banke and Tolu: Thank you.
Ladele: Well, SLM wants to struggle for an assurance of equity and social justice, pure and simple. Our committees will now give progress reports. Committee on News Magazine!
Ike: We have a lot of material fit for publication already! Injustices on campus, petty scandals, fraud in a government ministry and so on. But we are still looking for a good name – 'Searchlight', 'Eagle Eye'?
Ladele: Thank you, we'll pick a good one later. Now, I call on the chairman Committee on music.
Martins: We have a name – The Silver Lines Music Group. We acquire additional skill on our new instruments. We have composed many social satire songs. We practice every Friday evening. Please join us tomorrow.
Ladele: Thank you. Now, committee on Labour Interventions!
Simbi: We have invited Chief Tidimugigun Kẹsẹẹsin 'T.K' here today on the case of rape and exploitation of cleaners, his workers.
Ladele: We shall interview him later today at a different location. Now, any Intelligence Report? Chairman? Well, I am the chairman and there is something very urgent. The Heavy Weights want to harm Banke very soon.
Banke and Tolu: *(Scared)* Hah!
Martins: It is true. But we shall from now give Banke 24hrs cover. There is no problem.
Ladele: We are always at least one week ahead of them. We shall adjourn now. Some of us will go and interview Chief T.K.

8. Interior. Banke's room in the university. Night
(Under two beds) On campus, Martins, Banke and Tolu are hiding under the beds. Martins is alone under one bed, Banke and Tolu under the other.
Martins: We may have to be here for a long time. No one speaks and no light.
Tolu: I am scared!

9. Interior. A small room in town. Night
Some hard knocking on the door and before any answers, Dr. Damisa and Toks burst in.
Martins: What is the big idea?
Ladele: What do you mean bursting in on us like that?
Dr Damisa: Very good, very good. The game is up?
Ike and Simbi: What game?
Toks stands aside playing with a key and smiling self-assuredly.
Dr Damisa: So, you are the bunch of rascals trying to blackmail me? I have

come here just to identify you. Now let me assure you that your further stay on this campus is rather doubtful.

Ladele: What impudence! What makes you believe, Dr. Damisa, that you can come here, open your reckless mouth and abuse persons who are from all evidence, of higher moral qualities? You are very rude.

Toks stops smiling. He is looking at Dr. Damisa who is open mouthed, shocked by Ladele's speech.

Simbi: You are very dirty, Dr. Damisa.

Dr Damisa: God of thunder! Are you all aware that you are talking to P. A. Damisa. B.A. 1st Class Honours. Ph.D., now Senior Lecturer, and by the special grace of God, Acting Head of one of the most important Departments in this University?

Ike and Simbi: (*clapping*) Hear! Hear! Congratulations, Mr. H.O.D.!

Dr Damisa: All right. I have not come here to honour your presumptuous invitation. The tail cannot wag the dog. You are all very stupid.

Simbi: This is very serious!

Dr Damisa: Will you shut up your mouth when I am talking?

Ladele: Why don't you let us hear him out?

Dr Damisa: I will soon put all of you in your proper places. As far as I am concerned, Miss Denton's examination result is a closed affair. What I have marked, I have marked. The marks I have given are immutable. No external examiner has been able to alter them. As for you, meddling little minds, the battle line is drawn. You will explain how you got access to classified information, and what you mean by asking me to "settle" you. I shall destroy you to the last man in this organization. Toks, let's go.

Toks pulls out a gun and brandishes it before going out. Simbi is scared. They are all scared.

Ladele: You see what problems we have?

(*More*)

Ladele (*cont'd*): But like the flies in a spider's web, the more they try to struggle free, the more entangled they become.

Someone: Bring him out, take him to the field and burn him.

Crowd: No! Hand him over to the security.

Tolu: Hold him! He'll run away!

The porters are already there. Martins, the porter and many students lead Olu Ala to the Security Department

10. Interior. Decorated stage with huge lighting effects. Evening

The Silver Lines Club's concert in full swing. New song in performance (Talking about – 'wetin you use your eyes find na him you go see')

11. Exterior. Sports Centre Area. Day

Ladele, Simbi and Ike meet a group of workers. Some workers sit on benches, some on the grass. Ladele, Simbi and Ike sit on a bench.

Ladele: Good day ladies and gentlemen. Today, as we promised, we shall discuss some of your problems, and we shall try to find solutions.

Workers: Thank you o! You do well o. God go bless una o.

Ladele: Last month, we advised you to go on strike because your employer, the contractor reduced your salaries and victimized one of you.

One worker: Ha! Na wa o. This kind grammar! Wetin be fitimai?

Ladele: I mean that he did not treat one of you well.

One worker: Ooo o!

Ladele: Now that you are on strike, we understand that he has stopped paying you.

Workers: Na so o!

One man: Hunger no be man friend o. Make we kuku go back to work.

Ladele: No! No going back until contractor agrees to pay correct salary.

One woman: How we go do am? We no go chop?

Ike: Sebi you get union?

Woman: En. Union sabi fight, e no sebi pay salari!

Ladele: OK. Ibrahim is your leader?

One worker: Na our president!

Workers: Our chairman be dat!

Ladele: It's all the same! He is going to help us identify each one of you as we pay you some money to keep you going.

Workers: Heee! Thank you o! God beless una!

Ladele: OK you will come forward now one by one.

They all struggle to get in queue. Then Ike notices two men loitering. He walks towards them. They are Tika and Tiku of the Heavy Weights Club.

Ike: *(shouting)* Eh! Come and se o! These are Chief T. K.'s boys. They come do amebo for am!

Workers: Is that so? Make we teach them lesson.

As the workers move towards them, Tika and Tiku start running away and some men pursue them.

12. Interior. A room in the S.U.B. Day

The President of the students Union, the secretary and the treasure have invited officers of the Heavy Weights Club for discussion. Toks, Tika and Tiku are just entering the room.

President, SU: Please sit down. I have invited you here as officers of the Heavy Weights Club to respond to allegations or rather accusations against you of harassments, extortions and attempted rape...

Toks and his men show annoyance and restlessness. Toks stand up.

Toks: Mr. President! You are studying to be a lawyer and I thought you would be more cautious when talking about accusations and allegations! Anyway, we do not admit any wrongdoing and we cannot be asked to defend ourselves when no one has made any specific allegations...

President, SU: Well, as a matter of fact, specific accusations have been made against you all, and your accusers are here!

Toks, Tika and Tiku become very uneasy as they look around nervously.

President, SU: *(cont'd):* Please bring in the women.

Two young women are brought in and as soon as they enter...

Woman 1: En, en, en! Na dem be dis o! They say him too be president and we must to pay him.

Woman 2: Na so o! And one time for night, dis one (*pointing to Tiku*) say he wan do my thing. I say I get husband o! Na in he wan force me do. Na im I shout and he run away.

Tiku: Me? That is a lie! How can I touch a woman like you! Me! What do you take me for?

Woman 2: Na true o! You tink say I no go rekonise you? E don comot traosa sef. E say the thing press am too much!

Toks: Well, well. I don't know about attempted rape without witnesses, but I want to say that some shop owners were voluntarily paying what amounted to protection money when cases of burglary were becoming rampant...

Treasurer: (*angrily*) That is illegal! What protection can you provide? Are you security men? This is shameless fraud!

Tiku: What we were doing was to make sure that security men posted to the area actually report and stay there to do the securing.

Secretary: How about those who don't pay you? Who ensured that their shops were burgled?

Toks: (*angrily*) I beg your pardon! What are you trying to suggest? We were only trying to help! As friends!

President, SU: That is not the kind of leprous hand of friendship we would like to shake! It is a fraud. We will always thank you for your solidarity during the union elections, but you shouldn't go about collecting illegal levies as your reward...

Toks: I do not deserve all this you know? I have not come here to be insulted! Gentlemen, let's go.

Toks, Tika and Tiku walk out.

Treasurer: Mr. President, I think this matter should go to the Students Representative Council – 'SRC'.

President, SU: I agree with you.

Woman 1: So, you no go punish them?

13. Interior. Toks' room on campus. Night

Two men are standing in one corner of the room. Toks is writing something.

Toks: You thought I was joking when I warned you last week?

Men: We beg sa o!

Toks: Don't beg me o! Give me the keys!

The men prostrate before Toks.

Men: We beg sa. We go increase the return sa.

Toks: Out of the nine cabs, your own daily returns are the lowest....

Man 1: The reason be say cab don too plenty now! Before before we be only about 20. Now we more than one fifty!

Man 2: And before, your own and President S. U. cabs no queue for turn. Now di odas no gree agin. Efiribodi queue now. So we no get many trip again.

Toks: Is that so! I shall see to that. My cabs don't queue as a privilege. Take this as your last warning. I must have correct daily returns. I shall meet all of you at the usual place in the evening. Don't ever come to see me here again.

Men: Tank you sa.

They open the door and go out.

14. Interior. Governor's private office. Day

As Banke enters the office, the governor stands up, walks to meet her and embraces her hard. Banke is very embarrassed. Banke tries feebly to struggle free. The governor finally releases her.

Governor: Please, sit down.

Banke sits down somehow awkwardly. She tries to say something.

Banke: (*kneeling*) Your Excellency, on behalf of the ...

Governor: Banke! Before you say anything, for your sake, for the sake of this overwhelming beauty, I forgive the Silver Lines and all! Get up and sit down.

Banke sits down. Governor shakes his head in admiration.

Governor: Banke, I have a busy schedule today. Can I invite you to a drinks party on Friday in the evening? Do I have a date?

Banke: Well, well, yes. It's OK sir.

Governor: I'll send a car to pick you up at seven.

15. Interior. Governor's office reception. Day

After walking up and down the space along the wall Ladele sits down. Then an over-dressed woman with expensive make-up, ROLAKE enters.

Governor's secretary: Rolake, my dear sister! All the way from Rome!

Rolake: What can we do? Suffering and smiling!

Governor's secretary: Really! Let's change roles.

Rolake: I don't mind! You are making contacts! Who is with the Governor? A lady?

Governor's secretary: Yes, from the University.

Rolake: (*annoyed, forgetting the presence of Ladele*): Oh! These dignified prostitutes won't stay on their campuses!

Ladele: (*jumping up*) I beg your pardon? Will you control that frivolous tongue of yours? Let not the pot call the kettle black.

Rolake: (*turning to secretary*) Who is this dumb fellow?

Governor's secretary: He comes with the lady.

Rolake: (*turning to Ladele*) I see! Mr. Bodyguard! Listen. If you extend your spoilt children-type of freedom on campus to the real world, you'll get seriously hurt. I graduated five years ago and I have arrived. Don't cross my path, or I'll crush you.

Ladele: You...

Just then, the door of the Gov's office opens and the Gov. walks out with Banke, his left hand on her shoulder. They are laughing.

Governor: Thank you for calling Banke, and don't forget Friday.
Banke: (*pointing to Ladele*) This is our President, you remember him?
Governor: Oh yes! Your president! How are you?
Ladele: Fine, thank you sir!
He moves forward expecting a handshake. But the Governor does not offer his hand! Ladele cleverly steps aside squeezing his right hand fingers.

16. Exterior. Under an almond tree in a park. Day
Tolu is sitting alone. She is eating roasted corn and epa while reading some lecture notes. There is a soft drink bottle by her side on the concrete bench. Banke approaches from a short distance. Following well behind is Ladele.
Tolu: Heh! Banke! Welcome!
Banke arrives and sits on the bench close to Tolu.
Banke: Thank you Tolu
Tolu: Have the drink, I'll get another one.
Ladele finally arrives and sits some space away.
Tolu: (*cont'd*): Hai President! What's the matter? Move closer. How did it all go at the Governor's office?
Ladele: Why don't you ask Banke?
Banke: Will you stop this childishness or go away from here. What are you so moody about?
Tolu: Ladele, what's the matter?
Ladele: You asked me how it all went, but I don't know!
Tolu: You don't? You were there together?
Ladele: Yes, but only Banke met the governor!
Banke: You were there when he asked to see me alone. Here was a man who was still angry with you in particular. I apologized to him on your behalf and he has forgiven all of us. He may even give us more money. I have an appointment with him on Friday.
Ladele: You are not going back to him!
Banke: Are you talking to me?
Ladele: Yes. I, Ladele am giving you instructions.
Banke: As what?
Ladele: As President, Silver Lines Movement!
Banke: Oh that! You can have your Silver Lines back. I am neither your housemaid nor your little sister. I am seeing the Governor Friday afternoon.
Tolu: Now, now! This is getting out of hand. But I can see why Ladele may be perhaps jealous of the governor. The traces of a new development between you both are becoming evident! Sit down, think and talk about it. I will leave you. I have a lecture.
Tolu collects her books and leaves. Banke and Ladele remain silent. Banke is staring into space, Ladele, looking down.
Ladele: Banke, I am trying hard, but I don't understand you yet.
Banke: You, understand me! I wish I understood myself. Most of the time the spirit of adventure in me completely escapes my control.

17. *Exterior. University gate. Day*

Commercial Drivers Demonstration. The main gate is blocked. Various placards are carried:

> EVERY CAB MUST TAKE TURN
> TOKS TAKE CARE!
> PRESIDENT'S CAB - TOO MANY
> DAILY TICKET TOO HIGH, ETC.

As they demonstrate peacefully they chant:

> We no go gree o, we no go gree!
> President cab, we no go gree
> Toks cab, we no go gree!

18. *Interior. Dean's room. Day*

A big table full of piles of paper. The Dean is sitting at comfortable table at a meeting with President, Student's Union, Toks and Ladele.

Dean: Our intelligence report confirms all the allegations made by the commercial drivers. The University is not going to allow any student or group of students to take undue advantage of their positions or connections and disturb the peace on campus...

Toks: Sir, on a large campus like ours and with our population, social frictions and prompt resolutions are not uncommon. But our problem is that we have a group of students who make it their business to fuel those embers of friction and fan them into acrimonious conflagrations. The solution is to stop that group of students.

President, SU: I hope you know, sir, that the group is Silver Lines Movement led by Ladele...

Ladele: *(calmly)* The Silver Lines Movement is a registered club in this University. You all know that Toks heads a high profile partly clandestine but unregistered group. You have access to our own constitution. Groups that operate in secrecy are a threat to peace on campus. But this trend of argument may in the short run, be diversionary. The urgent thing now, sir, is to investigate the allegations made by those drivers. If they are true, appropriate measures should be taken.

Dean: Thank you all. I have listened very carefully to you. The panel that will look into this and other complaints will invite you again soon. I warn all of you to maintain the peace.

19. *Interior. Governor's private guest house living room. Day*

Banke walks about an exquisitely appointed room, air conditioned and well-lit. Dada enters the kitchen

Dada: *(V. O., shouting)* Kendy! They don come o!

Dada comes back into the living room, brings out his mobile and dials a number. Banke sits down.

Dada: *(cont'd)* We have come sir! Yes sir! Yes sir.

He passes over the mobile to Banke very respectfully.

Dada: (*to Banke*) They wan to speak to you ma.
Banke: Hello!
Governor: (*with phone-filtered voice*) My dear queen!
Banke: Yes sir!
Governor: (*phone-filtered*) Please feel at home. I'll be with you very soon
Banke: Yes sir.
Banke hands back the mobile to Dada.
Dada: (*going away*) O dabo ma
Banke: O dabo o.
Kendy rushes in with the day's papers and offers them to Banke respectfully.
Banke: (*to Kendy*) Oh! Thank you.
Kendy: Make I give you drink, ma?
Banke: Give me water.
Kendy goes away and brings in some water as Banke buries herself in the papers. But just then a car horn sounds. Kendy runs into the living room as if to announce to Banke:
Kendy: Oga is back!
He runs back into the kitchen. Dada enters with a heavy suitcase which he places on a table by the wall. The Governor comes in, Banke stands up.
Banke: Welcome sir!
Governor: (*hugging her*) My darling! How are you?
Banke: Fine sir.
Governor: Welcome to my little relaxing corner.
Banke: It is a beautiful place.
They both sit down. The Governor holds Banke's hand. He sees the papers on the stool.
Governor: You've read some papers. What news today?
Banke: The regulars. Politics! Ask any politician why they are so anxious to see the military go, they will never give the true answer.
Governor: I know why they want us to go away.
Banke: Why?
Governor: To ensure that they have their own share of the national cake!
Banke: What they want really is their own personal share. Money for their families to live on forever! Isn't it?
Governor: But really what's your problem? Why do you students rack your brains prematurely over solving political questions. Cracking political problems is the job of experts. You need to get trained first.
Banke: What kind of training are the next crop of politicians getting?
Governor: As a matter of fact, the training has just started. But you still need to get qualified to enter the training school. But, Banke, we shall talk later. I have a meeting in my office now.
Banke: But I too have an evening lecture, for 7.
Governor: I should be back before then, but just in case...
He opens his briefcase, brings out a bundle of naira notes and gives it to Banke. Banke is surprised.
Governor: (*cont'd*) That is your pocket money.
Banke: This is too much! Fifty thousand!
Governor: Dada will come back to take you back to campus. He will also

come back tomorrow to pick you. Can you drive?

Banke: Yes sir. I have a driving license.

Governor: Perfect! We'll get you a small car, so that you can come and go alone as you like. I'll reach you on your mobile. I have to go now. Kendy will get you something to eat.

The Governor hugs Banke and leaves. Kendy follows him out.

Banke: Thank you sirs.

Banke sits down and continues reading the papers. Kendy comes back.

Kendy: What shall I prepare ma? Amala or rice.

Banke: Nothing for me now. Don't worry. I don't have much time.

Kendy: Ha! I don prepare soup! Oga go vex o!

Banke: Tell me Kendy, do you also prepare food at home for your family?

Kendy: O ti o! God forbid bad tin. I get wife! We born pikin last week sef.

Banke: Really! So, the naming ceremony is this week?

Kendy: Yes! We de prepare small small.

Banke: (*brings out some money*) In that case, take this. Congratulations.

Kendy: (*counting*) Ha! I beg! This is too much! Faif tossan! I never see dis kin one before o. Ha! God go beles you o. You go get good husband and good pikin. Thank you o!

The door bell rings and Kendy goes to answer it. Chief Bongo enters.

Bongo: (*very cheerfully*) Hello there! How are you, my darling?

He tries to hug Banke, but she is cleverly trying to avoid him.

Banke: I'm fine, thank you sir. You are welcome, but His Excellency is not in sir...

Bongo: I know. I know! He just called me and I promised to come and see you. You are even more beautiful than reported! You shall know me well very soon. This place is for the inner circle only. Kendy!

Kendy: Sir!

Bongo: Give me a shot! Double!

Kendy: Yes sir!

Kendy enters with a double shot in a tall glass on a tray Bongo takes the glass.

Bongo: My daughter, what are you doing in the university?

Banke: I am reading law, sir.

Bongo: Law? Who wrote it? Not Soyinka again, I hope!

Banke: No sir. I mean I am studying to be a lawyer.

Bongo: Oro o! You want to be a lawyer! Very good.

Bongo looks at the glass in his hand very carefully, and drinks it up in one gulp.

Bongo: (*cont'd*) Well, my daughter. I have to go now. I just came to pay homage to our campus queen! Look, if His Excellency does anything you don't like, I am the one in charge here. Just tell me.

Bongo opens his briefcase, brings out a fifty thousand bundle and gives Banke.

Banke: No. no, sir! Thank you sir. Don't worry sir.

Bongo: What is wrong with you? If I am going to worry will it be over this paltry sum? Take it from my hand! Are you not an African? When an elder offers something to a small child, you do not refuse it.

Banke: (*taking the money and kneeling*) I am sorry sir. Thank you sir.

Bongo: You mean much to the governor. He has never felt this way about any girl. So, be a good girl.

Banke: Thank you sir.

Bongo: (*going away*) I'll see you again tomorrow.

Banke: Bye bye sir. Thank you sir. . . .

Kendy sees Chief Bongo to his car. Chief Bongo gives Kendy some money. Kendy comes in.

Banke: Kendy, who is that man?

Kendy: That na di man wey oga respect most for dis world. Northing he say, wey oga no go take.

Banke: I say who is he?

Kendy: Na business man, kontraktor. I think say e be Oga im relatif? Haba! He get money no for talk! Too much!

Banke: (*Standing up*) OK Is Dada back?

Kendy: Yes. The car dey outside.

Banke takes her bag and goes out.

Kendy: Bye bye ma! Good woman!

20. Interior. Banke's room in the university. Night

Tolu lies on her bed reading a magazine. Banke opens the door and comes in.

Tolu: (*excited*) Banke! Welcome! Just coming?

Banke: No I attended a 7 o'clock lecture.

Tolu: (*more excited*) How was your outing?

Banke: Fantastic! Absolutely. I met some very unique characters. The governor is more humane and readable than I had thought. I met a very big man living in the lap of luxury. They have surprised me today with their generosity. In addition, two lowly workers have impressed me with their diligence.

Tolu: (*still excited*) Yes, yes, but how about the real encounter with the governor, you being a "virgin"! I mean you don't have to tell me if you....

Banke: Oh. That! Nothing happened! He made no demands.

Tolu: Really! He is only biding his time. I think you are playing a dangerous game! I am afraid for you.

Banke: I am aware of the risks, but I continue to rely on my unusual good luck and mysterious womanly wiles that have helped me to escape the traps of many devils including the Lagos business executive, Toks and our own Ladele!

Tolu: Your date with the Governor has terribly upset Ladele.

Banke: He should know I am working for the SLM. I must also say that I love the adventure. You know I have brought one hundred thousand naira today!

Tolu: (*standing up and screaming*) No! A hundred what? A hundred thousand! That is unbelievable!

Banke: And only two people gave me the money! The governor is giving me a car of my own!

Tolu: (*Seriously*) Well Banke, seriously speaking, any time there is a party please take me along. Somebody will notice me I am not bad!

Banke: (*Smiling*) How about your S.U. morality?

Tolu: No problem. You will teach me how to escape the traps.

They both laugh.

21. Exterior. Front of a female hostel. Evening

Montage of several shots:

1. *Several young boys walk about between cars.*
2. *One boy accompanies a gorgeous girl to a car. The girl gives him some money. The man too gives him some money.*
3. *One boy walks to a man who has been sitting in his car for a long time. He asks him some question. The man shakes his head. The boy brings out about four photographs. The man picks one and the boy goes into the hall.*
4. *The boy comes back with a girl and leads her to the man in the car. The man comes out opens the door for the girl who elegantly takes her seat. The boy stands by the driver's door. The man gives him some money. The boy runs to the girl and stretches his hand. The girl gives an "I'll see you later" sign.*

22. Exterior. Front of a female hostel. Evening (int. car)

Banke, Ike and Martings are inside the car watching the events.

Banke: You see all that? If you stay long enough here and I hide myself at the back, one of these boys will approach you.

Ike: This is unbelievable! I know men come to pick girls, but I never realized it is so organized!

Martins: And to imagine that this is the market from where we are going to pick our wives!

Ike: We are in trouble.

Banke: But there are many good ones still.

Suddenly Martins gets out of the car to see if one boy will come to him.

23. Interior. Governor's private guest house. Day

Banke is sitting in the living room reading a newspaper. Kendy runs in from the kitchen.

Kendy: Madam, Oga is back!

Banke gets up, adjusts her buba and iro, sits down again to continue reading. The Governor comes in. Banke stands up.

Governor: (*hugging Banke*) My own darling!

They both sit down. Dada brings in the Governor's briefcase, put it on the table and goes out.

Banke: Welcome sir! I have a little. Surprise for you! I cooked something special!

Governor: (*surprised*) Cook! Where did you find the time? You cook. Besides I had lunch in the office. Not even my wife cooks. No one can tell where I have lunch or dinner any day. It is mostly in the office or on the road. (*Noticing that Banke is discouraged.*) Cheer up darling. That's a military Governor's life!

Door bell rings. Kendy goes to see.

Kendy: Na di commissioner for em .. .em... Work and em.

Governor: It's alright, let him come in!

Banke: (*standing up*) Let me go to my room to allow you to...

Governor: OK, please carry my briefcase along.

Works Commissioner: Good evening sir.

Governor: Good evening Lanre. That was fast!

Works Commissioner: Yes sir, our friend Mr Zuki has brought the whole thing in cash.

Governor: In cash!

Works Commissioner: Yes, I mean the part we want in naira.

Governor: Even that is a lot.

Works Commissioner: Well, we asked him to bring cash.

Governor: Yes! No cheques that can be traced! Well, where is the cash?

Works Commissioner: In a suitcase in the boot of the car.

Governor: Bring it in.

The commissioner goes out while the governor rubs his hands in satisfaction. The commissioner returns to hand over the suitcase which the Governor carries into the room.

24. Interior. Governor's private guest house, a room. Day

Banke is relaxing on bed, reading a paper. Governor comes in, rolls the suitcase to the foot of the table.

Banke: What is that?

Governor: (*in hushed tones*) Money!

Governor goes out. Banke gets up and goes to look at the suitcase. She tries to open it. It is locked. She goes back to lie on the bed. Governor comes in, Banke stands up.

Banke: Is he gone?

Governor: (*opening the briefcase*) Not yet. Just a minute.

Governor brings out a fat file, removes a document, drops the keys to the suitcase on the file and goes out. Banke gets up picks the keys, hesitates, and drops them. In the process she sees a document in the file; she looks at it, opens her mouth, removes it and quickly hides it in her bag. She lies back on the bed. Governor comes in smiling. He sits on the bed and holds Banke's hands.

Governor: (*looking pleased*) You are so beautiful!

Banke: Thank you sir. How much money is there in that suitcase?

Governor: You are always asking funny questions! Don't worry your head.

Banke: But what are you going to do with so much money?

Governor: One saves for the rainy day.

Banke: But there is only one rainy season in a year!

Governor: Yes, but so many years in a man's life! And so many lives in a family's many generations. Stop asking questions! Settle down to enjoy your life with me. I love you... you see, there are so many things you students don't know. Do you know that to get certain allocations released from the centre, I have to give some people a lot of money?

Banke: Really? Even in this military era?

Governor: Yes mam!

25. Interior. Governor's private guest house, living room. Day
Chief Bongo, Chief and T.K. and Dr. Damisa are seated. Governor enters and they all stand up.
Governor: Ah, Egbon! What is all this? Please sit down! I hope there is no problem.
Bongo: There is! Something is very wrong around us here!
Governor: Like what!
Bongo: Some people are spying on us like NSO people! We are not safe anymore!
Governor: For God's sake, where did you get all this from?
Bongo: We have this on good authority.
Governor: All right, gentlemen, please let us meet in my office in an hour.
Bongo: (standing up) OK.
They all stand up, ready to go.

26. Interior. Governor's private guest house, a room. Day
Banke sits down on a chair reading some document. Governor suddenly opens the door. Banke cleverly hides the document inside the newspaper in her lap. Governor does not notice.
Banke: Are you through with them?
Governor: (*taking a new handkerchief*) Yes, but I have a meeting in the office right now. I'll see you later.
Banke: I also have a 4 o'clock lecture...
Governor: You should be back by 5.30, 6?
Banke: Yes.
Governor: I should be back before six. I'll see you then
Governor goes out and Banke continues reading the document. She shakes her head, stands up and puts the document in her bag.
Banke: I have to make a copy of this!

27. Interior. Governor's private office. Day
The governor is seated at his special chair. Chief Bongo, Chief T.K. and Dr Damisa are ushered in.
Governor: Please sit down gentlemen. Egbon, this story is strange.
Bongo: We have concrete evidence to show that something is wrong. For example, do you know that some important documents have found their way into the hands of a dangerous group determined to discredit your administration?
Governor: No! What documents?
Bongo: Documents about certain enquiries, documents about certain deals, about certain monies that changed hands in suitcases!
The governor is shocked. He sits up and frowns.
Bongo: Reports of certain special committees marked "top secret". I was in London recently only to discover that some people have been tracing my account.

Governor: Really? But you still haven't told me the source of your information.

Bongo: Chief Tidimugi, you know works with the university. This group is based in the University. It is known as the Silver Lines.

Governor: The Silver Lines? I know about the Silver Lines!

Dr Damisa: I an not sure you do sir!

Governor: I beg your pardon! I am telling you I do!

Dr Damisa: Then you should know that they are bent on discrediting your administration.

Governor: I don't believe you.

Dr Damisa: Let Chief T.K. relate his experience in the hands of these blackmailers.

TK: They have ruined my business. They have infiltrated the ranks of my workers, sponsored a strike and took money from me.

Dr Damisa: Suddenly, their President and the girl called Banke are behaving like millionaires, driving about in a new car and checking into expensive hotels together.

Governor: (*angry*) Is that so?

The visiting group is encouraged by the Governor's angry mood.

Dr Damisa: And now, they want to start a magazine where they intend to demolish any credibility your administration may have using authentic documents! Look at this handbill.

Governor grabs one and springs up immediately he starts reading.

Governor: What! God of iron! "Contracts ride in suitcases"

Bongo: If this should get into the hands of our boss in the capital city! It is not going to be funny!

TK: These boys are devils!

Dr Damisa: We have to stop them before it is too late! We have other groups on campus who can promote a positive image of your administration.

Bongo: But you have to quickly seal that leak from your end.

Governor: (*in pensive mood*) Well,, thank you gentlemen for your interest. We shall take necessary action. Egbon, Bongo, please wait behind.

Chief T.K. and Dr Damisa go out.

Governor: Ègbón, I need to discuss certain things with you. We'll go back to my private place together.

28. Interior. Bank's room in the university, evening
Tolu and Simbi are reading a letter.

Simbi: This is what I got from the Students' Disciplinary Committee. We are charged with 'blackmail' and 'incitement' against Chief T.K. and Dr. Damisa

Tolu: I know who is behind all this. Olu Ala has been expelled from the University and Toks suspended for a whole session. Dr. Damisa and Chief T.K. are bitter. This is their counter attack.

Simbi: You are right. The Silver Lines have to meet tonight or tomorrow. You have to brief Banke today.

There is a knock at the door and Banke's mother comes in, looking rather troubled.
Tolu: Ah! Mama! Welcome!
Mrs Bandele: Thank you. Where is Banke?
Tolu: Eh, I.... Was not in the room when she left.
Mrs Bandele: Tolu! why are you lying to me?
Tolu: Ah? I am not lying ma!
Mrs Bandele: (*sitting down*) I received an anonymous call this afternoon. The caller told me that Banke no longer sleeps on campus! He called her an *asewo*! Tolu, did Banke sleep in this room last night?
Tolu and Simbi become nervous. They rock their fingers and do not know what to say.
Mrs Bandele: Tolu, you are Banke's best friend, and you could not advise her against this shameful behavours! Do you know where she is?
Tolu: She will come here after the lecture ma.
Mrs Bandele: (*sobbing*) Oh God, what have I done? Why should Banke become a harlot? Well, she will come and meet me here today.
A quick knock and Ladele enters.
Ladele: Hi, everybody Ah, good afternoon ma!
Mrs Bandele: Good afternoon, my son.
Ladele: Well, Tolu, Simbi must have told you about your invitation to testify. Here are your own letters and Banke's. We meet tomorrow morning. Tell Banke before she goes back to town.
Mrs Bandele: Why is she going back to town?
Ladele: (*surprised*) Eh.....
Tolu: That is Banke's mother.
Ladele: (*postrating himself*) Oh! Good evening ma! Em, you know we have to go to town to buy many things .... I am sorry I have to go ....
Ladele hurries out of his room.
Mrs Bandele: Hah! He e e! They are trying to cover up for her!
Tolu and Simbi want to go out to discuss something but before they reach the door Banke bursts in.
Banke: (*full of life*) Hi girls!
The girls receive her coldly and when she sees her mother she freezes. She quickly kneels.
Banke: (*timidly*) Good afternoon mummy.
Mrs Bandele springs to her feet and grabs Banke's clothes.
Mrs Bandele: Good afternoon Madam Asewo! Where are you coming from?
Banke: From lectures!
Mrs Bandele: And where did you sleep last night?
The two other girls are very uncomfortable, but there is no room to warn her.
Banke: In my room!
Mother starts beating her and shouting.
Mrs Bandele: Where is your room? Banke, Banke you have started telling me lies! I will kill you before you bring shame on me! I will kill you!
Banke: (*crying*) Please mother, forgive me! Please!
Tolu and Simbi try to separate them.
Tolu and Simbi: Please ma! Please! Spare her ma!
Mrs Bandele: You have to tell me where you now live!

Banke: Please mummy, don't shout so much … a crowd will soon gather!

Mrs Bandele: Ein, ein, ein! So, I am shouting? I will shout louder now. I want your friends to know what you are doing to me.

Tolu and Simbi: Please ma.

Mrs Bandele is now tired. She sits down and starts crying.

Mrs Bandele: You want to kill me, Banke! And you know my problems in your father's house! If your father should hear this, I will be the brunt of his anger. Now, pack a bag. You are following me home now. We have a few things to discuss.

Banke: Ah, mummy, please. I cannot follow you home today.

Mrs Bandele: You must be joking! If I have to shout and drag you, I will.

Banke: I cannot go home today ma, no no. I have to return an important book to the owner this night.

Mrs Bandele: You are joking!

Tolu: *(whispering to Banke)* Why don't you follow mummy home?

Banke: *(whispering back)* The documents must be returned tonight! Please mummy I'll come home tomorrow morning.

Tolu and Simbi: *(kneeling down)* Please ma, let her come tomorrow morning. Exams are so near!

Mrs Bandele: All right. If she cannot come today, I must see her first thing tomorrow morning. *(Turning to Banke).* You have disappointed me, but I now know what to do.

Banke follows her mother out.

Tolu: This is getting serious!

Simbi: It is the end of the experiment.

Banke rushes back into the room

Banke: *(holding a big envelope)* Lest I forget, please read this document. These are photocopies, I must return the original from where I stole it tonight. See you tomorrow night. Bye bye.

29. Exterior. Under an almond tree in a park, evening

Simbi and Tolu sit on the concrete bench reading the document brought by Banke. Martins join them.

Martins: This is the hottest document we have ever got.

Suddenly Ladele and Kendy approach running. Tolu, Simbi and Martins stand up and walk to meet them.

Martins: What is the matter?

Ladele: Where is Banke? Where is Banke?

Tolu: She has gone back to town.

Kendy: Hah! Them wan kill am o!

Ladele: Her life is in grave danger!

Tolu and Simbi: In grave danger?

Martins: Who wants to kill Banke?

Kendy: Na oga sef o!

Tolu: Oh God! What are they doing to her now?

Simbi: Has she got back home?

Kendy: No, she never reach home o. Na for road they wan kill am o.

Tolu: Oh! Let us do something now!

Ladele: OK. Now, Martins, you are a police officer. Please get one NSO man on campus and let us look for Banke before she is killed.

Martins: All right. Let Kendy join us in my car. We shall pick my friend and we shall go.

They all run towards Martins car. Tolu and Simbi also walk away.

30. Campus chapel premises. Night
Tolu and Simbi are praying for Banke's safety. They both stand.

Tolu: Almighty God! Father of our Lord Jesus Christ, our guard and guardian, our armour and our shield, please throw your strong arm of protection round Banke wherever she may be now!

Simbi: Amen!

As they pray Toks and Olu Ala appear behind them.

Toks and Olu Ala: Hello there!

Tolu and Simbi stop praying and move back in fear.

Tolu: What do you want here?

Simbi: Go away!

Toks: Why? We've only come to say goodbye

Olu Ala: You've succeeded in sending us out!

Tolu: We have nothing to do with you.

Toks: Take it easy, we are friends. We have come to obtain some souvenir from you.

Olu Ala: Like some piece of flesh or some blood stains!

Toks and Ala draw out sharp knives and move towards the girls. The girls shout hysterically.

Tolu and Simbi: Help! Help! Help! Everybody help!

A parked car nearby switched on its head lamps. The intruders quickly retreat, covering their faces.

Toks: Olu, let's get out of here!

They run away into the darkness. Some students around the chapel run to the girls to see what is happening.

31. Interior. Governor's private guest house, living room. Night
Governor sits alone drinking heavily. Two bottles of brandy are on the centre table. He grabs the telephone.

Governor: Chief Bongo! Don't forget the slight modification I demanded … Yes I would like to ask her a few questions … Yes! She should be brought to me first … yes … They'll take her away later.

32. Interior. Banquet hall of a new club house. Night
The audience is less energetic, reacting to a sorrowful song – apprehensive of the dangers, challenges and confrontations … (Sultan's song).

33. Exterior. Road (lonely stretch). Night
Two armed men sit down in a car parked by the roadside, watching keenly all approaching cars.

34. *Exterior. Road (lonely stretch). Night*
Banke is driving back to Governor's private guest house alone.

35. *Exterior. Road, Martin's car. Night*
Martins is driving. Ladele, NSO man and Kendy are watching both sides of the road carefully.

36. *Exterior. Road, Banke's car. Night*
Banke's car is abandoned on the roadside with the driver's door left open. There are no bloodstains and no evidence of any force being used. Martin's car approaches and Kendy sights Banke's car.

Kendy: Hah! They don kill am o! Oh God!

Martins: This looks like a kidnap! I think she has been kidnapped.

Ladele: She may still be alive! But what do we do?

Kendy: Make we go check the house now. May be dem take am go see oga first.

Ladele: Let's go! There is no time to waste!

They jump into the car and speed off, apprehension written all over their faces. Kendy is crying silently. As they approach governor's private guest house, Kendy advises them to stop.

Kendy: A beg, make we stop here o.

NSO: I was going to say that. The sound and headlamps can give us out.

They stop, park the car out of sight and move on foot. The NSO man is carrying a gun, Martins is carrying a pistol. Kendy leads them. There is light in the living room and in the bedroom. Kendy leads them into the compound through the small gate at the back. They hear voices from the living room.

37. *Interior. Governor's private guest house, living room. Night*
The governor in ordinary shirt and trousers and a glass of brandy in hand looks contemptuously at Banke in a pair of jeans and t-shirt, blindfolded, squatting on the floor. Two assassins with hand pistols stand by.

Governor: (*angry*) You really thought I was a fool, right? Now where are the documents you stole?

Banke: (*scared but bold*) I have returned all of them!

Governor: And the last one, this afternoon?

Banke: It is in my bag.

One of the assassins picks Banke's bag from the floor and hands it over to the governor. He opens the bag and brings out the sensitive report. He shakes his head.

Governor: (*to himself*) I have been careless! (*to Banke*) Well, now what have you been doing with all these documents!

Banke: Our movement is just collecting information...

Governor: To publish and blackmail me so that I can be sacked?

Banke: No, we never mention our sources ...

Governor: Anyway, don't worry, it is the end of the road for you. You'll be taken away now, and it is goodbye.

Suddenly Martins, NSO and Ladele storm the livingroom through the kitchen, behind the assassins and facing the governor.

Martins: Hold it! Stay where you! (*shocked silence*) move! Drop your guns, boys! This house is surrounded!

The assassins drop their guns and raise up their hands. Ladele pick up their guns.

NSO: Hah! Your Excellency! I didn't know! This is serious!

The governor looks temporarily dazed and embarrassed. But suddenly his anger overwhelms him.

Governor: (*pulling out a pistol*) But I cannot allow this ingrate to go scot free!

He aims the pistol at Banke. In swift action. Ladele rushes forward to attack the governor. He comes between Banke and the gun. His shot hits Ladele. At the same time, NSO wants to stop Ladele from harming the governor. He aims a shot at his thigh, but the shot hits the Governor's belly and he falls.

NSO: Oh! What have I done?

Martins: Why did you do that?

NSO: I wanted to stop Ladele. I have a duty to protect the governor.

Martins: But see what you have done!

In the confusion, one of the assassins makes good his escape. The other one is now handcuffed. Banke kneels down beside Ladele. The NSO man stoops by the governor.

NSO: He is dead! He is losing blood.

Banke: He is breathing! He is not dead yet! Please help!

The NSO man stays with the governor on the floor. He is trying to call the police on his mobile phone. He manages to move Governor into his own car.

38. Interior. NSO man's car
The NSO man drives off with Kendy sitting by the governor on the back seat.

39. Interior. Government clinic
The arrival of the wounded governor at the Government Clinic causes a lot of confusion. All the doctors assemble at the clinic to take quick decisions.

40. Exterior. A modest private clinic
Banke and Martins escort Ladele to see a private doctor.

41. Interior. Chief Bongo's living room. Night
Chief Bongo is drinking heavily. He is alone in the early hours of the day watching television.

Television announcer (newsflash): Reports reaching our studios and confirm that the Military Administrator of Zero State has been assassinated. The circumstances are still not clear. The police have commenced investigations.

Chief Bongo shouts and slumps, lying flat on his back.

42. Final credits.

Book Reviews

Colin Chambers, *Black and Asian Theatre in Britain: A History*
London: Routledge, 2011, 291 pp.
ISBN 978041537598-6 (pbk) £24.99

Colin Chambers needs no introduction as a chronicler and historian of British theatre. He has written on subjects ranging from Unity Theatre to the RSC, and on individuals from Peggy Ramsay to Charlie Chaplin. Much of his work has been on broadly modern theatre, with excursions into the nineteenth century, but in the present work the emphasis is firmly on the title's tag – 'A History'. At the beginning of the book, acknowledging recent work on Black and Asian theatre, Chambers suggests that 'there is little of detail …before the 1970s' stating that '[t]he aspiration of this book is to fill this conspicuous gap'. I admit that on picking up the book my initial assumption was that the focus would mainly be on the earlier part of the twentieth century, but in fact we are taken back to the sixteenth century (and with occasional glimpses even earlier), tracing Black and Asian presences in plays and personalities from the Indian servant boy in *A Midsummer Night's Dream* to the actor Lucy Negro, an actor Chambers suggests 'Shakespeare probably knew'. The research that has gone into this study may be judged by a 'Select Bibliography' that exceeds 500 entries. But, as with all of Chamber's excursions into theatre history, this is told in a style and manner distinguished not only by its scholarship but also by its enthusiasm, care and respect for its subject.

After the first chapter, 'The early era', Chambers moves onto the fascinating story of the American Ira Aldridge, 'the first black actor of note in Britain' (at the same time whetting our appetite for Bernth Lindfors' full-scale biography of Aldridge which is due to be published this year). Whilst much of Aldridge's success and reputation was made in continental Europe, his impact in Britain was substantial, playing Othello and Shylock, and Aaron ('the Moor') in *Titus Andronicus*. He encountered prejudice and intolerance, attempting to forge a theatrical career 'constrained by the legacy of stereotypes inherited from minstrelsy'. After Aldridge (itself the title of his hugely informative third chapter) Chambers chronicles an astonishing range of 'diasporic artists of colour', ranging from circus performers (William Beaumont, 'The African Lion King') to singers and dancers. He notes what was 'hailed as the first all-black musical comedy to arrive in Britain', *In Dahomey*, staged in 1903, and identifies Henry Francis Downing, an African-American, as 'probably the first person of African descent to have a play…written and published in Britain'.

The remaining five chapters of the book bring us into the twentieth century, tracing in detail Asian, African American and Caribbean companies, cultural organisations, actors, musicians, playwrights, cabaret artists, and venues. Paul Robeson's time in Britain during the 1930s is interestingly recorded, including the fact that as he was 'not part of the British empire's diaspora' there was sometimes 'resentment in the job market when British-based Caribbean and African actors were overlooked in favour of him or told they had to emulate him.' Like Aldridge, Robeson performed Othello (to Peggy Ashcroft's Desdemona), in a production that Chambers records was fraught with problems caused by a wealthy American producer (who decided to cast himself as Iago) and his wife, the director, who 'was issuing orders through a megaphone from the back of the stalls'.

It is one of the great strengths and, importantly, pleasures of this book, that it moves well beyond a mere chronicling of activities and individuals into a sensitive description of battles fought and prejudices encountered. Moving to more recent times Chambers offers detailed information and analysis of the work of such pivotal figures as Errol John, Mustapha Matura, Yvonne Brewster, and companies including Dark and Light Theatre, Indian Art and Dramatic Society, Tara Arts, Tamasha, Talawa and Temba.

There are many incidental pleasures to this study. It is enormously well researched, carries throughout a sense of respecting and caring for its subjects, offers a selection of informative and engaging illustrations, a theatre professional's insight into the demands and dangers of creating theatre, and - oh joy! – does not feel the need to wrap up its scholarship in critical jargon.

Chambers' closing paragraph is worth quoting as an illustration of his critical focus:

Black and Asian theatre has created a network of artists and groups distinguished by their own methods, their own values, and their own body of work. Black and Asian theatre has borrowed from, added to, and changed the dominant culture. Through a new aesthetic that draws strength from but transcends racial, geographical, and artistic boundaries, the canon has been re-envisaged and revitalized while new stories and players have been introduced. By doing this from the margins and restoring the challenging meaning of being on the edge, black and Asian theatre has added its weight to the reconfiguration of what was seen as peripheral. Black and Asian theatre has thereby transformed notions not only of British theatre but also of black and Asian theatre itself and notions of a new, devolving Britain, struggling to find a new 'we' and new ways of thinking and behaving.

Martin Banham
University of Leeds

Dominica Dipio, Lene Johannessen and Stuart Sillars (eds)
Performing Community: Essays on Ugandan Oral Culture
Oslo: Novus Press, 2008, 275 pp.
ISBN 9788270994991, $52

Dominica Dipio, Lene Johannessen and Stuart Sillars (eds) *Performing
Change: Identity, Ownership and Tradition in Ugandan Oral Culture*
Oslo: Novus Press, 2009, 230 pp.
ISBN 9788270995523, $64

The volume *Performing Community: Essays on Ugandan Oral Culture* is based on a collab-
orative project on Ugandan oral performances between researchers from the University
of Bergen and Makerere University, which aimed to 'record the oral cultural forms of
the diverse communities of Uganda, and to assist in their continuity and growth' (26) in
the contemporary post independent/post colonial moment. The book consists of an
introductory section, *Okutandika* with one essay, Stuart Sillars' 'Oracy and Belonging'
(23-32), and Saidah Namayanja's transcription and translation of updated Luganda
folktales, *Ssempeke ne Nampeke* (Ssempeke and Nampeke) and *Wankima ne Waggoonya*
(Monkey and Crocodile) (15-22). Section One contains essays on 'Kinship, Authority
and Resolution' and Section Two, 'Change and Assimilation', gives us two essays,
'Indices of Social Change in the Oral Literature of the Baganda' (149-169) and 'The
Symbolism of Music Festivals in Buganda' (170-188). Section Three evaluates parallel
formations in oral performance with two essays, 'Ubuntu Aesthetics in Welcome
Msomi's *Mabatha*' (191-212) and a comparative study of Okot p'Bitek and Rodolfo
Gonzzales, 'The Trails of "Stories-so-Far": Okot p'Bitek and Rodolfo Gonzales' (213-
232). Section Four, 'Children and Adults', centres on the evaluation of performative
cultures. The writers contend that in folk narratives, children and adult characters inex-
tricably intersect. Finally, Section Five contains the 'Afterword' (267-272) and a poem,
'Living Tales' (273-275).

In his Introduction, Sillars' explains that his aim is to underline the 'common
character of forms of ritual oracy as means of defining the individual and reinforcing and
extending community settings, and societies'. Sillars underlines that the research process
focused on rehearsal processes, performance and practice of oral forms while locating
them in contemporary ideologies. He argues that the research and recovery of the oral
performance forms is an essential stage in 'the process of genuine cultural awareness' for
both local communities and scholars (24). Austin Bukenya's 'Afterword' shows that
studies of 'oracy and literature' (267) and the 'social relevance of oral communication'
(271) are not new. However, previous essays have not done what these writers are
trying to do, initiating the compilation of 'an "atlas" of Ugandan orature' that adequately represents performative narratives from across the nation; and in addition,
'examining and re-examining them for new insights in the light of emerging realities
and experiences' (272). In an attempt to demonstrate the contemporary relevance of
these forms, for example in 'Children's Play Songs of the Baganda' (235-248) and 'The
Symbolism of Music Festivals in Buganda' (170-190), the contributors highlight the
transition from traditional oral performances to culturally relevant reworkings of the
stories and festivals while recognising gradual changes in the performance processes and
reception. The forms discussed in this volume rest on aesthetic and performative enact-
ments of societal beliefs and situations that radically pre-date any colonial infringements.
Although the first volume is poorly edited and translated in places, for instance, in

Namayanja's flawed Luganda spellings and inaccurate translations of Luganda folktales (*i.e.*, 16, 17, 19, 20, 87), these are nonetheless important contributions to contemporary studies in oral literature and performance.

The second book under review, Dipio, Johannessen and Sillars (eds), *Performing Change: Identity, Ownership and Tradition in Ugandan Oral Culture*, contains essays that 'address directly problems that are specific to the various societies of Uganda, but are also suggestive of larger human concerns' (17). This second book confirms oral performance as a dynamic form in Uganda. It contains an introduction and ten essays by eleven different authors, contained in three sections, 'Ownership and Recording', 'Gender and Change', and 'Society and Identity'.

The volume brings together a wide ranging survey of oral literature and performances outlining shifts in aesthetics influenced by social and political changes. Although sections of the books read like broad commentaries, the discussions draw in historical sources to demonstrate the development of oracy in the late twentieth- and early twenty-first centuries. Throughout the book, and in each of the four main sections, the contributors discuss folkloric performance forms, myth, ritual, marriage and popular festivals, the interrelationship between oral culture and digital media, and issues of performance and reception, and this underlines new analytical and methodological approaches to the study of oral performance.Once again this collection focuses on process but in addition, the contributors discuss various significant themes; for instance, ownership, gender and power, cultural identity, reception, and war and peace. In the chapters on society and identity the authors describe performance forms and styles that have become increasingly urban, transnational, and multicultural. The chapters, 'Mapping the Dream of Cultural Continuity: Songs at *Enkuukay'omwaka*' (209-230) and 'Reconstructing Traditional Heroism in Contemporary Context: The Case of Princess Koogere Atwooki of Tooro' (160-179) both offer new readings of this emerging area of approach.

Finally, the chapter exploring intellectual property issues is of particular of interest. Okello Ogwang examines how the Ugandan Copyright Act 1964 inadequately addresses the global 'appropriation of traditional forms'. He concludes that Uganda's 'local or indigenous conceptions of intellectual and cultural property stand at variance with the intellectual property regimes' (43).

Given the scope of the projects that inspired these collections, it is understandable that contributions vary in length and that they include translations and transcriptions of local performances. The introductions to the books are very useful, providing the reader with performance contexts. Despite the criticisms above, the editors have provided a significant collection of essays which offer a new reading of contemporary oral performances, and will be most helpful as a critical reference for more detailed studies of oral culture.

Sam Kasule
University of Derby

Gbemisola Adeoti, *Aesthetics of Adaptation in Contemporary Nigerian Drama*
Lagos: Centre for Black and African Arts and Civilisation (CBAAC), No 20 Occasional
Monograph Series, 2010, 74 pp.
ISBN 9789788406570, n.p.

Gbemisola Adeoti, *Voices Offstage: Nigerian Dramatists on Drama and Politics*
Ibadan: Kraft Books, 2010, 192 pp.
ISBN 9789788435106, n.p.

These are two extremely useful contributions to the ever growing publications on Nigerian theatre. Gbemisola Adeoti has a clear, original voice and brings new angles, concerns and playwrights to public attention.

Aesthetics of Adaptation is a single long essay of 74 pages considering why adaptation has proved so popular among Nigeria's leading dramatists, and going on to analyse key texts by Wole Soyinka, Femi Osofisan and Ahmed Yerima. Adeoti discusses how adaptation has long been a fruitful field for dramatists worldwide before considering why so many Nigerian playwrights have repeatedly been drawn to this mode of creation. He identifies a recognition of the repetition of human experience in different contexts and over millennia as a key factor here, but differentiates between when playwrights are emphasising the circularity of human experience – a mode he identifies with Soyinka; and when, like Osofisan, they utilise old and familiar stories to envision how society might be remade differently and better. He also differentiates between texts such as Yerima's *An Inspector Calls*, which are basically transpositions to a Nigerian setting, and a play like Soyinka's *King Baabu* which utilises Jarry's original *Ubu Roi* but then freely reworks it to fit his concerns with contemporary Nigerian society.

Adeoti looks not only at borrowings from other lands, but also considers how the playwrights have often incorporated elements of their own cultures in these plays. So he celebrates how Osofisan's *The Women of Owu* gains significant tragic power by utilising Yoruba *oriki, ekuniyawo, oku pipe* and *ofo* chant forms; and how in Yerima's version of *Othello (Otaelo)* contemporary resonance with the racism of the original is created by making the tragic hero of the Igbo outcast group: an *Osu*. Correlations with previous plays dealing with injustice, and particularly political abuse of power are seen as powerful motives for nearly all the adaptations.

All the plays considered are adapted from European texts. Indeed while Adeoti recognises that there are numerous inter-Nigerian adaptations, he calls at the end of his essay for more consideration of how the work of other African playwrights might create a fertile field for Nigerian reinterpretation. In each instance two plays are selected for consideration: so for Soyinka we are offered analyses of *The Bacchae of Euripedes* and *King Baabu*; from Osofisan's huge *oeuvre* of adaptations are selected *Tegonni* and *Women of Owu*; and he concludes by studying Ahmed Yerima's *An Inspector Calls* and *Otaelo*.

This is by no means the first time that attention has been drawn to the proliferation of adaptations from earlier works in Nigerian theatre, but Adeoti attempts both a consideration of why this has proved such a recurrently appealing strategy, and by looking at these plays in some depth explores how adaptations gain poetic power and relevance when playwrights reinvent the texts with reference to Nigerian cultural forms and specific socio-political issues.

Voices Offstage is an enormously valuable collection of interviews with eight contemporary Nigerian playwrights. This is a tremendous resource for all who are interested in Nigerian theatre. Femi Osofisan has of course been interviewed many times and there is quite an amount of material about Tess Onwueme and Ahmed Yerima in circulation, but some of the other voices are far less well publicised. This volume includes, besides the three named above, contributions from Esiaba Irobi, Emmy Idegu, Irene Salami, Akinwumi Isola, and a man much better known as a poet, Niyi Osundare.

In each case Adeoti has followed a similar trajectory of questioning. He asks about sources of inspiration, about major plays, playwrights' views about their role in society and the politics of Nigerian theatre, problems of publication and the future for theatre in the country, especially in view of the dominance of the Nollywood film industry.

Osofisan and Osundare are the senior figures here. Both emerge from a time when many Nigerian artists were strongly influenced by Marxist ideology and see their work as importantly related to the need to transform society. Osofisan particularly seems rather gloomy about future prospects for Nigerian theatre, arguing that after his generation 'art became a commodity rather than an ideological weapon' (p 32), while Osundare bemoans what he sees as a 'second phase of [cultural] colonisation' (p 160) I was particularly interested in Osundare's discussion of theatrical form and language, and how he seeks to make his plays 'accessible' to his audience (p 156-7). Indeed my greatest disappointment about these interviews was that so little was said about stagecraft and audience reception. This seems to be an area that is consistently overlooked in analysis of contemporary Nigerian theatre, and while Adeoti's title emphasises his focus on the politics of Nigerian drama, surely questions on theatricality would have been appropriate in the discussions with playwrights.

It is good to hear from two female dramatists, especially the lesser known Irene Salami. Both see a focus on female perspective as central to their work. Onwueme is possibly more assertive, saying she is a voice for the 'tribe' (44) of Nigerian women whom she argues are usually presented as secondary to powerful men even by relatively liberal male writers. Salami calls herself a womanist and argues for female solidarity to negotiate for equality with men. Salami discusses two of her plays, *Emotan* and *The Queen Sisters*, both of which are rooted in the history of her Edo people. And this strikes a chord with other writers: Emmy Idegu's *Inikpi* and *Omodoko* are both centred on historical stories of Igala heroic women, while Akinwumi Isola draws heavily on Yoruba mythology for his theatre. (A review of two of his Yoruba plays translated into English appears in timely fashion below). Generally these plays have allegorical messages for the present, but it is interesting that these 'third generation' Nigerian playwrights are still seeing the reclamation of history as a vital part of their theatrical mission.

As usual the iconoclastic Esiaba Irele, who sadly left us recently to take a little fire to the ancestors, is controversial in his misogyny, aggression and poetic brevity. Who could not be engaged by his description of himself as 'a retarded genius' (52).

Overall this collection tells those of us who seldom have access to the often only local publications of contemporary Nigerian playwrights much about the concerns and perspectives of a number of significant but lesser known theatrical voices. I do regret that no-one in this collection appears to be under fifty. Surely there are some young voices worth hearing from? And finally Martin Banham's suggestion in his Foreword that these playwrights band together to produce an anthology of Nigerian plays, given that all bemoan the lack of publishing opportunities, seems a simple but fabulous suggestion.

Jane Plastow
University of Leeds

Akínwùmí Ìṣọ́lá. *Efúnetán Aníwúrà, Ìyálóde Ìbàdàn and Tinúubú, Ìyálóde Ẹgbá: Two Yoruba Historical Dramas.* Translated from Yoruba by Pamela J. Olúbùnmi Smith
Trenton, NJ and Asmara: Africa World Press, 2005, 251 pp.
ISBN 159221228X, $24.95

Efúnetán Aníwúrà, Ìyálóde Ìbàdàn and Tinúubú, Ìyálóde Ẹgbá: are lively English translations by Pamela J. Olúbùnmi Smith of two Yoruba historical dramas by Akínwùmí Ìṣọ́lá. The original plays, *Efúnetán Aníwúrà* and Olúbùnmi are well known to Yoruba-speaking audiences. They dramatise the lives of two important and powerful women in turbulent nineteenth-century Yorubaland: Efúnetán Aníwúrà of Ibadan, and Tinúubú of Abeokuta; both Ìyálóde (Head of Women and Women's Affairs) of their cities.

Efúnetán Aníwúrà dramatises Efúnetán Aníwúrà's fall from power at the hands of the people after an act of vicious cruelty to a slave, while Olúbùnmi tells the story of how Tinúubú led the Ẹgba of Abeokuta to victory against Dahomey, and was subsequently awarded the Ìyálóde title.

Akínwùmí Ìṣọ́lá, author of the two plays, is a revered figure in contemporary Yoruba literature. His work, almost entirely in Yoruba with a few English exceptions, encompasses novels, plays, films and poetry, as well as scholarship and translation. Ìṣọ́lá makes full use of the suppleness of the Yoruba language, particularly its penchant for imagery, puns, allusions, jokes, rhetoric, ideophones and proverbs, and Smith has worked hard to bring this out in this translation. Crucially, Smith was able to work closely with Ìṣọ́lá, himself, and her translation retains much of the richness and playfulness of Ìṣọ́lá,'s original.

In her 'Translator's Notes', Smith discusses the difficulties posed to the English translator by Yoruba's 'penchant for tonal and semantic double-play', and its 'built-in rhythmic cadences and drum beat language'. Yoruba-English translation thus necessitates 'some inventiveness' (36). However, Smith has worked very faithfully with Ìṣọ́lá's original texts, such that the original and the translation are comparable, sentence by sentence. One of the few changes Smith has made is to add directions for characters' behaviour or emotions, where perhaps she felt the English doesn't entirely convey the emotional range or cultural nuances of the Yoruba.

Smith maintains a sense of the Yoruba cultural world of the original plays, while avoiding exotica or archaism in the English. For instance, a character in *Efúnetán Aníwúrà* proclaims, using well-known Yoruba sayings:

> Efúnetán has transformed herself into a crooked piece of green wood, a flame quencher; a fox let loose in a hen house. She has become the crooked hearthstone burner that tips the pot unexpectedly. (Scene 10)

Smith's translation retains the imagery drawn from nineteenth century Yoruba life without rendering it strange, while the careful assonance of 'crooked ... wood ... loose' replaces untranslatable echoes in the original between *wọ́rọ́kọ̀* and *wọ̀rọ̀kọ̀* (both meaning 'crooked', but with different nuances and intonation).

Smith's Introduction and footnotes provide a good amount of contextual information about Ìṣọ́lá's career, critical reception of the plays, Yoruba culture, the history of Ibadan and Abeokuta, and the history of the Ìyálóde institution. Smith makes much of Ìṣọ́lá's 'unique' and 'remarkable' interest in the history of Yoruba women, seeing these plays as 'major contributions to feminist and gender studies of pre-colonial Yorubaland'

(2-3). There is, however, little sense of the plays as literature or in performance; it would have been useful, for instance, to see some discussion of the plays' place in Yoruba drama, their relationship with oral literary forms, or their performance history. One of the few problems in the translation is Smith's rendering of Yoruba insults and slang. Earthy abuse is common in these plays: 'You are a dirty bastard. May your father be cursed. I hope you die like a dog' (*Tinúubú,* Scene 1) is a fairly representative example. Often, Smith admirably conveys the provocative and vivid spirit of the language, not straying too far from the literal meaning. In the above example, for instance, the Yoruba original is '*Ọmọ àle pátá gbáà ni ọ! Ìyá kan ọkùnrin mẹ̀ẹ̀ẹ́dọ́gbọ̀n! Yíò bá baba rẹ. O ò níi kúu re!*': a very serious insult which could be literally translated as 'You are a complete bastard! One mother, twenty-five men! May your father be cursed. May you die a lowly, unknown death'. However, Smith's English versions are sometimes unconvincing; for instance, she translates '*Jòwọ́ kó bí ó ti ńṣe ọ́ sọ́hũn o*' (a phrase used to express irritation) as 'Oh, go chase yourself, Bugger!' (*Ẹfúnṣetán Aníwúrà,* Scene 1) which reads stiltedly in English. Moreover, Smith sometimes uses a distinctively American-English idiom to convey colloquial speech: 'You're kidding me!' a character exclaims in *Tinúubú* (Scene 1). As a North American translator writing for a North American publisher, it is understandable that Smith would use this style, but it would have been interesting to see if more standard Nigerian-English equivalents could have been found for at least some of these phrases.

Unfortunately, the quality of the text is somewhat marred by editing and production errors. These range in gravity from typographical slips and formatting inconsistencies, to the absence of footnotes 114 to 123 for *Ẹfúnṣetán Aníwúrà.* Photographs of Ibadan and Abeokuta in the Introduction have been printed at a surprisingly low resolution, rendering them fairly poor quality.

Overall, however, *Ẹfúnṣetán Aníwúrà* and *Tinúubú* are faithful, playful and intelligent translations of Ìṣọlá's important works. Their verve with language offers plenty of scope for compelling performances, while the contextual material will prove useful for both academic and general readers. These plays join a small body of translations of Yoruba literature into English, including Wole Soyinka's 'free' translation of Fagunwa's *Ògbójú Ọdẹ Nínú Igbó Irúnmalẹ̀* (1938) as *The Forest of a Thousand Daemons* (1968) and Karin Barber and Òládèjo Òkédìjí's translation of Òkédìjí's play *Aájò Ajé* (1997) as *Running After Riches* (1999). It is to be hoped that translation of such an extensive African-language literature as Yoruba will continue to grow, and that Smith's proficient translations will reach new audiences as both performance and text.

Rebecca Jones
Birmingham University

Anton Krueger, *Experiments in Freedom: Explorations of Identity in New South African Drama*
Newcastle-upon Tyne: Cambridge Scholars Publishing, 2010, 264 pp.
ISBN 1443814253, £39.99

Anton Krueger has provided a comprehensive account of developments in South African theatre from 1994 to 2004. He has navigated the crisis of identity that was deeply felt in South Africa after apartheid ended when there was, to some extent, an impasse in theatre making. The years of anti-apartheid or protest theatre had ended with the deleterious effects on theatre of the Culture Desk of the then United Democratic Front or Mass Democratic Movement. The Culture Desk had functioned as a gate-keeper in relation to the cultural boycott, but also for South African artists wishing to take their work abroad. Their guidelines caused Breyten Breytenbach, for example, to declare that South African arts existed in a state of 'cultural and intellectual terrorism where we have Stalinist jackasses manning "cultural desks" to tell us what a "people's culture" is supposed to be like?' (*Weekly Mail*, 22 June 1990). Many people were taken by surprise by the quickly shifting political arena, and after years of theatre that reflected the period of struggle, practitioners seemed hesitant to embrace their newfound freedom. There was also some truth to the assertion that for a few years in the early 1990s, the real drama was in the streets with protests, in the negotiation halls of CODESA and in the Truth and Reconciliation Commission.

Albie Sachs' paper, 'Preparing ourselves for Freedom' (1988) had been crucial in instigating a move in the arts away from, *inter alia*, depictions of the four pillars of the struggle (which the African National Congress in the 1980s had declared were mass mobilisation, armed struggle, underground organisation and international solidarity). Sachs was adamant that South Africans needed to escape the ghettoised, one-dimensional thinking that characterised the arts as a 'weapon of the struggle'. Krueger, in consequence, discusses the dramatic experiments of a wide array of male theatre makers (with the addition of Reza de Wet), through the lenses of masculinity, nationality, ethnicity and identity. Krueger argues that in most of the work he reviews, except for that of Brett Bailey and Reza de Wet, there are imprints of the good-bad binary that was prevalent in anti-apartheid theatre (184), even though many of the practitioner/writers suggest that clinging to fixed ideas from the past is unhelpful to the project of nation building. He suggests that this is most evident in Athol Fugard's *The Captain's Tiger* and in Jane Taylor's *Ubu and the Truth Commission*.

In his research, Krueger has raised the issue of 'the authorisation of information' (23) as it pertains to identity. He raises this in terms of his own position as commentator, arguing that few people in contemporary South Africa feel able to 'speak for the group' (23). He describes at some length for example, the criticism of Brett Bailey, not based on his theatre but on his being white, and presuming to tell 'black stories' (161). In analysing Greig Coetzee's *Happy Natives*, Krueger subtly shifts the argument towards how ethnicity entitles black South Africans to an 'authentic' heritage, but white South Africans are perpetually cast as the colonial 'leftovers'. By the time Krueger analyses Mpumelelo Paul Grootboom's *Inter-Racial* (which ends, 'Fuck these white people man! Fuck white people! Fuck them! Fuck them! Fuck these motherfuckers!'), he is able to assert that white practitioners have tended to question national (or racial) identity through working with multi-racial casts. Krueger argues that the impulse of black South African practitioners, for example Mbongeni Ngema, Ronnie Govender, Aubrey Sekhabi and Grootboom, has been to consolidate a racial, national identity. He argues that it is the small moments of transgression in, for example Reza de Wet's work (the only woman he discusses), that provide some hope that eventually South Africans will just be part of the human race.

In the conclusion to his work, Krueger touches on the ever-expanding area of physical theatre and dance. He argues that since this theatre is not reliant on language it bridges the divides in a multilingual society, and cites Mark Fleishman (221) in saying that 'it contains the idea of untranslatability, of being able to house things that language can't'. Krueger doesn't go into great detail on physical theatre and dance, but offers brief descriptions of Sylvaine Strike's and Mark Fleishman's work as tantalising glimpses into a future experimentation where South Africans let go of their racial identities.

Krueger returns to his theme of experiments in freedom at the end of the book, arguing that artist practitioners need to 'abandon the pursuit of who we think we are' (xv). He cites Ashraf Jamal (225) in arguing that South Africans are still caught in defining their world and the theatre according to the identity structures of apartheid and the struggle. These identities to some extent remain trapped in binaries – while apartheid may be over, people are not yet exercising their freedom. The issue theatre of the past is replicated in the present – where once it was about imprisonment, pass laws or migrant labour, it is now about child rape, HIV/AIDS and sexuality. The practitioners Krueger examines are different precisely because they are standout examples of experiments in freedom. He suggests that their works are examples of the 'unlearning' (230) that needs to be done; they are explorations in liberating people from their previously over-determined identities.

If there were a criticism of the work, it would be that the book packs too many practitioners in, but I would be hardpressed to suggest who should have been left out. It is also a great relief to read about more contemporary artists and work after what seems like decades of scholarship only about the 1950s to the early 1980s. South African theatre is in great need of further scholarship, and Krueger's book is a welcome contribution.

Catherine M. Cole, *Performing South Africa's Truth Commission: Stages of Transition*
Bloomington: Indiana University Press, 2010, 227 pp.
ISBN 978025335390, $24.95

Performing South Africa's Truth Commission reviews a part of the Truth and Reconciliation Commission (1996–1998), namely the Human Rights Violations Committee (HRVC) hearings. Catherine Cole has framed the HRVC hearings as performance, or as Richard Schechner (1985) suggests as 'twice-behaved behaviour'. In this sense Cole is contributing to the body of narrative about the TRC performance, taking into consideration the pejorative meanings of the TRC as a 'drama' or as 'theatrical', or a spectacle of hysterical misery.

Cole's analysis includes a discussion of the precedents for the TRC, for example, the Nuremberg and Eichmann trials, and she discusses the importance of the South African choice to conduct hearings rather than trials. She has contextualised the hearings by describing performance elements in previous trials in South Africa, including the infamous Treason Trial (1956-1960) where 156 Congress movement activists were accused. Cole also discusses the importance of the role of the interpreters (translators) in the multilingual proceedings, and the difficulty of deciphering meaning in live translations. She briefly points to the performance project *Truth in Translation* (Dir. Michael Lessac, 2006) and *Rewind Cantata* (Composer Philip Miller, 2006) as examples of how the TRC hearings have been reinterpreted.

As part of her research, Cole watched all 87 episodes of the *TRC Special Report* that were broadcast as summaries of the hearings each Sunday on South African television, and she makes a compelling argument for this series to serve as another reinterpretation of the TRC (and to a lesser extent the radio broadcasts). She describes some of the generally felt ambivalence (in South Africa then and now) about the TRC's actual accomplishments because of its 'toothless' mandate to seek the truth but its powerlessness to prosecute individuals or provide meaningful reparations to victims. But Cole evaluates the success of the TRC in contrast to previous trials that were conducted in relatively private spaces, whereas the HRVC and Amnesty Committee hearings were not only open to the public, but also highly mediatised performance events. The book does not discuss the Amnesty Committee hearings in any detail, other than tangentially.

I was perfectly prepared to hate this book, written by a foreigner and an *umlungu* (white) to boot. However she has been able to do this work precisely because she has a critical distance that a South African may lack, and because she did not have to navigate the unwritten rules of 'permission to speak' that permeate the South African academy – although Cole makes it clear that she encountered hostility more than once. I was prepared to dislike the book and the author for daring to write about that which I could not, for being willing to read and watch testimonies when I could not, and for being able to comment on a process of sharing national pain when I could not. I feel that Cole has achieved a compelling narrative, even if I am partly engaged in order to see what she will get 'wrong'. In this vein I could mention that she should have looked at the features of secondary orality (Ong 1982), in order to understand the importance of spoken language and testimony in South Africa. I could have pointed her towards the rhythms and structure of soap operas on South African television and radio for ideas on how drama and 'acting' are appropriated by ordinary people. She could have examined the performative acts of transgression by women during the struggle, to contextualise the shoe-throwing incident at the Gugulethu 7 hearings. I could take issue also with Cole's unproblematic acceptance of testimony as authentic. But this would detract from her real accomplishment in this book.

Catherine Cole views the TRC public hearings as being an important part of South Africa's coming to terms with its painful past – and although her last chapter suggests that the notion of transitional justice was possibly not served by the TRC – there were aspects of the entire process that were significant opportunities for remembering the past and bearing witness. What is often revealed in these narratives is not only the extraordinary suffering and courage of the ordinary person, but the powerlessness of the entire system in South Africa to do anything about it in the present time. The important issues around redress, reconciliation, justice, reparation, were not part of the process.

The HRVC was stage-managed to provide select testimony in a suitable presentation style – to keep the lid on the tensions that were simmering beneath the quasi-religious ceremony. Cole mentions the reactions of the commissioners to the shoe-throwing incident as one of wanting to assert control, to prevent spectacles, to rule out surprises. In this sense, I think that Cole suggests that the TRC and the media offshoots of it were initiated and directed for cathartic purposes. Pity and fear were meant to be exorcised in an elaborate staging, so that South Africans could have something tangible to 'put behind' them, something to 'move on' from. I would argue that the purpose of the TRC was to grieve ritualistically for the past, but not to dwell in it.

Cole strongly argues that there is merit in further mining of the material, although for now most of the TRC documentation remains inaccessible in the archives of the Department of Justice. However, I would question for how long South Africa will re-rehearse its pain nationally and internationally, even while the TRC is touted as an example to all for its open hearings and performance of suffering. Cole amply demonstrates in the final chapters how this performance of pain and suffering took its toll on the interpreters of the TRC, as has the *Truth in Translation* and the Philip Miller *Rewind: A Cantata* pieces and several other publications including Antjie Krog's *Country of my Skull* (1998).

I would suggest that recycled pessimistic accounts of atrocities in South Africa is potentially damaging for a public that is inured to hearing about apartheid, the current carnage of HIV/AIDS, xenophobia and crime. Perhaps, rather, the real success of the South African Truth Commission would be if South Africans could leap forward from it into the future. However important the scholarly pursuit of further excavation of the TRC documents may be, I feel convinced that South Africans have served their time in the past. This is not to suggest that the past yields no lessons, but rather that continual rehearsal of it can lead to paralysis, inertia or pessimism.

Postscript

In 2010 I was struck by the responses of the audience members and performers at a London performance of *Rewind: A Cantata*, which illustrates my point. The performance moved the audience greatly – the repeated, grief-stricken cry as a leitmotif in the cantata, songs which plumbed emotional identification with mothers and victims, while the evocative projections underscored human frailty. At the end of the performance, there was a hushed silence before applause broke out. Performers bowed, after which the Black performers re-emerged and gave an impromptu performance of freedom songs from the struggle era, including a bit of *toyi-toyi* (a rhythmic protest dance), and the hymn *Thula Sizwe* (Quiet Down Nation). Those of the audience who knew the songs joined in the singing, and the Southbank Centre jumped to very different style of music to what had preceded it. While I appreciated the performance of the *Rewind: A Cantata*, it was the impromptu performance which I believe demonstrates the courage and authentic spirit of South Africa to go forward.

Veronica Baxter
University of Leeds

Adele S. Newson-Horst (ed.), *The Dramatic Literature of Nawal El Saadawi*

London, San Francisco, Beirut: Saqi, 2009, 240 pp.
ISBN 9780863566837 UK £9.99, US $15.95

The book starts with a Foreword by Adele S. Newton-Horst, and is comprised of two plays by Nawal El Saadawi: *Isis*, translated from Arabic and introduced by Rihab Kassatly Bagnole and *God Resigns at the Summit Meeting* translated by Sherif Hetata and introduced by Jane Plastow.

In her Foreword, Adele S. Newton-Horst states that the two plays included in this edition are 'works of recovery', in the sense that they both take on the arduous task of defending the mythological and historical reputations of a number of great female religious/mythological icons: Isis, Eve, the Virgin Mary and Hagar; and in so doing stand up for all women whose rights to power and veneration have been stripped away from them since the dawn of history as a result of misogyny. Thus the two plays presented in this work pose the same issues: social (in)justice and patriarchal oppression. Anyone who is acquainted even faintly with Nawal El Saadawi's writing realises that these two specific points are paramount to her in real life and in her fiction. As a blend of radical and socialist feminist, El Saadawi constantly advocates for both oppressed women and the struggling poor classes, but, typical of radical feminists, she also vilifies patriarchy in all its forms: from its ultimate manifestation – as God – to the average father figure and common man. As a domineering figure overflowing with confidence and belief in her own perspectives, El Saadawi's voice dominates the overall body of her novels and dramatic productions as she frequently places herself in the centre of her narratives; a pattern for which she is sometimes criticised.

The first point that catches attention in the work is its title. It gives two faulty impressions: first that Nawal El Saadawi has a prolific playwriting opus when she does not. She has only written seven plays: the quality of some of them is debatable. Second, the title allows the reader to expect more than two plays to be included. A more accurate title would have mentioned that only two plays are being introduced and translated into English. This oversight does not by any means diminish the importance of the book or its contribution to the library of translated world drama, particularly those written by (non-western) women. Therefore, this work is important on many levels, supremely because it gives the English-speaking world a chance to read the dramatic output of a leading Arab feminist – who typically does not write for the theatre but is rather better known for her contributions to the novel. This work also enriches the library section of translated comparative literature with Arab works which is an endeavour that is always appreciated greatly amongst Arabists and Arabic literature scholars when planning their course work. Last, but not least, it provides theatre artists two additions of translated texts from the Arab world that could be utilised for production. So, from all these perspectives this work is a valuable contribution to both literature and theatre.

In the introduction to *Isis*, Rihab Kassatly Bagnole provides a warmhearted account of her longtime admiration for and personal encounter with El Saadawi. She declares that after meeting El Saadawi in person she made the decision to translate the play. Bagnole admits that the undertaking was challenging, but her admiration for both El Saadawi and the goddess Isis induced her to go forward with the project. In her introduction to the play Bagnole focuses more on Isis as an ancient Egyptian/Mediterranean deity than on her presence in the play as a dramatic character. In fact, Bagnole says little about the dramatic structure of the play or whether she perceives it as successful for a stage production or not, which is surprising since the play does have obvious weaknesses in plot construction and language. In the original Nawal El Saadawi makes little effort to produce dramatic language pretending to be representative of the dramatic period of the play and uses modern overtones in the dialogue – unlike al-Hakim, who uses poetic language is his play, *Isis*, about the same protagonist. As a result the translation, which also for the most part sounds very contemporary, comes through as lacking any sense of faithfulness to the period or the mythological figures represented in it. Obviously, this is the reason why al-Hakim's *Isis*, while misogynistic, as many of his works are, is perceived as a 'superior' dramatic achievement to that of El Saadawi.

The second play included in the book, *God Resigns at the Summit Meeting*, is a one-act play, and is effectively introduced by Jane Plastow who provides an excellent synopsis of the plot. Unlike Bagnole's introduction of *Isis*, which reflects personal admiration towards El Saadawi and at times veers away from academic objectivity, Plastow places Nawal El Saadawi within the wider context of international feminism as well as within the scope of Middle Eastern and African women's writing. She comments on El Saadawi's unique choice to create a female character as the offspring of God, saying, 'The idea of Allah having a daughter is both transgressive and teasing – and a beautiful counterpart to Christ as the Son of God.' Plastow is accurate in this account as El Saadawi's objective in writing this play seems to be to shock and break taboos. From this point of view, the dramatic structure, which is essentially dialogue, is used only as a practical *modus operandi* by which to construct a (pseudo-)dramatic conversation with God, and to break the tacit rule of the imperative silence and concealed face of God in the Abrahamic tradition, not as an aesthetic end or choice in itself.

The play itself bears the same dramatic shortcomings as other plays written by El Saadawi; typically, her drama is spurred by dialogue not action. The premise of the play is based on the single notion of shock value provided by way of the physical imperson-ation on stage of God Himself and his four revered and larger-than-life prophets: Abraham, Moses, Jesus and Muhammad, not to mention Eve and the Virgin Mary, all of whom are strictly forbidden to be portrayed on stage (or on the screen) in Muslim countries. The play is full of naïve questions rather than mature and philosophical con-templation – in fact, its reputation rests solely on its provocation and transgression of everything 'sacred' to El Saadawi's Muslim/Coptic community in Egypt. Successful scenes in the play appear more clever than dramatically adroit. Generally speaking, the play presents a barrage of questions and attitudes about and towards God – from this point of view it could come through as liberating for readers sharing the same theological quandaries and discontent with God's distance and invisibility. Jane Plastow expresses this point skilfully in saying 'Imagination and reality, truth and ideas, are coming together in the struggle for control of, or liberation from, coercive concepts of the divine'.

While El Saadawi's main concerns, as a feminist writer, are usually women's issues, in this play she combines feminists' resentment of patriarchy, represented in God and his prophets' sexism, with a strong critical stance towards organised religions. Her criticism implies that religions are all man-made constructions that the modern person should interrogate. On reading the play, one immediately suspects that the rage expressed in the play is El Saadawi's own (and not the characters') distrust of the Abrahamic tradition, which is known to place men at the centre of power and to marginalise women, but in so expressing herself, she affirms and reinstates the feminists' belief – indeed, dogma – that 'the personal is political'. In translating *God Resigns at the Summit Meeting*, Sherif Hetata, a long-time translator of El Saadawi's works into English, succeeds in reflecting her style and phrasing, but this particular play loses some of its humour and irony in the translation.

Finally, El Saadawi maybe imaginative, provocative, inspiring and daring, but she is certainly not a skilful dramatist and writing for the stage is apparently not her forte as the essential quality of dramatic writing is the art of condensation, of which she seems to be incapable. In the two plays presented in this work, she is unconvincing in the art of plot construction and characterisation, and her didacticism lacks subtlety and is largely used to express her own opinions and concerns. Moreover, with such large casts, staging her plays would not be an easy undertaking for low-budget productions by NGO and women's organisations who might wish to use El Saadawi's theatre to promote feminist and human rights agendas.

Dina Amin
Villanova University

SERIES EDITORS' NOTE

Anthony Ackerman contacted the author of the doctoral thesis 'Role-Play in South African Theatre', Haike Frank, because he felt accused of plagiarism in a footnote in her book from the thesis. He wanted to know how the footnote came about and asked for clarification in distinguished publications. The following is Haike Frank's reply:

> In the book *Role-Play in South African Theatre*, which appeared as No. 70 in the Bayreuth African Studies Series, the author Haike Frank comments in footnote 18 on page 108 on identical passages printed in two articles in the 1970s. These are 'South African Blacksploitation' by Russell Vandenbroucke, printed in *Yale/Theatre* 8.1 (1976), pp. 68-71 and 'Why Must These Shows Go On? A Critique of Black Musicals Made for White Audiences' by Anthony Akerman, printed in *Theatre Quarterly* 28, pp. 67-69. It turns out that several passages in Akerman's article which are word-for-word copies of passages in Vandenbroucke's article were actually interpolated by Vandenbroucke himself - who also acted as the overall editor of the feature on South African theatre in *Theatre Quarterly* 28. Vandenbroucke refers to this interpolation in the introduction to the feature on page 43, but does not include a footnote in Akerman's article. This is unfortunate as it causes confusion and misleads readers, who only look at Akerman's article, into missing a traditional academic reference. Therefore, Haike Frank and Anthony Akerman ask all scholars who work with the latter's text to include the introduction to the feature by Vandenbroucke in their research.